THE ISRAELI DIASPORA

Israelis form a unique case in the field of diaspora studies. When the State of Israel was founded in 1948 it was seen as the longed-for end to the wandering and oppression which had characterized the Jewish diaspora over the centuries. For various reasons, however, 1 percent of the Israeli population chooses to live abroad despite the condemnation of those who see emigration as a threat to the ideological, demographic, and moral viability of Israel itself.

In this fascinating study, based on extensive field work in the major Israeli communities of New York, Los Angeles, London, Paris and Sydney, Steven J. Gold looks at emigrants' reasons for leaving – existing links abroad, political and economic dissatisfaction at home, the lure of world-class career opportunities and cultural environments in global cities, and, in the case of the Sephardim or Israelis of non-European origin, often a feeling of being treated as second-class citizens. He also examines the tensions, compromises, and satisfactions involved in their relations with Israelis who have not left and with the Jewish and non-Jewish communities in the countries in which they settle. In the final chapter, he talks to Israeli men and women who after years as emigrants have made the decision to return. The end result is a major contribution to the study not just of the Israeli diaspora but also to our wider understanding of migration and transnational identity.

Steven J. Gold is Professor of Sociology at Michigan State University.

GLOBAL DIASPORAS
Series editor: Robin Cohen

The assumption that minorities and migrants will demonstrate and exclusive loyalty to the nation state is now questionable. Scholars of nationalism, international migration and ethnic relations need new conceptual maps and fresh case studies to understand the growth of complex transnational identies. The old idea of "diaspora" may provide this framework. Though often conceived in terms of a catastrophic dispersion, widening the notion of diaspora to include trade, imperial labour and cultural diasporas can provide a more nuanced understanding of the often positive relationships between migrants' homelands and their places of work and settlement.

This book forms part of an ambitious and interlinked series of volumes trying to capture the new relationships between home and abroad. Historians, political scientists, sociologists and anthropologists from a number of countries have collaborated on this forward-looking project. The series includes two books which provide the defining, comparative and synoptic aspects of diasporas. Further titles focus on particular communities, both traditionally recognized diasporas and those newer claimants who define their collective experiences and aspirations in terms of diasporic identity.

This series is associated with the Transnational Communities Programme at the University of Oxford funded by the UK's Economic and Social Research Council.

Already published:

GLOBAL DIASPORAS
An introduction
Robin Cohen

NEW DIASPORAS
Nicholas Van Hear

THE SIKH DIASPORA
Darshan Singh Tatla

ITALY'S MANY DIASPORAS
Donna R. Gabaccia

THE ISRAELI DIASPORA

Steven J. Gold

University of Washington Press
Seattle

First published 2002
by Routledge
11 New Fetter Lane, London EC4P 4EE

and in the United States of America by
University of Washington Press,
PO Box 50096, Seattle, WA 98145-5096
www.washington.edu/uwpress/

Routledge is an imprint of the Taylor & Francis Group

© 2002 Steven J. Gold

Typeset in Baskerville by Exe Valley Dataset Ltd, Exeter
Printed and bound in Great Britain by
TJ International Ltd, Padstow, Cornwall

British Library Cataloguing in Publication Data
A catalogue record for this book is available
from the British Library

Library of Congress Cataloging-in-Publication Data
A catalogue record for this book has been requested

ISBN 0–295–98280–2 (hbk)
ISBN 0–295–98261–6 (pbk)

CONTENTS

PLATES

PREFACE

The State of Israel was founded so that Jews could cease their long saga of wandering and oppression in the diaspora. Since 1948, almost three million have settled there. While the founders of Israel believed that the in-gathering of exiles into a Jewish homeland would bring about an end to Jews' existence as a minority group in other peoples' lands, a fraction of the Israeli population retained aspirations and connections associated with life outside of the Jewish State and chose to leave. As time passed, it became apparent that emigration was not strictly a first generation phenomenon caused by the lingering influence of the diaspora on recent arrivals. On the contrary, some number of those born in Israel also elected to go abroad. True, the total number of emigrants from this small nation is modest. However, the fraction of the entire Israeli population overseas – over 1 percent – is comparable to that of major source countries of international migration (Cohen 1989: 267).

Precisely because Israel is a country of immigration, Israelis and Israeli emigrants are characterized by a complex array of identities as well as multiple connections to social groups within and beyond Israel. As both Jews and Israelis, Israeli emigrants are part of two diasporas – the age-old Jewish diaspora as well as the recently established, but more personally consequential, Israeli diaspora. (The experience of Israeli Arabs is especially complex. While they sometimes maintain relations with Jewish Israelis in points of settlement – especially between the 1993 signing of the Oslo Peace Accords and the start of the Al Aksa Intifada in 2000 – they are also linked to the Palestinian diaspora. The emigration of Israeli Arabs is a topic deserving of serious scholarly consideration, but it is not the subject of this book).

As a small-sized, generally middle-class, and highly westernized migrant population, Israeli emigrants have generated relatively little interest in their points of settlement. However, they have provoked extensive concern and not a little indignation in the country of origin (and for Israel's overseas supporters as well), who see out-migration as a threat to the ideological, moral and demographic viability of the Jewish State.

While going abroad subjects Israeli emigrants to the condemnation of co-nationals, they nevertheless retain strong and durable connections to the country of origin. Despite their lengthy stays abroad and generally successful adaptation to host societies, they seldom concede the permanence of their emigration, refuse to identify with the country of settlement, and express a longing for Israel, which they often visit and sometimes return to. As they build lives in one country while identifying with another, Israelis can be included within a growing number of migrant populations – sometimes called transnationals – whose behavior corresponds to neither of the categories of settler or sojourner long used to classify migrant behavior.

Despite (or perhaps because of) the controversy surrounding Israeli emigration, this topic has not been the subject of a large body of academic scholarship. Moreover, most of the studies that do exist have been concerned with a single matter – estimating the size of the emigrant population, most commonly in the United States. Accordingly, a wide range of issues and many points of settlement associated with the Israeli diaspora have not been studied.

This book examines Jewish Israeli emigrant communities in several countries, as well as their on-going relations with the country of origin. It focuses on their reasons for emigration, patterns of economic adaptation, familial and communal lives, bases of identity and experience of return. While the primary concentration is on the group in question, the project is informed by theories from the broader field of migration, ethnicity and diaspora studies. Accordingly, researchers interested in these topics should find the book a useful case study.

Research on diasporas has commonly been undertaken by historians who have relied on archives and other published sources. Since Israel is a young nation, I follow a different approach, relying primarily on ethnographic materials – including in-depth interviews and fieldwork – collected over a period of ten years among Israeli emigrants in several points of settlement, as well as with returned migrants in Israel.

ACKNOWLEDGMENTS

I wish to thank Debra Hansen, Michal Shachal-Staier, Lilach Lev-Ari, Irit Gordon, Jonathan Miran, Khaled Furani, and Brikena Balli for research assistance. I am especially grateful to Rona Hart for her interviewing, insight, and knowledge.

Naama Sabar, Bruce Phillips, Stanley Waterman, Silvia Pedraza, Nancy Rosen, Moshe Shokeid, Gabriel Sheffer, Andrea Louie, Pini Herman, Ruth Seldin, Roger Waldinger, Mehdi Bozorgmehr, Yoav Ben-Horin, Ivan Light, Edna Bonacich, Khachig Tölölyan, Luis Guarnizo, Alejandro Portes, Eran Razin, Georges Sabaugh, Hilla Israely, Sergio DellaPergola, Pierette Hondagneu-Sotelo, Nazli Kibria, Rubén G. Rumbaut, Yinon Cohen, Jonathan Friedlander, Michael Rubner, Natan Uriely, Mary Waters, Nancy Foner, Sally Frankental, Rina Cohen, Gerald Gold, Brian Fry, Tom Kuecker, Marie Anderson, Ian McCutcheon and Ruth Minster provided advise, contacts, materials and many useful suggestions. Robin Cohen, the editor of this book series, encouraged me to examine the experience of Israeli emigrants as a global diaspora. Mari Shullaw gave valuable aid with publication.

The Wilstein and Whizin Institutes, John Randolph Haines and Dora Haines Foundation, ASA/NSF Fund for the Advancement of the Discipline, Social Capital Interest Group at Michigan State University and the Michigan State University Non Profit Research Initiative provided funding for the project.

Tammy Dennany, Marvey Olson, Sandy Cummings and Maxine Bazzy did photocopy and Vivek Joshi solved computer problems. Carol Oberg and Theresa Doerr cut through reams of red tape to make sure my research assistants were compensated.

My children, William and Betty Gold, cheerfully accompanied me on numerous fieldwork trips. Finally, Lisa Gold helped me with my writing, and clarified many organizational problems. The book is dedicated to her.

1

INTRODUCTION

From Jewish diaspora to Israeli diaspora

The idea of diaspora – a group's forced dispersion or exile from their homeland – is a focal theme in the long history of the Jewish people. The bible tells Jews that they were sent out of the Promised Land for violation of God's law (Patai 1971). Each year, during the Passover Seder, they commemorate their exile and express their desire to return to the Promised Land with the phrase "next year in Jerusalem."

Post-biblical Jewish history also resounds with themes of homelessness and insecurity. During the Crusades (1096–1291), Christians seeking to capture the Holy Land from Muslims attacked Jews as non-believers. Before they were done, the Crusaders had terrorized, massacred and forced the conversion of Jews from England to Palestine. On the Feast of All Saints in 1290, the entire Jewish population of England was expelled, and Jews remained banished from the British Isles for the next 367 years. French Jews met a similar fate in 1394. During the late 1400s, the Spanish Inquisition deported thousands of Jews from Spain and Portugal to North Africa, Turkey, Brazil, Holland and other settings. Through the late nineteenth and early twentieth centuries, Jews in Russia and Poland suffered from state-sanctioned attacks called Pogroms. In response, millions fled to the Americas and Western Europe. A few decades later, six million were exterminated by the Nazis. In the 1950s, thousands of Middle Eastern and North African Jews took leave of their homelands. Finally, since the late 1970s, most of the Jewish communities of the former Soviet Union and Iran and a sizable number of South African Jews departed from the countries of their birth.

Despite this record of persecution and exile, from early times to the present, Jews also enjoyed periods of good relations with their neighbors in various diaspora settings. During these intervals, they developed lively and sophisticated communities and made important

1

and wide-ranging contributions both to Jewish culture and to the societies in which they lived. Consequently, as Robin Cohen (1997: 21) notes, "the diasporic experience in all areas has been enriching and creative as well as enervating and fearful." Similarly, Zvi Sobel (1986:43) asserts "Exile might have been 'foisted' upon the Jewish people – but the Jewish people embraced it. The Jewish people endowed it with a certain aura of positive immutability."

The term diaspora has been used to describe a wide variety of groups and situations and as such is imprecise. Moreover, even when speaking of a single diaspora (such as that of the Jews) we see widely varying forms, reflecting the authors' particular ideologies, religious orientations and historical contexts (Patai 1971; Levine 1986; Sheffer 1986; Safran 1991; Clifford 1994; Cohen 1997). In order to clarify the concept, in his *Global Diasporas*, Robin Cohen (1997: 26) identified a list of criteria defining diaspora. Diaspora involves: dispersal or travel from an original homeland to two or more foreign regions; a collective memory or myth of an idealized homeland; a commitment to the maintenance of the homeland, including a movement for return; a strong, long-term, group consciousness and identity; a belief in a shared fate; a range of possible relations (from troubled to enriching) with the host society; and finally, a sense of empathy and solidarity with coethnics in other places of settlement.

These characteristics apply to Jews – the archetypal diaspora group – and hence to Israeli emigrants. Despite their separation from the Jewish State, Israeli emigrants probably do not qualify as a diaspora *per se*, largely because of the short duration of their exile and the relative ease of return (Safran 1999: 265–6). Nevertheless, having been socialized in Israel, they are intimately familiar with the language of diaspora and often describe their experience and identity as such. Accordingly, Israeli emigrants sometimes see themselves as encountering yet another phase in their group's long record of displacement. As Jonathan Boyarin (cited in Clifford 1994: 305) observes, "Jewish experience often entails 'multiple experiences of rediasporization, which do not necessarily succeed each other in historical memory but echo back and forth.'"

The origins of Israel

The origins of the Israeli diaspora can be traced to the formation of the state of Israel, itself a product of the Jewish condition in nineteenth century Europe. The late 1800s were a difficult time for European Jewry, who saw their earlier hopes for enlightenment-based acceptance dashed by growing anti-Semitism. In an effort to end their legacy of exile and persecution, in 1897, Jews in Russia and Romania developed a movement called Hovevei Zion (Lovers of Zion) whose goal was to establish a political entity in the Land of Israel (Goldstein 1995: 104). The movement's leader was Theodore Herzl, a secular native of Budapest who worked as journalist for a Viennese newspaper in Paris. As he reported on a series of anti-Semitic incidents, culminating in the Dreyfus affair,[1] he became convinced that "the Jewish problem was intractable, emancipation had failed, and that a new approach was urgently needed" (Goldstein 1995: 111). Herzl and the other founders of Zionism were influenced by the political ideals of their time and place – especially socialism and nationalism – as they sought an opportunity for Jews to build their own lives on their own land. A half century later, in 1948, their dreams were realized, and the State of Israel had been formed. Its presence is justified by the Balfour Declaration of 1917, the League of Nations, and the United Nations (MFA 1999).

Over the next fifty years, Israel would overcome a variety of political and economic obstacles and survive several wars. Its Jewish population would swell from about 500,000 in 1948 to over 5,243,000 in 2001 – the result of natural growth and in-migration from many nations. In addition to these five million Jews which, ironically, includes about a quarter of a million recent immigrants from the former USSR "who are not regarded as being Jewish," there are 1,215,000 Israeli Arabs (*Jerusalem Post* 2001). While Zionists asserted that all Jews share a common nationality, the practical challenge of uniting an incredibly diverse and often traumatized population in a new state – including Jews from countries as disparate as Yemen and Germany, together with indigenous non-Jews – was enormous. A consciously created system of culture, education, military experience and language (ancient Hebrew rejuvenated for use in a modern society) was devoted to the task (Zerubavel 1995). A mere two years after Israel's independence, the nation's first Prime Minister David Ben Gurion stated:

> The transformation of this human dust into a successful nation . . . is not an easy task. We need to resort to enormous educational and moral efforts, accompanied by genuine, deep and pure love of these forsaken brothers . . . in order to imprint in these incoming and defeatious diasporas the values of our proud culture, language and creativity.
> (Ben Gurion 1964: 34, cited in Yiftachel 1998: 41)

While many external differences did decrease, Israeli society continues to be stratified along the lines of ethnicity, class, religion and ideology. Further distinctions, having evolved within the particular social, political, religious and economic context of the Jewish State, continue to challenge national unity and consequently, the ideological basis of Israeli society, in a number of ways (Goldscheider 1996; Yiftachel 1998).

Israel and the diaspora

In order to recruit Jewish citizens, Zionists redefined the meaning of diaspora. Before the formation of the Jewish State, diaspora was largely a religious concept. The desire to return home involved a spiritual rather than a geographic journey. Residence in the diaspora was the Jewish reality. Good, bad or indifferent, it was simply the place where the vast majority of Jews lived (Levine 1986: 3).

The early Zionists proclaimed a radically different view. "In the case of the Jews, the term diaspora itself – which essentially and neutrally means a dispersion of an ethno-national group – acquired an utterly negative meaning and became synonymous with detested 'exile'" (Sheffer 1998: xix). Zionists depicted the diaspora as a place of isolation, degradation and suffering – "Jewish life in exile constituted a recurrent history of oppression, punctuated by periodic pogroms and expulsions, of fragile existence imbued with fear and humiliation" (Zerubavel 1995: 18). Moving from the diaspora (or golah, exile) to Israel was "making aliyah" or going to a higher place. In nation-building texts and rituals, the achievements of Jews in the diaspora were denigrated or repudiated by early Zionists. According to Oz Almog, author of *Sabra: The Creation of the New Jew* (2000: 77), "The Diaspora Jew was described as the diametric opposite of the pioneer of the Land of Israel and was portrayed along the lines (and to a large extent under the inspiration) of anti-Semitic stereotypes." Even the biographies of heroes of Israel's War for Independence were recast to obliterate their "life as a child and adolescent in eastern Europe," thus separating Israelis from the millions of Jews who continued to reside outside of the Jewish State (Zerubavel 1995: xv).

While early Zionists depicted the diaspora as a place of degradation and exile, they failed to convince the majority of the world's Jews – especially those in affluent and democratic nations of the West – to make aliyah. Instead, diaspora Jews chose to stay put, contributing political and financial backing from afar. As sociologist Steven Cohen (1991: 123) writes, they are more supporters of Israel than true Zionists. "While the claim that American Jews are overwhelmingly pro Israel has some merit, only a very small number accept some of the very basic premises of classical or contemporary Israeli Zionism."

Although this attitude among diaspora Jews would appear to displease Zionists, they realized the practical benefits provided by having supporters abroad. There is little doubt that the Jewish State would not have survived without the financial assistance of diaspora Jews, as well as the political and economic aid of Western nations that resident Jews, together with their allies, lobbied for (Sobel 1986; Evron 1995). In sum, although some forms of early Zionism hypothesized that the formation of the State of Israel would bring about the end of the Jewish diaspora, in reality, the two locations became mutually enmeshed and inter-dependent as sources of support and continuity for Jewish life.

If Israel learned to accept the practical benefits extended from diaspora communities, it was far less tolerant of its own citizens joining those populations. The official and informal condemnation of Israeli emigration, however, did not fully prevent Israelis from going abroad. According to the *Israel Bulletin of Statistics*, between 1948 and the end of 1992, 438,900 Israelis were living overseas and had not returned (*For Those Returning Home* 1995). This group includes persons born abroad as well as native Israeli Jews (sabras). The largest fraction resides in major Jewish communities, including New York, Los Angeles, Paris, London and Toronto.

From the Israeli point of view, migration from the Jewish State threatens the assertion that Israel is the best place for Jews to live. And practically, Jews are needed to populate the Jewish State and to ensure its military, economic and demographic viability in a hostile world region. In contrast to the Hebrew term aliyah that refers to Jews' move from the diaspora to higher place of Israel, yeridah describes the stigmatized downward path of Israelis who descend from the Promised Land into the diaspora. Emigrants are the yordim. "There is an implication that the citizen who has left Israel is guilty of a subtle form of betrayal of the shared obligation to protect the land of Israel" (Linn and Barkan-Ascher 1996: 7). During the 1970s, Israeli politicians such as Prime Minister Yitzhak Rabin were especially vitriolic on this issue, calling Israeli emigrants "moral lepers," "the fallen among the weaklings" and "the dregs of the earth" (cited in Ritterband 1986: 113; Kimhi 1990). However, by 1992, Rabin had recanted these statements (Rosen 1993: 3).

If Israelis have been hostile to the emigration of their countrymen, Jewish communities outside of Israel have been ambivalent about these newcomers. Following the lead of the Israeli government (which wanted to discourage settlement), diaspora Jewish communities offered little of the support that they have customarily extended to immigrant Jews. However, since the 1980s, in accordance with evolving Israeli policy towards expatriates, and realizing the value of this energetic, Jewishly-conscious and Hebrew-speaking population in their midst, Jewish communities in settlement countries have established outreach programs for recently arrived Israelis. Jewish population studies in New York (1991), Los Angeles (1998), England (1998) and South Africa (1993) all enumerate Israelis, their presence one of the few positive tendencies in a general trend of aging and shrinking Jewish demographics.

Moreover, regardless of the policies of their communal agencies, diaspora Jews (and Israeli émigrés as well) discern that the arrival of former Israelis bears marked similarities with earlier Jewish migrations to Western Europe, North America or other "lands of opportunity" in order to acquire education, affluence, individual freedom, family unification and security. Their support of Israel not withstanding, Western diaspora communities are generally patriotic and satisfied with life (Wolitz 1991; Bershtel and Graubard 1992). And for good reason. They have achieved the goals that motivated their predecessors' migration – education, affluence and political influence – to a degree that exceeds that of other ethnically defined populations in many countries of settlement (Pollins 1984; Waterman and Kosmin 1986; Lipset 1990; Gold and Phillips 1996b; Hyman 1998; Schmool and Cohen 1998; Cohen 1999; Gold 1999). Further, for many diaspora Jews, the appeal of Israel is not as strong as it once was. Since the 1980s, Jewish communal surveys have found that young diaspora Jews are less inspired by the image of a secure, powerful, Likud-led[2] and ethnically polarized Israel than was the case during an earlier period (Cohen 1991; Tobin et al. 1995; Shain 2000; Nir 2001; Shamir 2001; Halle 2001). A small but influential movement questions or rejects Zionism altogether (Boyarin and Boyarin 1993; Finkielkraut 1994; Azria 1998; Safran 1999).

Paradoxically then, while Israel and Jewish communities beyond its borders are mutually involved, interdependent and maintain good relations, the two settings uphold distinct assumptions about where Jewish people, especially Israelis, belong. Having been socialized in Israel, but living in the diaspora, Israeli emigrants confront this paradox of membership and belonging as individuals and within the communities they create in places of settlement. Moreover, while the idea of diaspora has a long and important history for the Jewish people, Israeli émigrés are among the only members of the Jewish diaspora who have the actual experience of being separated from known relatives and real life experiences in the land of Israel. Gabriel Sheffer (1998) made just this point in his provocatively titled article in *The Jewish Year Book* (of England) "Yordim (Emigrants) Are the Authentic Diaspora."

This book concerns the experience of Jewish Israeli migrants. Drawing on in-depth interviews, fieldwork and other data, it describes their motives for exit, patterns of adaptation – family arrangements, means of earning a living, religious involvement, interaction with other Israelis and host community Jews – and plans for eventual return to the Jewish State. The purpose of this book is twofold. First, it offers a detailed picture of the experience of Jewish Israeli emigrants. Secondly, it seeks to contribute to the broader understanding of migrant groups, such as Dominicans, South Asians, Turks, Armenians, Caribbeans, Mexicans, Palestinians, overseas Chinese and Filipinos, who like Israelis, maintain social, economic and political ties and a sense of identification with nation states and social groups beyond their place of immediate residence. Social scientists and scholars in cultural studies describe these populations as diasporic or trans-national (Basch *et al.* 1994; Goldring 1996; 1998).

Perspectives on Israeli emigrants

Because of the controversial nature of Israeli emigration, a wide range of theories are useful for understanding the experience of Israeli emigrants as well as its meaning to various interested parties. However, drawing from both existing literature and available explanations, I propose that three distinct bodies of work fit best. These approaches employ common conceptions of migration and similar research methods. However, each reflects a unique set of concerns, ideological outlooks and national locations. These positions, in turn, determine the guiding assumptions, methods, comparisons and conclusions drawn by the scholars involved.

Social scientists and philosophers have long debated objectivity and the place of bias in their work, and despite intensive critiques, impartial investigation still has ardent advocates (Lincoln and Guba 1985; Allan and Turner 2000). However, in the investigation of Israeli emigration, researchers' value judgments about this human movement are so central to their conclusions that to ignore them would be naïve (Shokeid 1989). Yes, these three outlooks are ideologies, but so are Zionism, nationalism, anti-Semitism and other social movements and perspectives that are central to the understanding of Israeli society. Accordingly, I discuss the nature of these assumptions at the outset, as a means of organizing relevant literature.

The first approach considers the phenomenon from the point of view of the country of origin. Since Zionism, the philosophy that underlies the existence of the Jewish state, calls for return home of the world's Jews, the opposite movement – Israelis leaving the Jewish state to reside elsewhere – clearly presents an ideological and demographic problem. Reflecting the negative evaluation of Israeli emigration from the Israeli point of view, I call this the "yordim" perspective.

A second approach – migration studies – is most closely associated with scholars in Western Jewish communities (especially in North America, but also Europe, Australia and elsewhere) that have been the destination of significant migrations of both Jews and gentiles in the last century. Drawing from the larger body of migration research, this outlook sees Israeli emigration through theories of agency and self-interest, most commonly in the form of neo-classical economics, where profit-maximizing individuals move across borders in order to exploit available opportunities and rewards (Massey *et al.* 1993; Portes and Rumbaut 1996). An alternative formulation centers upon neo-Marxist world systems theory, wherein migration takes place in response to macro-level economic and political circumstances (Burawoy 1976; Portes and Borocz 1989; DellaPergola 1992).

Finally, a third perspective associated with transnationalism and what Robin Cohen (1997) calls cultural diasporas examines the collective experience of Israeli emigrants as an effort of this group to maintain a degree of freedom to negotiate within the rigidity and limitations of nation states, cultural agendas and economic systems that would force them into restrictive categories and social structures not of their own choosing (Glick Schiller *et al.* 1992; Appadurai 1996; Cohen 1997; Smith and Guarnizo 1998).

As we shall see, in examining the phenomenon of Israeli emigration, each of these positions imposes its own moral evaluation. The yordim perspective sees Israeli emigration as a social problem; the migration studies approach is (at least explicitly) value neutral, and the transnational/cultural diaspora model celebrates Israeli emigrants and other transmigrants as innovators who develop creative means to resist social and economic systems that would limit options available to them.

Migration from the source country perspective

Israeli emigrants share many social features with other contemporary, skilled migrant groups. These include settlement in world cities of the developed West; concentration in typical immigrant occupations such as service industries, retail sales, light manufacturing, construction and technical and professional jobs; creation of ethnic enclaves; possession of cultural skills, resources and networks that allow them to function in various settings; and relations with native-born proximal hosts (Gold 1994a; Portes and Rumbaut 1996; Cohen and Gold 1996;

Warner and Wittner 1998). However, in contrast to many current migrant groups settling in North America and Europe, the existence of the Israeli migrant community is much more likely to be examined from the vantage point of the country of origin than the host society.

Because Israel is a small country, the total number of Israeli exiles in any place of settlement is minuscule in contrast to populations hailing from many other source nations. Further, because Israelis are generally white, well educated, employed, competent in the language of the host society and highly integrated into its institutions, they have low visibility, receive little notice in the media and are neglected by the politicians, academics and social agencies that generally attend to migrant communities. Even host country Jewish organizations that are aware of the Israeli presence are ambivalent about it. While seeking to comply with the Israeli policy of discouraging settlement, they also wish to assist these fellow Jews. Consequently, the communal response is low key (Cohen 1986; Rosen 1993).

Rather than attracting the attention of the country of settlement, Israeli emigrants are a topical issue in the country of origin. Israelis have long been interested in their expatriate countrymen. They are the subject of novels, films, comedy sketches and political speeches, as well as scholarly, journalistic and official inquiries (often featuring wildly exaggerated estimates of their numbers, indicating the seriousness with which this social problem is treated). Israeli sociologist Zvi Sobel (1986: 8) – who admits his own "recognition of the threat – personal and communal – suggested by large scale 'desertion' on the part of thousands of countrymen," describes Israelis' anxiety about emigration:

> While a demographic emergency in a purely objective sense might not exist, it is clear that a psychological emergency does. Whatever the 'facts' of the matter, large numbers of Israelis – the man in the street as well as establishment figures – *perceive* emigration as a problem and one of serious dimensions.
> (Sobel 1986: 14, italics in original)

Faced with the threat of exit by its Jewish population, Israel has undertaken a series of actions to counter emigration. Unlike those societies that prohibit emigration as a crime against the state, Israel, as a liberal democracy, has not closed its borders to the departure of Jews (Lahav and Arian 1999). Rather, it generally relies on collective pressure, speeches by prominent officials and the creation of anti-emigration cultural productions to discourage exit. "In keeping with the goal of increasing the Jewish population, Israel, unlike other Western states, has persistently discouraged emigration (of Jews) primarily by exerting moral and ideological pressures on potential leavers" (Cohen 1988: 909). The findings of yordim scholarship are consistent with this agenda in several ways – by repudiating the diaspora as a setting for Jewish life, by condemning emigration as immoral and by describing actual emigrants as unhappy and unsuccessful.

The methods and concerns of yordim work are compatible with the broader literature on migration as it describes the social, cultural, familial and economic reasons that motivate Israelis' emigration (Greenberg 1979; Sobel 1986; Shokeid 1988). However, what is unique about this body of research is its focus on the difficulties and travails encountered by Israeli exiles. This despite the fact that according to almost any measure – education, income, labor force participation, naturalization – Israelis can be counted as among the most successful migrant populations in their countries of settlement (Gold and Phillips 1996a).

Much yordim research assumes that Israeli émigrés have been affected by their socialization in the Jewish State to the extent that they are ill-suited for life outside of it. For example, Israelis are depicted as more collectivist, less materialistic, more outspoken and less willing to tolerate life as a minority group than is the case for diaspora Jews. "It is often suggested that for most Israelis individual identity is embedded in their national identity, so that separation from the nation may result in identity conflict" (Linn and Barkan-Ascher 1996: 7; Cohen 1991). These studies generally conclude that émigrés' feelings of guilt and disorientation with regard to being outside of the Jewish State prevent them from creating viable and supportive ethnic communities – a pattern associated with immigrant adaptation in general and especially with Jewish migrants. Since statistical data and comparative research depict Israeli emigrants as successful, much of yordim work focuses on the individual and communal troubles of the group – disillusionment, loss of Jewish identity, family breakdown, poverty, unethical behavior, alienation from host-country Jews and loneliness. "Yordim are described by the media in negative terms, and where failure to adjust overseas can be cited, this is reported with great relish" (Greenberg 1979: 55).

Illustrative of this tendency, Moshe Shokeid (1988: 39, 49) records an obscene acronym with which American Jews label Israelis and goes on to describes émigrés' difficulty in establishing social ties in the US: "As noted by many Israelis, not only did American Jews make no effort to facilitate the Israelis' entry into American society, but they themselves appeared to be no less reserved and unapproachable than gentile Americans." Countering the image of affluence and career advancement available to Israeli émigrés, Naama Sabar (1996; 2000) describes former Kibbutzniks in Los Angeles who speak broken English, live in squalor and support themselves as archetypal middleman entrepreneurs – by selling shoddy, overpriced remodeling services to slum-dwelling African-Americans and Latinos. Suggesting the unwelcoming environment in another point of settlement, Cohen and Gold (1996: 22) report that Canadian Jews portray Israeli émigrés with the same stereotypes that Canadian Gentiles see Jewish Canadians: loud, dishonest, arrogant and rude. (Israelis respond by describing Jewish Canadians with the identical platitudes that Canadian Jews attribute to their non-Jewish neighbors: formal, lazy, naïve, and beer-drinking.)

From the yordim perspective, Israeli emigration is fundamentally unlike other forms of migration. Several studies make this point explicitly. "Israelis in the homeland and Jews in the diaspora exhibit attitudes towards Israeli emigrants that are markedly different to those that other homeland societies have shown towards their emigrants" (Sheffer 1998: xix). For example, in his book on Israeli emigration, Zvi Sobel asserts that other models of migration are of little use for examining the experience of Israeli émigrés:

> Thus, from the starting point of our analysis [of Israeli emigration] – defining and labeling the act or process as well as the actors – we are confronted by a rather singular situation with little parallel material to provide guidance.
>
> (Sobel 1986: 223)

Similarly, Gabriel Sheffer (1998: xix) alleges "until recently, immigration to and emigration from Israel were not regarded as connected to the current world-wide phenomenon of migration." Israelis' reluctance to regard the emigration of their own countrymen and women as being like that of other migrants reveals an interesting paradox in terms of Israeli ideology. The ultimate hope of early Zionists was to create a "new Zionist person" who would transcend the consciousness of the diaspora Jew, limited as it is by minority status and the constant threats of assimilation and anti-Semitic oppression (Zerubavel 1995; Almog 2000).

By leaving Israel to return to the diaspora, the Israeli emigrant would appear to be defying this goal. However, through his or her inability to function in the diaspora, the Israeli sojourner actually validates the Zionist hope. Israelis *are* different, after all. Unlike other immigrants and especially diaspora Jews, who readily adapt to life in exile, they cannot thrive outside of the homeland.

Israeli emigration is an enduring concern. However, many of the most critical studies on the topic appeared in the 1970s and 1980s, when the problem was viewed as especially threatening. Since that time, social and political changes in the Jewish State, including economic growth, the arrival of almost a million Russian newcomers, and – at least until fall 2000, when the Al Aksa Intifada began – improved relations with many of Israel's Arab neighbors, have resulted in Israel's enhanced political, economic and demographic security. As a consequence, both Israel and the Jewish communities of host societies have taken a more benevolent stance toward Israeli emigrants (Rosen 1993; Gold and Phillips 1996a).

Migration studies

In contrast to the yordim perspective elaborated above, most of the literature in the broader academic and policy-oriented fields of migration studies tends to be economic in focus. It assumes that migration occurs to pursue goals of increased or more stable income, education, career options or an improvement in lifestyle (Massey *et al.* 1993). Leftists often supplement this individualistic model with macro-sociological analysis that sees people as compelled to relocate as part of the social and economic realities – notably uneven development – associated with the world economic system (Portes and Borocz 1989; Castles and Miller 1998).

Rather than concentrating on Israelis' difficulties in adjustment and feelings of displacement, this perspective emphasizes the many resources that Israelis use to facilitate their relatively easy adaptation to host societies. These include cultural and occupational skills, networks, and relatives in host societies, as well as the high level of social, political and economic cooperation between Israel and major hostlands like the US, Canada and Great Britain (Sobel 1986).

In contrast to the Israeli-based perspective, the migration studies model does not emphasize a special relationship between a person's ethnic or national identity and a particular nation state. While Zionism argues that Israel is the true, historical homeland for all Jews, the migration studies view suggests that ideally, people should be able to freely choose their place of residence according to their own prerogatives and available opportunities, and that any one nation is as good as another. For example, economist Jorge Borjas (1990; 1996) asserts that nations compete in a world market for the most economically desirable (skilled and productive) migrants.

Transnationalism and cultural diasporas

Finally, a third perspective on the experience of Israeli emigrants emphasizes their ability to combine resources, networks and identities available from multiple locations in order to maximize their freedom and independence from the confines of any one nation state and to minimize obligations and limitations connected with patriotism, citizenship, military service, religious or cultural projects, racial hierarchies, gender ideologies, restrictions on sexuality and the like. This perspective is associated with the recent scholarly concern with transnationalism. Most transnational writing has addressed the experience of "postcolonial" groups, including African-origin peoples, South Asians and Latin Americans who have worked to develop fields of social membership that transcend the limited options available either in ancestral countries of origin, or diasporic settings where they are subject to cultural isolation, racialization and economic exploitation (Appadurai 1996; Portes 2001).

In contrast to the more conventional definition of diaspora associated with a long history of dispersion from a single homeland, and essentialized, primordial notions of identity, postmodern scholars discuss what Cohen (1997) refers to as cultural diasporas. These involve fluid bases of identity in which points of origin and settlement become blurred and associated with loose, multiple connections to various groups, settings and practices. Cultural diasporas and transnationalism draw upon the language of diaspora and the feelings of displacement and cosmopolitanism associated with it. However, unlike established studies of diaspora, this new paradigm does not privilege fixed relations with coethnics and a single homeland. Rather, it emphasizes the feelings of alienation, and new identities and subjectivities generated as individuals and groups cross borders of culture, nation, ideology, gender and imagined community (Safran 1999: 284).

Transnationalism and cultural diasporas are grounded in environments variously called transnational social spaces, transnational communities or transnational fields. Such environments are not fixed in geography. Rather, they include people and networks in points of origin and settlement who exchange outlooks, expectations, resources, and agendas that are a product of their unique interaction and experience (Faist 2000). For example, Dominican and Mexican communities in both the country of origin and the US are bonded by common styles of consumption, political agendas and even gender roles. Their transnational social fields include persons who have never traveled, because these network members are immersed in social and economic environments and forms of subjectivity that are produced by migration (Goldring 1998; Smith 1998; Hirsch 1999; Levitt 2001a). In order to make this rather amorphous, if creative, concept more concrete, Portes *et al.* (1999: 219) define transnationalism as "Occupations and activities that require regular and sustained social contacts over time across borders for their implementation." According to this definition, only a fraction of Israeli emigrants are true transnationals. Others, who travel less frequently, fall into the more traditional categories of settlers and sojourners.

For political, cultural and economic reasons, Israelis and Jews (who are often associated with "the West") have not been commonly included in the post-colonial discourse of transnationalism and cultural diasporas, nor have they seen themselves as a part of it. However, given Jews' legacy of dispersion, oppression, marginality and cosmopolitanism, their experience not only corresponds to this position, but in many ways has inspired it. In fact, transnational and diaspora scholarship can be traced to earlier work on middleman minorities, pariah capitalists, cosmopolitans and marginal personalities, all of which drew on the experience of Jews (Wirth 1928; Schuetz 1944; Becker 1956; Simmel 1971; Bonacich 1973; Marx 1978; Weber 1978; Zenner 1991; Reid 1997; Safran 1999).

Accordingly, a growing number of writers have begun to describe the relationship between the Jewish diaspora and the State of Israel in terms of the transnational model (Cohen 1997; Gold 1997; Galchinsky 1998; Sheffer 1998).

> Recent theorists have begun to understand Jews' history and theories of diaspora as crucial to postcolonialism's attempts to subvert identity politics of all kinds . . . The postcolonial adaptations of the concept 'diaspora' emphasize the transnational, hybrid, and fluid communities created by both forced and voluntary migratory flows and suggest that . . . these diasporic communities can be subversive of the brutally homogenizing ideologies and practices of nations and empires.
>
> (Galchinsky 1998: 186)

Taking an anti-Zionist position, Boyarin and Boyarin (1993: 719) contend that Zionism is both ethically flawed – because it yields the unequal treatment of Gentiles, especially Palestinians – and a violation of "Rabbinic Judaism." Instead, they posit permanent commitment to life in the diaspora as a means of sustaining Judaism and supporting tolerant and multicultural societies. While committed to the diaspora, they strongly reject assimilation, which was often a major goal of diaspora Jews prior to the Holocaust, and which continues on as a reality in contemporary Jewish life (Patai 1971; Kosmin 1991; Kadish 1998). Moreover, while Boyarin and Boyarin renounce the creation of a Jewish nation state, they do not repudiate Jews' connections with the Land of Israel:

> [If] Jews are to give up hegemony over the Land, this does not mean that the profundity of our attachment to the Land can be denied. This must also have a political expression in the present, in the provision of the possibility for Jews to live a Jewish life in a Palestine not dominated by one ethnic group or another.
>
> (Boyarin and Boyarin 1993: 715)

While Boyarin and Boyarin reject Zionism, other writers privilege neither the diaspora nor the Jewish State, but instead, put both settings on equal footing as important and interdependent spaces for Jewish life. For example, Galchinsky (1998) contends that both Israel and the diaspora offer challenges to and benefits for Jews, and that involvement in both settings offers the greatest possibilities for connecting with the full diversity and intensity of Jewish life. Like other writers with transnational leanings, Reginé Azria suggests that modern technology allows contemporary identities to transcend the boundaries of time and space that once made nation states constraining and confining. Because of easy, affordable and rapid international communication and travel, the distinction between Israel and the diaspora is no longer very important.

> Thus, today, some Jews are simultaneously Israeli Jews and diaspora Jews without being concerned about either this or which passport they carry. They travel around the world simply because they feel like it, or because they need to for professional, academic, family or vacation purposes.
>
> (Azria 1998: 24)

Similarly, social scientists including Gabriel Sheffer (1986; 1998) and Robin Cohen (1997) assert that whatever the spiritual and ideological implications, interdependent Jewish communities exist both within and beyond Israel, and that individuals, ideas and resources continually oscillate between them. "Decades after Israel's independence it is still not clear which is the dominant component in world Jewry" (Sheffer 1998: 10). Gold (1997; 1999) and Gold and Phillips (1996a) have described Israeli transnationalism as an inevitable by-product of the cultural, economic, familial, institutional and political links between Israel and other Jewish communities.

Given the multiple locations of Jewish life, transnational scholars realize that some Jews and Israelis will maintain on-going links to several settings. Consequently, they conclude that nationalist ideologies that privilege any single location as the center of Jewish life are impractical and exclusive. "Many Israelis and Jews realize that the Israeli diaspora is a now a permanent feature in the nation's existence" (Sheffer 1998: xxviii).

Discussion of perspectives

As this brief summary has shown, literature on Israeli emigration reflects three distinct perspectives, each of which emphasizes contrasting assumptions about where Jews and Israelis should live. Because of the different bases of these bodies of work, to elevate one over others would require celebrating one set of assumptions and value judgments over the other two – an exercise that would contribute little to an inclusive understanding of the topic. To a considerable extent, the experience of Israeli emigrants reflects their relationships with the contexts from which the three per-1spectives have arisen. Accordingly, the tension between these perspectives should be explored, not resolved by fiat. Eclecticism, however, does not preclude critical thinking. As I point out in the following critique, each approach is marked by strengths and weaknesses.

The yordim perspective on Israeli emigrants is richly detailed. Generally written by Israeli scholars who are familiar with the cultural background, formative experiences, language and way of life of émigrés, it reflects the migrants' feelings of loss and separation from the homeland. In my many interviews, I found that these feelings were commonly and spontaneously articulated by emigrants representing a very wide array of social categories including the young and old, the long established and recently arrived, and the affluent and impecunious. As such, these accounts exhibit the real difficulties and feelings of ambivalence that migrants – even economically successful ones – encounter. This issue is too often glossed over in much of the social science literature on migration that often assumes that quantitative descriptions of migrant adaptation are sufficient and self-evident facts, while migrants' personal accounts are less worthy of consideration.

The yordim perspective reminds us that immigration is a process, not an event, and that ties with the country of origin often endure. While popular myths and nation-building ideologies in countries of settlement would have us believe that migrants stop identifying with the country of origin and cast their lot with the host society soon after arrival, historical and contemporary research contains ample evidence of immigrants' longing for home. Moreover, the fact that many immigrants repatriate demonstrates the power of such sentiments. Individually and collectively, Israelis do seem much more concerned with the country of origin than many other immigrant groups, and especially other Jews, who had very low rates of return migration and often did not consider themselves to be members of their societies of origin (Gold and Phillips 1996b). As a case in point, Stanley Waterman writes:

> Comparing Israelis and South African Jewish migrants in London, the Israelis are more likely of the two to engage in return migration . . . most Israeli emigrants will tell you that they still intend to return . . . or hope that their children will. Very few, if any, of the South Africans will echo those sentiments.
>
> (1997: 152)

In addition, because it emphasizes Israelis' *collective* connections with and obligations to the Jewish State, the yordim research offers an instructive and sociological alternative to the individualistic approach of migration studies, and indeed, of social science in general (Bellah *et al*. 1985). Drawing from psychology and neo-classical economics, migration research is heavily immersed in individualistic, cost/reward evaluations of social relationships and human behavior, even if they are examined in aggregate at a macro level. These assumptions make this outlook poorly equipped for dealing with issues of collective loyalty and national membership that are central to understanding Israeli émigrés' feelings of ethnic, national, religious and family connection and identification (Blumer 1958; Zhou and Logan 1989; Portes and Sensenbrenner 1993; Light and Gold 2000). Finally, the historical experiences and values of Israeli society are quite distinct from those of established and secure countries of the West. Most notable of these is the concern with collective survival (Dowty 1998). Accordingly, the meaning of social membership is quite different in Israel than it is in many other nations (Goldscheider 1996). Hence, there are valid reasons for considering Israel emigration as, in important ways, unlike that from other countries.

While yordim studies offer valuable insights, they also have flaws. In depicting Israeli emigration as a social problem, they often downplay the successful adaptation of Israeli emigrants, oversampling pathologies while eschewing accomplishments. In asserting that

Israelis are fundamentally unlike other migrant populations, these authors fail to engage in the sorts of comparisons that would demonstrate Israelis' successful adjustment in relation to that of other migrant groups. In so doing, yordim studies conveniently avoid addressing evidence that detracts from their assertion that Israelis' adaptation is difficult and painful. While some emigrants may be unhappy and disoriented, they are neither poverty stricken nor, as a rule, subject to the harsh treatment confronted by large numbers of contemporary migrants and refugees.

Finally, those who contend that Israel's negative view of emigration is unlike that of other countries are only partly correct. From the perspective of industrialized Western countries where Israelis tend to settle (and to which Israel often compares itself), it is true that emigration is not stigmatized. Yet from the perspective of developing countries and states maintaining ideologies of national liberation and development, emigration – especially by the young, the capable and the well educated – represents both the loss of human capital and a rejection of the national project in favor of personal comfort. Accordingly, such human movement is seen in a negative light and often described as brain drain. (In fairness, Harold Greenberg makes this very point in his book *Israel: Social Problems* [1979].)

An alternative to the yordim perspective is found in migration studies. Rejecting the premise that Israelis are unlike other migrants, this view holds that they bear marked congruity to numerous groups. It follows that the most useful comparisons should be made with groups with whom they share clear similarities, including common levels of skill and education, high rates of entrepreneurship, shared locations of settlement, similar gender patterns and close regional origins (Razin 1991; Bozorgmehr *et al.* 1996; Waterman 1997; Gold 1999).

The findings of this more universalistic and generally more macro level approach are quite different from those produced by the yordim research. Rather than seeing the presence of Israeli emigration as pathological, its authors conceive of it as the predictable outcome of prior events. "One would expect that the major streams of immigration to Israel would produce counterstreams of emigration, if not to the country of origin, then to areas of better economic opportunity" (Goldscheider 1996: 57). While admitting that Israeli émigrés long for home, this reaction is seen as both predictable and common to various groups (Linn and Barkan-Ascher 1996; Gold and Phillips 1996a).

Further, not only is re-migration from Israel likely, from a demographic perspective, it poses little threat to the Jewish State. Rates of emigration "from Israel are relatively unimportant at the societal level and do not threaten the longer-term social demographic consequences of immigration [to Israel]" (Goldscheider 1996: 59). From the migration studies view, the attention given to the subject is the result of its ideological, not demographic consequences. Israeli emigrants "challenge the ideological basis of one form of Zionism that negates the viability of Jewish communities outside of Israel. When native-born Israelis of the third generation emigrate, the ideological challenge intensifies" (Goldscheider 1996: 59).

Moreover, in contrast to the social pathology perspective offered in yordim scholarship, the migration studies approach sees Israelis as well-adjusted members of host Jewish communities. Writing in the *Harvard Encyclopedia of American Ethnic Groups*, Goren (1980: 597) states: Israelis "have successfully established themselves in the professional life of the greater society and have contributed to the Jewish community as teachers and communal functionaries." Reports from South Africa, the UK, the US and Canada characterize Israelis as having made exceptionally successful adjustments. They are well educated, entrepreneurial, prosperous, fluent in English, have high rates of naturalization, make important contributions to economic and cultural life and are likely to reside in comfortable neighborhoods, near other Jews (Frankental nd; Cohen and Gold 1996; Bozorgmehr *et al.* 1996; Waterman 1997; Herman 2000). For example, Israelis are the fifth most affluent and second most entrepreneurial of all nationality groups tabulated in the 1990 US Census (Yoon 1997: 20, 22).

In contrast to 1970s-era yordim literature, more recent studies – including those highly critical of Israeli emigration – have documented the organizational vitality of Israeli emigrant communities in several nations (Rosen 1993; Gold 1994b; Cohen and Gold 1996; Shor 1998; Teitelbaum 2001a). Finally, when put in a comparative context, assertions about Israelis' inhospitable reception by host communities seem quite minor in contrast to the hostile treatment received by many contemporary migrant groups who are the targets of violence, hostile legislation and anti-immigrant social movements (Calavita 1992; Castles and Miller 1998). Moreover, while Jews in and beyond Israel have a long record of aiding newly arrived co-religionists, intergroup relations between greenhorn and veteran have invariably been marked by conflict and tension (Howe 1976; Sowell 1981; Pollins 1984; Markowitz 1994; Hyman 1998; Siegel 1998; Gold 1999). Hence, if Israeli emigrants have sometimes contentious relations with host country Jews, this is hardly a unique pattern (see Chapter 5).

From the vantage point of Western Jewish communities, the migration studies perspective appears more accurate than the social pathology view maintained by Zionists. The emigration of Israelis is highly consistent with a large body of knowledge about migration and demography. People with a personal history of migration are likely to continue to migrate. This is especially the case for Jews, who have extensive contacts with sizable and secure coethnic communities abroad. According to the owner of one of Israel's largest international shipping companies,

> Israelis are considered people who adapt to new surroundings with record speed. They learn new languages quickly, they are mobile, and there is an Israeli community in every large Western city that helps them acclimatize. The Israelis are migrants in their souls.
>
> (Shavit 2001: 8)

The Zionist ideology, while powerful, is not strong enough to convince every Israeli that life outside the Jewish State is intolerable. Instead, a considerable number of foreign and native-born Israelis continue to move overseas for a variety or reasons.

As noted above, a strength of the migration studies tradition is that it emphasizes comparative research, which allows us to contrast the experience of Israeli emigrants with that of other migrant populations. While this provides many useful insights, at the same time it is based upon the idea of universalism. In recent years, a growing body of criticism has attacked universalism as a tool for exploring culturally diverse groups. The critique's first claim is that universalism is impossible since supposedly universal assumptions, values and ideas about humanity are not universal at all, but lodged in the cultural traditions and ideologies of specific groups while absent from the worldviews of others (Smith 1990; Marcus 1995). A second criticism asserts that it is inappropriate to examine anything as unique as Israeli emigration – embedded in the Jewish religion, the singular history of the Jewish people, Zionism, and anti-Semitism – from a universalistic perspective. Since Israel's very existence can be attributed to the distinguishing experience of the Jewish people, we can go only so far in examining it from a perspective of universalism. Suffice it to say that migration studies appears to embrace universalism while the yordim perspective is more committed to essentialism. Depending on how used, each can enlighten or obscure.

Our third perspective, that of transnationalism and cultural diasporas, offers several valuable insights into Israeli emigration. One advantage of this approach is that it is broadly synthetic. While yordim studies emphasize the micro dimensions of Israeli emigration, the migration studies perspective highlights macroeconomic factors, such as opportunities for jobs or education in host societies. However, transnational approaches consider both macroeconomics and phenomenology in their examination of human movement (Basch *et al.* 1994; Gold 1997; Faist 2000; Portes 2001). Similarly, while yordim studies see Israel as the appropriate setting for Israelis, the migration studies approach suggests that Israeli émigrés would receive the greatest economic rewards in the highly developed nations that are the centers of the global economy (DellaPergola 1992; Massey *et al.* 1993). However, the transnational/cultural diaspora perspective understands that Israelis may reap social and economic benefits by maintaining social relationships with multiple settings and membership statuses (Portes 1995b; Levitt 1998; Kivisto 2001).

While raising important issues and generating insight, some versions of transnationalism are marked by problems as well. Much work on transnationalism and cultural diasporas emphasizes abstract motives such as subverting identity politics and "deploying imaginations" as the major engines of migration (Appadurai 1996: 5). As suggested by the following quote, some texts are plagued by hyperbole:

> [B]y means of strategies of transnational mobility, Chinese have eluded, taken tactical advantage of, temporized before, redefined, and overcome the disciplining of modern regimes of colonial empires, postcolonial nation states, and international capitalism. These mobile practices have intersected with the imposition of modern regimes of truth and knowledge to take the form of a guerrilla transnationalism.
>
> (Nonini and Ong 1997: 19)

One may ask how often do such esoteric motives or enigmatic practices actually enter the minds of migrants planning their lives? In contrast to this finding, both my own research and a broad body of scholarship on migration suggests that much more practical matters having to do with getting an education, earning a living, maintaining family relationships or avoiding mistreatment are foremost in migrants' minds when they decide where they wish to live (Sobel 1986; Massey *et al.* 1993; Hondagneu-Sotelo 1994; Portes and Rumbaut 1996; Gold 1997; Levitt 2001a).

Moreover, despite their references to Marxist formulations such as exploitation and global capitalism, several styles of transnational theorizing fix on the social psychological aspects of migration – subjectivities, identities and imagined communities – while neglecting the structural basis of resources that are required to accomplish goals in the real world. For example, a recent article contends, "Through transnational processes everyday people can generate creole identities and agencies that challenge multiple levels of structural control" (Mahler 1998: 68). However, as Guarnizo and Smith (1998: 11) point out, "transnational practices cannot be construed as if they were free from the constraints and opportunities that contextuality imposes." It is clear that the transnational approach generates valuable insights and brings up a whole range of new processes for scholarly consideration. At the same time, as an emerging outlook it requires further refinement. Finally, as Portes (2001) notes, only a relatively small fraction of contemporary migrants are transnationals. The status of a significant majority is accurately depicted by existing categories of settlers, sojourners, refugees and the like. Hence, while innovative and instructive, theories of transnationalism often overstate the extent to which border-crossing populations are involved in this pattern.

In sum, each of the three perspectives have their own merits and flaws. Moreover, they reflect distinct ideological and national positions, and accordingly, are concerned with distinct sets of issues. Rather than attempting to prove the superiority of one approach over others, I will apply them eclectically as warranted, in order to best understand the topics under discussion.

Identifying Israelis

In order to reflect upon the experience of Jewish Israeli emigrants, one must first identify those whom he or she intends to study. This is no easy matter, as Israeli demographer Sergio DellaPergola has remarked "the problem of 'Who is an Israeli' is no less and probably quite more complex than the issue 'Who is a Jew.'" (Gold and Phillips 1996a: 51). There are three ways to become an Israeli, which is a necessary prerequisite for becoming an Israeli emigrant. The first is to make aliyah or move to Israel from another nation. The second way to become an Israeli is to be born there. Native-born Jews are identified as sabras, in contrast to this young nation's many foreign-born citizens. In turn, established immigrants are vatikim while recent arrivals are olim. The third way is to be born outside of Israel to Israeli parents. This basis of identification is transnational in that it reflects the reality of a growing number of migrants in the world today – Jews and Israelis among them – who maintain strong connections to one nation state while residing in another. While such persons may be legally citizens of their country of birth, many Jewish and Israeli leaders as well as their own parents think of them as Israelis. In fact, the Israeli Bureau of Statistics estimates that 100,000 Israelis have been born abroad (*For Those Returning Home* 1995). For example, a study of the Jewish population of Los Angeles found that while the city is home to about 14,000 sabras, 26,200 people in the study claimed to be of Israeli nationality (Herman 1998: 14; Herman 2000). These include former residents of Israel as well as children of immigrants and spouses of Israelis with minimal connection to the Jewish State.

Another definitional issue involves the distinction between temporary visitors – tourists, students and scholars spending time at educational institutions, business travelers and government emissaries – and longer-term settlers (who may themselves eventually return to Israel after spending more than a decade abroad, perhaps to leave again). Like co-nationals with a longer tenure in the host society, short-term residents are often active participants in émigré communities. In fact, several informants in London told us that they had learned to avoid building deep relationships with short-term co-nationals because they find it deeply depressing to lose a valued friend when his/her two-year assignment is complete.

For the purpose of this study, Israeli émigrés are defined as those who identify themselves as such. Non-Israeli family members as well as children born in countries of settlement are also included if they are active participants in the Israeli emigrant community.

Demographics of Israeli emigration

In any study of migration, questions regarding the numbers and characteristics of the populations involved always arise. Without this kind of information, it is difficult to determine who is migrating, the size of the groups involved, the impact on countries of origin and settlement, prospects for adjustment, patterns of selective emigration, motives for emigration and other issues. However, while such information is useful, for a variety of technical reasons, the enumeration of migrants is subject to difficulty (Heer 1968; Anderson and Fienberg 1999). Because of these contingencies, scholars of migration are accustomed to studying immigrant populations with imperfect data.

That being said, debates about the size of Israeli emigrant populations tend to be more pervasive and heated than those linked with most other groups. Academics, journalists and communal activists affiliated with Israel, host societies and émigré communities continue to dispute these estimates, commonly claiming that the local population is three to four times as large as indicated by census or survey-based tabulations (Herman and LaFontaine 1983; Herman 1988; 1994; Gold and Phillips 1996a; Cohen and Haberfeld 1997; Cohen 1999). Despite the manifold ideological and religious controversies associated with Israeli emigration, by far the most contentious issue surrounding this group involves estimates of their numbers in diaspora communities.

It is certainly important to obtain sound demographic data about Israeli émigré communities. However, this study is not a demographic report. It draws most heavily from interviews and fieldwork in various Israeli émigré communities. Accordingly, the following brief outline of Israeli population characteristics is intended to be descriptive, not definitive. I attempt to use the best data available from respected demographers, while also acknowledging the limitations in existing demographic information about Israeli émigré populations.

To save time and space, I sometimes rely on US-based tabulations of Israeli emigrants' social characteristics as a general representation of the entire émigré populations' characteristics. While recognizing the problems inherent in this approach, I do this because the US population is the largest group of Israeli emigrants, US data are the most detailed available, and because a precedent for this kind of generalization exists: English demographers Schmool and Cohen (1998) adjust their estimates of Israelis in the UK according to figures derived from the US census. I encourage readers with special interests in the demographics of Israeli emigration to consult the web site of the Israeli Central Bureau of Statistics[3] as well as various studies on this topic cited in the bibliography (Eisenbach 1989; DellaPergola 1992; Dubb 1994; Herman 1994; 1998; 2000; Cohen 1996; Gold and Phillips 1996a; Goldscheider 1996; Cohen and Haberfeld 1997; Schmool and Cohen 1998).

Population estimates

The 1990 US Census enumerated 144,000 people living in Hebrew-speaking homes "almost all of which can be assumed to be Israeli" (Fishkoff 1994). According to the British Census, there were 12,195 Israeli-born persons in the UK in 1991. However, because Israel's population includes numbers of people who were not born there, the number born in Israel accounts for only a fraction of all Israeli Jews in England. Using the ratio of Israeli-born to all Hebrew speakers determined in the US Census, Schmool and Cohen (1998: 30) estimate that approximately 27,000 Israelis live in England.

Drawing from South African census data, Dubb (1994: 17) estimated that the legal-resident Israeli population of South Africa in 1991 was 9,634. France has a significant population of Israelis, many of whom trace their ancestry to former French colonies in North Africa. Because of their possession of French citizenship, or their birth outside of Israel, only a small fraction of these are enumerated in the French Census. Based on official national population censuses, the figures for Israeli citizens permanently living in France were 3,500 in 1981 and 2,900 in 1990 (Council of Europe 1998; DellaPergola 2000). According to the 1996 Canadian Census, 21,965 Canadian residents indicated that they possessed Israeli citizenship, regardless of their country of birth. Finally, the 1996 Australian Census enumerated 5,923 Hebrew-speaking people in Australia.

It would be incorrect to assume that Israelis in these points of settlement will remain permanently. Rather, data suggest that a significant fraction of Israeli emigrants eventually return (*For Those Returning Home* 1995; Cohen 1996; Chabin 1997). In fact, the "failure to consider Israeli's high rates of return migration may be one of the reasons for the popular perception that the number of Israelis" overseas is as high as assumed (Cohen and Haberfeld 1997: 200).

Age, sex and family composition

Israeli emigrants are a young population. The 1990 US census shows that 79 percent of Israelis in New York and 70 percent of Israelis in Los Angeles were under age 44. On both US coasts, there were more males than females. New York's community was 55 percent male, while Los Angeles' was 54 percent male. A 1990 survey of Jews in greater New York City found that 67 percent of Israeli emigrants were part of married couple families, a fraction that exceeds other foreign-born and native-born Jews (Horowitz 1993). Fifty-five percent of Israeli households in New York City consist of a married couple with children under age 18 (Horowitz 1993). Similarly, over 50 percent of Israelis in England are married (Schmool and Cohen 1998: 30). Finally, Cohen (1999: 129) reports that 94 percent of Israelis in Toronto live in husband-wife families. At the same time, New York-based Israelis' divorce rate – of between 2 and 5 percent – is lower than for other New York Jews, whose rate of divorce is 10 percent. Finally, Israelis tend to have larger families than American Jews (Ritterband 1986: 120–1).

Occupational characteristics

Journalistic reports sometimes depict Israeli emigrants as employed in menial occupations, such as cab drivers or furniture movers (Ben-Ami 1992; Sabar 1996). However, every study based on systematic analysis of census or survey data demonstrates that emigrants are far more educated and skilled than Israelis generally, and among the very most highly educated of all arrivals in countries of settlement. Moreover, this trend is long-standing and has been observed for several decades (Toren 1980). Analyzing 1980 US Census data, Zvi Eisenbach (1989: 261) found that among Israelis in the States, "education is much higher than among the relevant source population [Israelis] . . . [and] also much higher than among the white population there." Yinon Cohen (1996: 78) agrees, stating "regardless of the data and methodology used, Israeli Jewish immigrants in the US were found to be more educated and to hold higher status occupations than both US and Israeli populations." Drawing from US Immigration and Naturalization Service data, Herman and LaFontaine (1983: 63) found that "over 70 percent of employed Israeli immigrants work at white collar occupations . . .; of these, about half are professional, technical and kindred workers (doctors, engineers, etc.). Only five percent are employed as service workers." UK Census data reveal that Israeli emigrants in Britain are also marked by high levels of education and occupational prestige. "The Israeli-born form a skilled professional work-force, 56 percent were in professional, management or technical occupations" (Schmool and Cohen 1998: 30).

While Israeli emigrants are already a highly educated group, they tend to further improve their educational credentials while abroad (Toren 1980; Rosenthal and Auerbach 1992; Schmool and Cohen 1998). Their emigration is, to a high degree, economically motivated. "Emigration rates of Jews from Israel are thus governed almost solely by the economic conditions in Israeli and potential receiving countries" (Cohen 1996: 76).

Ethnic and national origins

Drawing from 1980 Census data, Paul Ritterband (1986: 121) reported that in New York City, 16 percent of Israeli-born immigrants were of Mid-East or North African ancestry. Forty-five percent of Rosenthal's (1989: 64) respondents from Brooklyn and Queens reported themselves as Ashkenazi, 42 percent as Sephardic/Oriental and 13 percent as a mixture of both. Herman and Lafontaine (1983: 102) found that 58 percent of naturalized Israelis in Los Angeles were of Ashkenazi origins while 37 percent were Sephardic/Oriental, and 2 percent were mixed. Herman (2000) found a similar distribution in 1997: 53 percent of the Israeli born populations percent were Ashkenazi while 38 percent were Sephardic.[4]

About 20 percent of Israel's population is made of up of non-Jewish Arabs (otherwise known as Palestinians) and a fraction of Arab Israelis have also gone abroad. One demographer estimated that about 27,000 Israeli Arabs left between 1949 and 1979 (Cohen 1996: 77). While relatively little research has been conducted on this group, existing reports suggest that they reveal many similarities to Jewish Israelis, including lofty educational profiles, settlement in major cities of North and South America and Australia and a very high level of self-employment. Arab emigrants from Israel tend to be Christian, and are unlikely to return (Cohen 1988; 1989; 1996).

Research methods

Sources of data

Data for this book were collected in the form of in-depth interviews and participant observation fieldwork with Israeli immigrants in several settings. A major source was 194 interviews (conducted in both Hebrew and English) with a socially diverse sample of Israeli immigrants and others knowledgeable about their community in Los Angeles between 1991 and 1996. In addition, interviews with thirty returned migrants were conducted in Israel in 1996, 1997 and 2000. We interviewed fifty Israelis in London between 1998 and 2000, and fourteen in Paris in 1999. Finally, Naama Sabar generously provided her transcriptions of interviews with twenty-four Kibbutzniks living in Los Angeles. Most interviews were tape-recorded, translated into English (if conducted in Hebrew) and transcribed. All names of respondents in this report are pseudonyms.

To supplement in-depth interviews, we also conducted participant observation research at a variety of religious and secular community activities and other Israeli settings such as parties, restaurants, Israeli-oriented synagogues, schools, youth programs, shops and the pool of a San Fernando Valley apartment complex with many Israeli residents. We visited numerous meetings of communal organizations in Los Angeles and London as well as Yom Hatzmaut (Israeli Independence Day) festivals in Los Angeles and Detroit. While our most intensive data collection was conducted in Los Angeles, London, Paris and Israel, we also did interviewing and fieldwork among Israelis in New York and Detroit. In addition, the sample includes Israelis who have lived in Argentina, Australia, Holland, Hong Kong, the Philippines, Japan, Italy, South Africa and Canada. Their accounts inform us about Israeli emigrant communities in these settings. Field observations were recorded in written field notes and sometimes with photography. We also conducted a descriptive survey with a separate sample of Los Angeles Israeli migrants (N = 100) at various Israeli community events and in neighborhoods where Israelis frequently congregate (Gold 1994a).

Referrals to subjects were obtained from a variety of sources, including Jewish communal agencies, Israeli Consulates in several cities, representatives of various Israeli associations, published lists of Israeli organizations and ethnic businesses, and snowball referrals (whereby the people we interviewed referred us to additional respondents from their social networks). To facilitate rapport and openness, we did not use a closed-end questionnaire. However, questions were selected from prepared lists of interview issues (Gold 1994b). Interview quotes are presented directly from interview transcripts (with most grammatical errors intact) in order to reflect the speech patterns of respondents. Pseudonyms are used throughout to protect interviewees' identities. Unless otherwise specified, the quotations used throughout the book were selected because they represented what appeared to be a widely held position among the respondent population.

We sought to contact respondents who would represent various social subgroups and categories. Because visible activists, professionals and self-employed business people are among the established elite of the Israeli emigrant community, we also interviewed the recently arrived and those of humble means to gain a more rounded picture of the population. Our sample intentionally includes Israelis from a variety of backgrounds – including Ashkenazi, Mizrahi (Yemenite, Iraqi, Turkish, Moroccan, Syrian, Egyptian and Persian), Kibbutzniks, persons from multinational families (Israeli/American, Israeli/French, Israeli/Canadian, Israeli/British, etc.) and those maintaining both secular and religious orientations, and right- and left-wing ideologies.

Long-term and in-depth contacts with Los Angeles' Israeli population, together with the results of data collected by the US Census, Jewish Population Surveys and feedback from Jewish and Israeli community leaders, give us a degree of certainty regarding the size and nature of this population. However, even in this setting, there is some reason to question the inclusiveness of our sample. Population estimates are imprecise and Israelis are especially difficult to identify because, beyond fluency in Hebrew, they lack distinctive names or other defining social features, and a sizable proportion were not born in the Jewish State. For these reasons, extensive reliance upon random sample surveys would be impractical. Accordingly, involvement in Israeli émigré networks became a major means of identifying and contacting Israelis. However, given the diversity of the Israeli population, members of one subgroup of Israelis may have very limited connection with others, to the point that they may be all but unaware of their existence. We made concerted efforts to contact diverse subgroups, but cannot be sure how inclusive or representative our sample is.

While I devised the interview guides and conducted most of the interviews in Los Angeles, five Israeli women and one Hebrew-speaking American woman did extensive interviewing and fieldwork in Los Angeles, London, Paris and Israel. In all cases but one, these researchers were themselves involved in or had completed graduate training in social science fields and were involved in their own scholarly research about the experience of Israeli emigrants. Fluent in Hebrew, well versed in the study of migration and ethnicity and themselves part of Israeli emigrant communities, they had excellent rapport with the communities they were studying and offered many insights into their characteristics and dynamics. Their keen observations were invaluable to my understanding of Israeli emigrants and the communities they create. As women, they had access to and comprehension of aspects of the Israeli emigrant community, that I, an American man, did not. At the same time, because I was a non-Israeli, community members may have felt free to express certain perspectives to me that they might have not shared with co-nationals. Hence, by relying on multiple methods and a team of field researchers characterized by diversity in terms of age, gender and nationality, I sought to generate a well-rounded view of Israeli emigration and return.

Plan of the book

Chapter 2 summarizes Israelis' motives for exit, especially in light of their involvement in ethnic networks. Chapter 3 reviews Israeli émigrés' approaches to supporting themselves. Much of the discussion concerns forms of economic cooperation involving Israelis and established Jews. Chapter 4 addresses the gender and family patterns of Israeli émigrés in communities of settlement as well as their connections with relatives in Israel and other countries. Chapter 5 describes communal life among Israeli emigrants in various settings. While Israeli émigrés often live and work with diaspora Jews, many prefer to interact with co-nationals. The strongest links are among subgroups of Israelis who share commonalties of religious outlook, gender, ethnicity, ideology, background and cohort of arrival. Chapter 6 considers Israeli emigrants' religious, ethnic and national identities. Finally, Chapter 7 examines the experience of return and draws conclusions.

2
MOTIVES FOR ISRAELI EMIGRATION

From self-evident to problematic

Largely neglected within the vast literature on international migration is the topic of motives. Until recently, migrants' motives were not seen as deserving of extensive examination because they were so easily explained by existing social science theories, common-sense thinking and national ideologies. The principles of self-improvement and self-preservation were seen as the driving force behind international migration. People leave one country and settle in another to improve their standard of living and enjoy a better life (O'Sullivan See and Wilson 1988: 231; Borjas 1990). In the remaining cases, people are forced to depart because of social or political upheaval, oppression or natural disaster. Finally, people may travel abroad because they are attached to a family or other social unit (village, social movement) that has migrated (Peterson 1958; Lee 1966).

Recently, the question of migrants' motives has become a much more interesting and challenging one as the number and diversity of migrating populations has expanded. Explanations involving obvious self-improvement still hold sway for many. However, new sets of migrants appear to be leaving home for reasons that defy ready explanation. For example, current research reveals that employed, middle-class migrants sometimes give up the relative security, stability and clear-cut roles of their countries of origin for the uncertain rewards, low rank jobs, undocumented legal standing and ethnic minority status (occasionally to work as inner city entrepreneurs) in host societies (Ong *et al.* 1994; Margolis 1994; Lessinger 1995; Bates 1997; Min 1998). Massey *et al.* (1993) note that rural Mexican families sometimes send members to work in the US (an undertaking that involves a substantial risk of financial loss, bodily harm and incarceration) not necessarily to increase their income, but rather, in pursuit of a much more subtle end: to "control risks to their well-being by diversifying the allocation of household resources" (Massey *et al*. 1993: 436).

Established assumptions about the motives of migration have also been brought into question because many contemporary migrants reveal patterns of travel, settlement and adaptation that violate the basic premises of the "sojourner-settler model" (Pessar 1997; Gold 2000). Given the rapidity and low cost of international communication and travel, changing economic conditions and people's growing familiarity with the cultures of many countries, it is increasingly evident that many forms of migration involve neither a single voyage resulting in permanent settlement, nor a temporary stay abroad for the purpose of work. Instead, growing numbers of people travel across borders on multiple occasions, for various reasons, while retaining affiliations with multiple groups and settings (Basch *et al*. 1994; Findlay 1995; Appadurai 1996; Portes *et al*. 1999; Gold 2000). For these reasons, motives for contemporary migration would appear less transparent than those cited during earlier periods.

Finally, making matters even more complex, our understandings of the personal experience of migration have recently become much more subtle and humane than those prevalent in previous times. This is because numbers of migration experts – social scientists, journalists and the employees of policy-making agencies – have become less explicitly racist, andocentric and jingoistic. As a consequence, they are more attuned to the voices and aspirations of migrants themselves. Rather than paternalistically imputing motives and perspectives to today's migrants, at least some scholars, activists and policy makers actually listen to migrants' reflections about their experience (Foner *et al*. 2000). Generally, such accounts include mixed feelings.

Scholars informed by these new understandings of the complexity of migrants' motives have not jettisoned established models. Rather, recent and established approaches have generally been synthesized, so that contemporary scholarship on migration addresses both traditional concerns – such as the economic incentives for migration – as well as more contemporary topics, including the ways in which subjective, contextual, cultural, and identificational issues are implicated as people cross national borders. Scholars in various disciplines now discuss a much wider variety of factors as shaping patterns of migration to and adaptation in new settings – ranging from macro-level social processes, to gendered economic strategies, to the invention of new group identities and communities (Faist 2000).

Understanding Israeli emigration

Israeli emigrants rank among those contemporary groups whose motives for migration have been especially complex and ideologically loaded. Complex because Israelis generally possess skills, resources, social ties and aspirations that connect them with both Israel and their countries of settlement; ideologically loaded because, as noted in the last chapter, their travel abroad is considered to have profound implications for the legitimacy and demographic viability of their homeland (Sobel 1986; Shokeid 1988; Sabar 1989; 1996). As William Peterson (1958) noted long ago, there is little evidence to suggest that human beings are predisposed either to settlement or constant migration. Accordingly, assertions about the inevitability of settlement are especially problematic with regard to Jews, who have a singular history of geographical mobility (DellaPergola 1994).

Contemporary social science offers three approaches for understanding migrants' motives. The first is the micro tradition. It attends to the accounts that migrating individuals and groups present to explain their behavior. The second approach is macrosociological. It documents the large-scale political, economic, social and environmental developments that encourage or require large groups of people to leave one place for another. The third approach focuses on networks. It emphasizes the links that migrating people or institutions can access in locations of settlement. The network approach is the most synthetic of the three perspectives because it generally addresses the widest array of factors, ranging from ties maintained within specific families, to patterns of economic, political and cultural engagement between world regions.

In my opinion, each of the three approaches offers valuable insights into Israeli emigrants' motives, but no one model is conclusive. In keeping with C. Wright Mills' (1959) famous injunction for sociologists to attend to both history *and* biography (or in other words, broad trends and personal circumstances) in exploring social phenomena, this chapter explores Israelis' motives for emigration in terms of evidence mobilized within the three traditions – micro, macro and network – cited above.

The micro tradition: migrants explain their motives

Much existing research on Israelis' motives for migration has applied ethnographic and/or open-ended survey methods (Sobel 1986; Shokeid 1988; 1993; Uriely 1994; 1995; Sabar 2000). This study collected these types of data as well. When asked why they came to the hostland, most Israelis referred to one of three overlapping responses – economic opportunities (including education), family factors and a need for broader horizons. Others described their presence in the diaspora as a reaction against the social constraints or limitations inherent in living in a small and isolated country. Finally, a third group discussed issues associated with disillusionment, discrimination or a search for meaning and connectedness.

David offers a typical explanation, describing how his short-term plans to get an education turned into a permanent stay, and how his ties to Israel actually extended his tenure in the US:

> I came here about 18 years ago. It was in 1975, right after the Yom Kippur War. I went to UCLA for about a year and a half. I had no money, so I worked and went to school, studying economics. I didn't know if I wanted to stay at that time or not. The thing is, I might have gone back to Israel. However, every time I called, all my friends said "Don't come back, there's nothing happening here." So I stayed another year and then I met my wife and that's how I started. I got into the clothing business and I stayed. Since then, I haven't done anything but clothing. That's all I've done.

Yossi, who now works as a building contractor, alludes both to "broadening his horizons" and increasing economic opportunities as he describes his desire to come to the US:

> I came here in February '78 as a student. Back in Israel, I see and hear so much about America and I figure America is somehow the final place in the progression of the world. Whatever happens in the world, somehow, America has a good hand in it. And so I decide that maybe it is the main source and I want to learn about America and open up my mind. And also, back home, there was not adequate opportunities.

A fairly large number, generally women and children, came to accompany husbands and fathers who sought economic betterment and educational opportunity (Lipner 1987; Kimhi 1990). In the words of Rachel:

> For most of the people that came here, the men came and the women came after them. Like when I came, my husband came for a job. I had to leave my job and I had to find a new job and it was very painful. I think now there are women

coming on their own, but if you look at most cases, it is the men coming after jobs and it means that the women are the ones that have to take care of finding an apartment, finding schools for kids. As a result, they get depressed, very badly depressed.

In a similar manner, an Israeli teenager described moving to Los Angeles with her parents:

NARDIT: No, I am not angry with my parents because it's something that they like to do. The major thing that was difficult for me was that for 16 years, I was educated in a certain way. I was in a certain kind of mood and atmosphere. All the education system was toward your country, toward patriotism. You were taught about wars and about great leaders. And suddenly you come here and it's like a slap because here it's all materialistic. You don't learn about leaders in the schools, you don't learn service in the schools. You don't learn the Bible in the school. And it's very contradictive to everything I known before.

Another family-based reason for immigration was for unification with relatives already living overseas. In a chain-migration process, several respondents were influenced by contacts in host societies who initially made them consider moving and, once they did, facilitated their adjustment. Such links included the presence of friends and/or relatives in countries of settlement and having been stationed in western countries as employees of international or Israeli companies (Sobel 1986; Shokeid 1988).

Family relations often provide Israeli emigrants with legal status in a host society, thus making their migration there that much easier. Such was the case for a couple I interviewed in London. They met on a Kibbutz when both were passionately committed to Israel. However, as time went on, they began to desire a change of scene. Through family connections, both had legal resident status in the UK and knew English. As is often the case among Israeli émigrés, their initial plans to stay for a short period kept getting extended. They now acknowledge that their settlement may be permanent:

I was originally born in a kibbutz and all my three children were born in a kibbutz. We came here at the end of 1984, for maybe a year. We didn't come because we didn't like Israel. We came to try [life here]. We realized that the kibbutz life –

although very nice and beautiful and everything else – in a way, it is suffocating. You know exactly where you are going to be when you're 50, 60.

The kibbutz gave us six weeks' time to visit my husband's family in England, which was very nice and generous – they paid for it. But then we realized that [because of limited resources] it will be every ten, twenty years that we can visit our family. So we took a leave of absence. We were both very happy in the kibbutz. I think happier than here, all in all.

Ideally, if we could afford to have a small place in Israel and maintain this [house in London] as the family unit here, it would be great. But we don't really know. I mean, you pay a price for staying and I'm aware of it. You can pay the same price back in Israel in a kibbutz and your children are scattered all over the world. It's a free society today and everybody goes their own direction.

Couples wherein the husband or wife was a native of the host society are well represented within the Israeli émigré population, the result of a relatively high rate of marriage between Israelis and host-society Jews (Shokeid 1988). In his survey of naturalized Israelis in Los Angeles, Herman (1988: 20) found that of the 80 percent who were married, 35 percent were married to American Jews. (Of the remainder, 49 percent were married to other Israelis, 8 percent to European or South American Jews and 8 percent to non-Jews.) As the following quote suggests, marriages between Israelis and host-country Jews can foster immigration among the extended families of those involved:

My older brother met his wife in Israel. She is American. After they got married, she wasn't willing to stay in Israel. All of her family was here [in Los Angeles]. And he followed her back here to the United States. He solicited me many times to join him after I finished at Technion [an Israeli College of Engineering]. I said "What the heck, maybe I should? Life is short and why not get this experience?" Basically we planned to be here for two or three years. But we are now in the seventh year and it looks like now we are going to stay.

Another reason for emigration was to escape from a bad relationship. A London restaurant owner explains this:

I had a disappointing love affair . . . laughing (embarrassed). I had a relationship – a very close relationship actually before

I came here. I met her, and we became very close and it was assumed that we would get married. I didn't want us to become any closer. I got out of it and came here. It's a complicated story. We met in the army, and then slept together . . . and that is it. I came here to get away from all that.

Among a certain group of Israelis who were self-employed prior to emigration and retained their entrepreneurial pursuits beyond the Jewish State, their motives were clear and direct: Western countries are simply better locations for capitalistic endeavors (Uriely 1994; Gold 1994a). This is reflected in the following exchanges, the first with Nissan, a garment manufacturer in Los Angeles, and the second with Dan, a restaurant owner in London:

NISSAN: For the people who were in business in Israel, you don't even have to ask. We just know that they came to do business. America is a better country for business. Less regulations, taxes and controls. They want you to do some business. Israel, it's too much socialism.

DAN: In Israel, I owned the first pub in Petah-Tikva. I had the pub for two years and it was really difficult. It was very successful, but it was all work and very hard work around the clock. I thought having a pub would mean going to work at 7 p.m. and cleaning up at 3 a.m. The reality was different. It was working twenty-four hours per day. It wasn't only the first pub in the area, but also the biggest – 300 places and a stage for performers, so I had to work before and after the shows. After two years, I sold the place and I took a flight to Japan.

I stayed there for two years. I worked there in the market. I sold watches and other jewelry. I had a company – we bought things from the factory in the country and sold them in Tokyo. The work was easy and we made good profit. We made about $30,000 per month per stall – and I had a few stalls. Life there was very good, everything was incredible. Much better than here [London]. The nightlife was very rich. Tokyo doesn't really sleep at night. There's always something interesting to do.

But after a time, I felt I had enough. There was a lot of quarreling and conflicts among the Israelis in the market, and although I was making tremendous amounts of money, I felt unpleasant there. When things became really unpleasant, we decided it's time to leave.

> We wanted to go to Australia. But because there was a real problem with a work permit and visas in Australia, we decided to try it out here. So we came to London.

Especially in Los Angeles, a fairly large fraction of Israeli emigrants describe their presence outside the Jewish State as being somewhat unintentional, resulting from an extended layover during the international travel – known as "the secular pilgrimage" – that is almost a right of passage for young Israelis who have recently completed their military service (Ben-Ami 1992). Since military duty is compulsory for men and women alike, this pattern of post-duty world travel includes a sizable fraction of the Israeli population.

> I served three years in Lebanon. Then I feel real tired. When I finished the army, I go to vacation. My friend convinced me to come here because we had visas and everything. We came to see Los Angeles for two or three weeks, that's it. But you know what happens here in Los Angeles. You come and you rent a place and then you start to work because you need money to spend, and your life starts running. You don't realize you are here two, three, five, six years. That is what is happening to most of the people here.
>
> All the time, all the Israelis, they keep in their minds, to go back to Israel. But you know, you start to work here, you have a good job, you have a nice house, [then] comes two or three babies and the life is running. All the time [we say], "Next year we are going back."

Disillusionment and limitations

An additional explanation for Israeli emigration is the desire to be outside of the confines of the Jewish State. As C. Wright Mills (1940) points out in his article "Situated Actions and Vocabularies of Motive," groups construct motives for action that are socially acceptable. For supporters of Israel, direct criticism of the Jewish State by those living beyond its borders is seen as disloyal, and as such, is relatively infrequent among émigrés. However, in explaining why they left the Jewish State, some described feelings of disillusionment or a general attitude of not being able fit into the particular social order.

Some Israelis mentioned "burn-out" or unhappiness with the general direction of the country. Such sentiments were more openly discussed following the assassination of Prime Minister Yitzhak Rabin, the election of Benjamin Netanyahu as his successor in 1995–6, and after the start of the Al Aksa Intifada in 2000. Ethnic conflicts were also brought up. Eastern and Sephardic Jews sometimes claimed that ethnic discrimination contributed to their exit, while secular, western-oriented Jews occasionally complained about the increasing power of religion and eastern Jewry in shaping Israel's cultural life. Finally, some émigrés felt out of place – that they simply could not achieve their goals or find their niche in the small nation.

According to an LA-based Israeli psychotherapist with many co-national clients that I interviewed in 1992, one group of disillusioned exiles are war veterans:

> Those who come to my office now are the [result of] the first Lebanon War [in 1982]. This is a wounded group. For them, the idealism, the Zionist goals are gone. Now they are saying "I want to make money. I need time out, [away from] the pressure cooker [atmosphere]. How many more times am I going to go to war? I am sick and tired of going to the army, reserves and everything."

A journalist described his feelings of burn-out rooted in an earlier Middle East conflict:

> Those of us who have been politically involved in the peace camp in Israel usually suffer from battle fatigue. And we say, "Look, I've gone to demonstrations. I've written to politicians. I've debated. I've done it all. It's going nowhere. It's going to self-destruction or whatever. I've had enough. I'm taking a sabbatical."
>
> I left Israel in 1972; ten months before the '73 War. I knew there was going to be another war. I saw no one trying to do anything to prevent it. I'm not going to die for a war that other people are not trying to prevent.

David, a young man who emigrated with his Holocaust survivor parents in the early 1970s, cites the constant threat of violence as his family's motive for exit:

> Why did my parents decide to leave Israel? My father immigrated to Israel in 1949. They went through the war, the [Nazi concentration] camps and everything. [Later] he had a business . . . so he was a very successful entrepreneur. But in 1960, he started traveling to the United States and to Europe and each time when he would come back, he liked more the

lifestyles and the quietness of living here rather than in Israel. We were four boys and the army scared him. We lost a very close relative, a young guy. It was by a terrorist attack in the border patrol.

My feeling is – he never elaborated on it – but my feeling is that in coming here, my father was getting away from living in Israel with all the pressure. He wanted to have quiet. He said "two sons were in the service, I don't want to worry about two more." It was me and my younger brother. And I really think that was the reason for leaving Israel because economically, we were very well off which was a bit different at that time from most of the Israelis who immigrated here. Most of them at that time were people who just didn't have any money and wanted to find better luck. I guess after you survive a thing like World War II in the concentration camps, you want security and quiet.

Ana, an Argentinian woman residing in Haifa, has traveled back and forth between her country of birth and Israel several times. She confirms David's claims about the role of "tension" as she explains why Israelis move to South America:

INTERVIEWER: What do you think attracts Israelis to Argentina?

ANA: Argentina is a very rich country, very comfortable. You can make a living and have fun in it. Israel is also undoubtedly beautiful. Why then do Israelis still want to leave? They, of course, seek some escape. It is suffocating for them. What is here, I feel, is lots of tension, lots of pressures . . . nationalist and so forth. It is not a country like other ones in reality. This is a country that is not so easy to live in. There is tension all the time. This country is always on the news. So, if you are looking for a motivation for leaving the country, I would say it is tension.

The vicissitudes of the Israeli political climate are sometimes implicated as motives for both exit and return. At the outbreak of 1967 and 1973 Wars, Israeli émigrés returned to contribute to the war effort. During the early 1990s, when the Los Angeles economy was depressed by recession, riot and earthquake, and prospects for peace in Israel seemed enhanced by Yitzlak Rabin's election as Prime Minister and the Oslo Peace Accords, Israelis returned home (*For Those Returning Home* 1995). Following Rabin's assassination in 1995, secular Labor Party supporters in London and Paris expressed their disillusionment, claiming that they had "lost the country" to the political right and the ultra-Orthodox. Such was the case for a London psychologist:

INTERVIEWER: Do you consider coming back to Israel?

SHULA: It is a dilemma. We are against Bibi [Netanyahu – Likud Party Prime Minister from 1996–9]. I said before he was elected that if he would win, we will go. But it is a problem because we have not been brought up to escape [to leave Israel when times get hard].

    If we will stay here, it will come back to [haunt] us. My mom was the first generation of female soldiers in the Israeli army. They built the country and now people are talking about [criticizing them as] the elite. Nobody knows how much they gave for integrating with the others. I am getting very insulted by that. My dad always did public service. He did so much without getting paid and now they blame people like him.

    I feel that the country is slipping from my hand. The Orthodox are everywhere, everyone is busy with money. I do not know if we should come back. But both my parents are old. They miss me, they are not healthy, they will feel sorry if I will leave the country [permanently].

A couple living in Paris discuss general feelings of disillusionment with Israel's political and cultural environment:

We did not come to Paris because we had work awaiting us, or because we're students. We came because we wanted to leave Israel. I'm not saying for good, because there is no such thing, but, we came because we didn't want to live there any more. Why? Because of many reasons. Not only the current government [led by Benjamin Netanyahu], there are other reasons. We started thinking about this when Rabin was the prime minister. It was more about the cultural gaps in Israel which really bothered us. We started to feel them in our teens, when we were about 13. We decided to go for Paris, because of my Aunt. We knew she'd help us with work and stuff, and she did.

While both research literature and our interviews suggest that political concerns are not the primary cause for Israeli emigration, changes in the Israeli political environment may offer those already considering exit additional encouragement to go abroad, and may also influence plans to either stay on overseas or return (Goldscheider 1996; Sheffer 1998).

Most recently, the economic decline of 2000–1, coupled with the ever-more violent conflict following the Al Aksa Intifada, has increased interest in emigration in some parts of Israeli society (Curtius 2001). Between fall 2000 – when the uprising began, and fall 2001, applications for travel abroad have increased about 13 percent (Derfner 2001b). For example, requests for permanent residency in Canada's Tel Aviv embassy increased 50 percent during that time. (However, the overwhelming fraction of these, over 90 percent, came from recently arrived Russian Jews, and Palestinians. Only 4 percent were requested by veteran Jewish Israelis (Shavit 2001).)

Ethnic discrimination and conflict

As a nation of immigrants, Israel is ethnically diverse. A major distinction exists between the higher-status Ashkenazi (European origin) group, and the lower-status Mizrahi Jews (also called Eastern, Oriental or Sephardic Jews), who trace their origins to North Africa and the Middle East (Smooha 1978; Uriely 1995; Goldscheider 1996; Yiftachel 1998). Most Israelis assert that ethnic discrimination against Mizrahi Jews has reduced significantly since the 1950s. However, this ethnic distinction remains an important one in Israeli society, and for émigrés as well (Ben-Ami 1992; Uriely 1995). "The ethnic factor does play a role of some importance in some departees' decision to move" (Sobel 1986: 217). In the words of a Los Angeles Israeli psychotherapist: "The Yemenites and the Moroccans come here from Israel with a chip on their shoulder because they are black in Israel. Here, the Americans really don't know the difference and accept them as equals." A Yemeni-origin Israeli woman described her contacts with discrimination as shaping her interest in things outside of Israel, and ultimately contributing to her decision to exit:

> I remember one time my brother came to my mom and he asked her "What is Ashkenazy?" And "What is Temany?" [a term for Israelis of Yemenite origins]. Another time, we went to visit my aunt in Tel-Aviv. And there, the kids were telling us, "black, black, you guys are black, go from here, go from here." And my mother saw it from the balcony and she was very upset.
>
> I don't think I ever internalized that into my life in any way. But, I remember that when I entered junior high and

high school, they started these integration programs where they had people from all different part of the neighborhood go to the same school. Ashkenazies were simply the majority. It was a class of about 38 students. We were only six students in my school.

I was the most advanced student in my class. And so I was put in a very bad position because I didn't know how to assimilate. I could not break that cohesiveness that they had and I could not be with the students I grew up with either.

I was trapped between the two worlds and I really had a rough time. I think all my junior high was bad. Academically, in the beginning I made a big drop in my achievements. And then I caught up and it was all right. But, socially it was terrible for me. I did not find myself.

INVESTIGATOR: Do you think that was one of the reasons maybe you thought about coming to America?

I think that in a way I was afraid to face [Israeli] society. I was afraid not to fit in. Even though I had the knowledge and education, I was afraid of not being accepted because it wasn't part of my childhood. I didn't have a support system around me to fit me in. If I want to be honest with myself, discrimination was part of it. I just did not see myself teaching in Israel. I just thought that America would be better. I did not know too much about it, I just decided to come.

Israelis of Oriental heritage complain of discrimination from co-national Ashkenazi Jews. In contrast, secular Israelis steeped in western culture (who comprise Israel's elite) sometimes object to the growing influence of Mizrahi culture in Israeli life (Goldscheider 1996; Siegel 1998). From his apartment in Paris, Shai explained that Israel has become "too Middle Eastern" for him. "I can't find myself in this Oriental place." His wife Esther agrees, saying that the cultural forms that she values – Western and classical music, "good" theater, European manners and the like – are currently devalued in Israel by the Mizrahim. "They give the tone [of Israel] now," Shai asserts:

Listen to the radio. You can't get a non-Oriental song on the main stations. See the stuff the TV channels are giving us – trash – either American trash or our own Israeli-made trash. Nothing of value. The talk shows are the lowest. The language is terrible, and the manners are even worse.

Social constraints

Some émigrés maintained that they simply felt uncomfortable within the Israeli environment and that the nation is too small, conformist, competitive and socially demanding for their liking. In his book on Israeli emigration, Zvi Sobel (1986: 77) asserts "Repeatedly I was struck by the extent and depth of frustration expressed by a wide range of individuals with respect to this factor of limited opportunity that is tied to a natural and unassailable limitation of smallness – physical and demographic."

Such was the case for Ella, who grew up on a Kibbutz. Her chosen occupation – to become a physical education teacher – was not needed by her Kibbutz, so she was pressured by its administration to choose another career. Further, because of the small size of the Kibbutz community, she was "lonely and had few prospects of finding a boyfriend." In Los Angeles, however, she was able to pursue her field of choice, and had a boyfriend and an active social life with a network of Israeli émigrés – many of who were former Kibbutzniks like herself. Ella elaborates:

> For singles, the loneliness on the Kibbutz is hard. From my class, there are two married [male] pilots, and one girl is married. Two others are on other Kibbutzim and all the rest are in Tel-Aviv. Going into the dining room alone at the age of 22 or 23 is terrible. The social pressure put on me was very hard to take: "How is it that that pretty redhead who serves in the officers' training camp hasn't found herself an officer?" And I was very sensitive and depressed by every remark. What terrible pressure. Naturally, the depression caused by the arguments about studying slowly moved me farther away from the Kibbutz. Here, of course, I don't have that. Here I can do whatever I like, and the freedom is wonderful.

At first glance, émigrés' personal accounts of why they left Israel seem credible enough. However, further examination reveals certain limitations. First is the fact that they are post-migration reconstructions of reasons for exit. Such interpretations may be distorted by these persons' current experience and context, selective memory or various kinds of social influence: "As a number of researchers have found, motives adduced by migrants for motives in the past may hide, rather than reveal underlying causes for movement" (Bedford 1975: 30, quoted in DeJong and Fawcett 1981: 44).

Another problem with after-the-fact explanations for migration is related to the broader critiques of social science methods that fix their analysis solely on respondents' accounts of their own situation: these characterizations are inherently limited to actors' own understandings of their circumstances, and often overly "concern[ed] with the transient, episodic and fleeting" matters (Weinstein and Tanur 1976: 106) and "minimize or deny the facts of social structure and the impact of the macro-organization features of society" (Stryker 1980: 146; Ritzer 1988).

Migrants may be largely unaware of broader historical, economic, structural and demographic developments that influence their behavior. At the same time, they are apt to echo interpretations of their conduct circulated by social networks or media, regardless of their validity (Mills 1940). Accordingly, if we rely only on such personal accounts, we will come up with an image of the migration experience, which while strong in phenomenological detail, is lacking in macro interpretations and comparative insights of the kind that sociologically informed observers can generate. The world system perspective fills many of these gaps.

The world system and migration

In contrast to the microsociological accounts above, most of the literature in the broader field of immigration tends to be economic in focus, and depicts immigrants as either maximizing their available income and rewards (in the neo-classical version) or being forced to relocate abroad as part of the world economic system, due to underdevelopment of certain regions and the like, in neo-Marxist models (Castles and Kosak 1973; Sklar 1991; Guarnizo and Smith 1998). World system theorists argue that recent history reveals a series of events, some unplanned and some intentionally devised, that have had the effect of redistributing, capital, labor, extraction, production and consumption among countries and regions. Accordingly, world system theorizing sees emigration as part of a larger social and historical process, not simply the result of individual decisions to go abroad. As William Peterson cogently remarked "when emigration has been set as a *social* pattern it is no longer relevant to inquire concerning the *individual* motivations" (1958: 263, emphasis in original). This kind of macrosociological analysis offers much to our broader understanding of Israeli emigration.

While the world system perspective acknowledges that immigrants have some ability to plan their actions, it also asserts that many aspects of their experience – including the nations from which they originate, their legal rights, the degree of disadvantage and discrimination that they encounter and the jobs for which they are eligible – are the result of the larger social structure and usually out of immigrants' direct control. In this way, the world system perspective connects the experience of Israelis with the broad flows of international migration that have been major avenues of social change for decades.

The individual cannot be conceived of as a rational actor maximizing interests under market forces. Instead, the flow of labor is directed by supramarket institutions beyond the control of an individual or even a group of migrants.

(Burawoy 1976: 1051)

World system theorists emphasize the benefits accrued by industrialized nations as they acquire workers from other countries. For example, the cost of training an engineer who will take a job in an Canadian corporation is many thousands of dollars. However, if such a worker is educated in Russia, Israel or India and then moves to Toronto, the Canadian economy benefits from his/her skills, but at little cost. Further, while skilled migrants are relatively well paid, nevertheless, due to disadvantage and discrimination, they often accept less desirable jobs and earn lower wages than their native-born peers (Parlin 1976; Castells 1989: 80; Alarcón 1999; Light and Gold 2000). Since Israelis are often skilled, their migration represents a huge net gain in human capital for the economies of their host societies.

Especially appropriate for understanding the experience of Israeli migrants are those recently developed theories that address what has been called "the new immigration" – the movement of skilled and educated persons from less developed societies to Western Europe, North America and affluent Asian countries (Sassen 1991; Findlay 1995; Nonini and Ong 1997). Governments, business interests, educational institutions and organizations in various locations understand the value of what Nonini and Ong (1997: 10) call "transnational functionaries associated with the globalization of capitalist production" to the furtherance of political and economic integration and capital growth. Incentives to attract such workers have been implemented in various host society settings. "Excellent research, working and living conditions have attracted a large number of foreign professionals to seek employment in advanced countries. All of these have laid a solid foundation for the flow of the highly trained" (Cheng and Yang 1998: 649). The immigration laws of the US, Canada, Australia and New Zealand reflect this, as they all include special provisions to attract international entrepreneurs (Marger and Hoffman 1994).

Ong *et al.* (1994: 26) describe a world migration system contributing to the presence of skilled Asian migrants in the United States. Their model involves "stressing the importance of placing the immigration in the context of the restructuring global capitalism" and "contributes to the expansion of migration theories by including the movement of professionals and managers and examining that movement in terms of global restructuring" (Ong *et al.* 1994: 5). In this model, the flow of skilled migration is both a product of and a contributor to the social and economic restructuring of the world order.

> To understand the characteristics of the new immigrants, as well as the role they are playing within the US political economy, one needs to place this immigration in the larger context . . . [I]mmigrants are not only shaped by this context but are themselves shapers of it. They are among the actors who are helping change the face of Los Angeles, the United States, and the world.
>
> (Ong *et al.* 1994: 31)

While the Asian immigrant experience is in some ways distinct from that of Israelis, it is marked by enough similarities to offer beneficial insights. For example, like Asian immigrants, many Israelis are skilled and educated, arrive with families, take advantage of Western countries' "higher salaries or possibilities for profitable investment" and have substantial rates of self-employment. Business owners often hire migrants from other nations – notably Latinos in the US or South Asians in Britain – as a work force (Ong *et al.* 1994: 27; Gold 1992b; 1994a). Others enter to obtain an education and afterward, stay on. Like Israelis,

> not all Asian businesspeople fall into the petty capitalist class. Others are owners, executives and investors of major Asian transnational business that are establishing bases in the US economy. In other words, these Asian immigrants are manifestations of a globalizing economy, in which national boundaries no longer confine business activity.
>
> (Ong *et al.* 1994: 27)

Today's elite, transnational migrants often obtain citizenship with relative ease, and use it for different reasons than the permanent immigrants of an earlier epoch. In fact, while social scientists have traditionally considered naturalization to be an indicator of loyalty to a country, transnational migrants sometimes take on citizenship in order to facilitate their access to other societies. For example, travel to and from the US becomes much easier if one holds a US passport. Accordingly, a resident alien who is content to live his/her life within US borders has far less incentive to acquire US citizenship than does a co-national who wishes to make regular trips to the country of origin. At the same time, in order to retain a degree of access to the loyalty, skills and resources of expatriates, a growing number of origin countries (Israel included) provide dual citizenship to their overseas citizens and even extend it to their foreign-born children (Cohen 1997).

The world system perspective does a good job in helping us understand the economic trends and state policies that result in the emigration of affluent entrepreneurs and highly skilled workers. This model also explains social and economic patterns that foster the emigration of the less skilled. Applying world system theory, Douglas Massey *et al.* (1993: 441) contend "market economies create a permanent demand" for those "willing to labor under unpleasant conditions, at low wages, with great instability and little chance for advancement." Such workers are often supplied through migration, although generally under less secure and pleasant circumstances than available to the highly skilled (Sassen 1991; Guarnizo and Smith 1998). The possibility of a job does foster the emigration of working-class Israelis who pursue higher earnings and new ways of life in London, New York, Toronto and other settings.

As these developments suggest, the world system perspective understands migration not simply as involving isolated individuals moving from one place to another, but instead, sees it as part of a large scale, interconnected processes wherein shifting social, political and economic realities yield fundamental changes in relationships both between and within nations. Migrants, who bring skills, innovation, new international links and resources into an economy but lack the expectations of native-born workers and entrepreneurs, can play a vital role in facilitating restructuring because they are not attached to the outmoded social and economic relations which established groups are reluctant to abandon (Sassen 1991; Gold 1994b).

For a number of macrosociological and historical reasons, Israelis can be considered likely candidates for international migration. Geographical mobility is a fundamental element of the Jewish experience. In *Jewish History in Modern Times*, Joseph Goldstein (1995: 6) writes "Jewish migration and the establishment of Jewish communities all over the world have existed since the emergence of the Jewish people as a religious and ethnic identity." Moreover, "The dispersion of the Jews throughout many countries was a major factor in ensuring their continued existence." Similarly, demographer Sergio DellaPergola (1994) sees migration as so central to the Jewish situation that he refers to a "World Jewish Migration System." While noting that Jewish migration is a "product of a complex chain of explanatory determinants" rather than a primordial disposition towards travel (as suggested by the stereotype of "the wandering Jew"), DellaPergola (1994: 3) nevertheless concludes "the Jewish case [with regard to migration] appears to extend over a longer time span and is geographically more complex and articulated" than that associated with "other ethnoreligious or sociocultural groups." This legacy of migration perpetuates itself among the Jewish people. "The likelihood of migration at any time appears to be significantly determined by the existing geographical distribution of the Jewish population worldwide which, is in turn, to a large extent the product of previous migrations" (DellaPergola 1994: 2).

In "The Jewish People as the Classic Diaspora," Daniel Elazar asserts that Jews have always been characterized by a

> strong tendency to gravitate to the center of whatever universal communications network exists at any particular time and place. . . . The conventional view of Jewish history is that of shifting centers of Jewish life, so that the Jews themselves have the self-image of a people on the move. These constant migrations were, on the one hand, disrupting, but, on the other, they offered the Jews as a group opportunities to renew life and to adapt to new conditions.
>
> (1986: 214–15)

Applying world system theory, Sergio DellaPergola (1992; 1994) has shown that the post-World War II migration of Jews has generally followed a pattern of movement from less developed areas of the world (the periphery) to more economically central, advanced regions, indicating that economic improvement ranks with nationalism as a major force behind Jewish migration. Since the US and other Western nations are more developed economically than Israel, Jews' emigration from Israel to the US, Canada, the UK, Paris or Australia is consistent with the general trend in Jewish migration.

An examination of the origins of Israel's population since 1948 suggests that most came because Israel offered immediate asylum for Jews who lacked other options. Consequently, their numbers include potential candidates for further movement if advantageous circumstances become available. The largest fraction of Israelis hails from Eastern Europe, North Africa and the Middle East. They came because political developments in their countries of origin forced them out. In contrast, relatively few of the millions of Jews in the more secure and affluent nations of North America and Western Europe made aliyah (moved to Israel). Of the approximately 3.1 million Jewish immigrants who settled in Israel between 1919 and 1997, 95 percent came from Eastern Europe, North Africa, the Middle East or Asia, while only about 5 percent (160,000) came from the UK, France, Australia, New Zealand, the US and Canada (Central Bureau of Statistics, tables 5.1; 5.3).

Further suggesting Israel's status as location of temporary residence is the steady stream that have left the Jewish State for other countries. This group accounts for about one-fifth of the number who has entered Israel from 1948 to 1976 (Greenberg 1979: 49). Finally, the post-World War II emigration of Jews from North Africa, the Middle East, the Soviet Union, South Africa and Argentina reveals "significant sociodemographic self-selection. In broad aggregate generalization, more of the culturally more traditional and socially lower strata emigrated to Israel; more of the better educated, entrepreneurial and professional strata preferred France, the United States and other Western countries" (DellaPergola 1994: 12). As some of these economically disadvantaged Israelis increase their ambitions and resources, they too may to follow co-nationals abroad to what appear as greener pastures.

Hence, both theoretical and empirical evidence indicates that Israelis would be likely candidates for migration to Western countries. Accordingly, the world system model gives us a much broader understanding of this migration and its possible causes than does the social psychological, micro perspective that tends to view their migration simply as the sum of purely individual decisions.

However, like microsociological understandings of migration, the world system model also offers an incomplete image of Israeli migrants' motives and behavior. One major flaw is that the world system perspective generally focuses only upon capitalism as shaping international relationships. A recent formulation asserts: "migration is inextricably linked to the changing conditions of global capitalism and must be analyzed within the context of global relations between capital and labor" (Basch *et al.* 1994: 22). Whereas, as the above statistics about Israelis' origins reveal, only a rather small fraction come from fully capitalistic nations. Instead, a large component is from what was the socialist block of Eastern Europe and the former Soviet Union or from Iran and Arab states. Generally, they entered Israel not because of labor market issues (although these may prompt their eventual exit from the Jewish State) but in order to escape persecution at the hands of the non-capitalist elites of their former countries (Gold 1994c). Further, if capitalism was the driving force behind Israeli emigration, why then have so many Israelis stayed in the Jewish State rather than following other Jews to the West? As the authors of "Motives for Migration" query: "Addressing the question why people do *not* move is as significant as the analysis of why they do in understanding migration decision making" (DeJong and Fawcett 1981: 29, emphasis in original).

Second, because the world system perspective often verges on economic determinism, it downplays ethnicity and nationalism as forces in shaping social membership: "World systems theorists have tended to reduce migration to labor migration and immigrants to workers, eliminating all discussions of the many different racial, ethnic or national identities which shape people's actions and consciousness" (Basch *et al.* 1994: 12). Since Israelis are Jews, leaving from the Jewish State and settling into diaspora Jewish communities, and are as we have seen, actively concerned with the meaning of their migration in terms of their ethnic, national and religious identities, world system theory's disregard of ethnic and national identities is a major liability in terms of understanding Israeli emigration. For the same reasons, the world system approach is also limited in its ability to account for forms of migration that are not economically determined – for example, those driven by expulsion, family unification, pursuit of education, cultural preferences, religious yearnings, political aspirations or romance.

Finally, while the world system perspective indicates why persons may migrate, it does not tell us much about the process of migration nor the chosen place of settlement. For example, why do Hebrew-speaking Israelis with family origins in Central Europe so heavily favor English-speaking countries (including South Africa) as points of destination? As I suggest below, network-based models do a better job of accounting for these patterns. In conclusion, while aspects of global capitalism play important roles in shaping Israeli migration, such issues cannot fully account for this process.

Networks and social capital

A more complete understanding of Israeli emigration is offered when it is considered in light of this group's links to both host societies and Israel. In her book about Israeli immigrants in Los Angeles entitled *Kibbutz L.A.* (1996), Naama Sabar describes how a combination of established co-national friends, a Hebrew-speaking ethnic economy, and an immigrant-friendly legal system allow a just-arrived Israeli to acquire a job, a driver's license, a car and a feeling of social orientation within a few hours of his flight's arrival at Los Angeles International Airport. Sabar's example demonstrates the analytic power of a network-based understanding of international migration. The micro approach would have focused on the personal relationships alone, while the macro model may well have stressed the US economy's demand for undocumented labor. A network-oriented model appreciates the importance of these factors and more. It also helps us comprehend why Israelis are familiar with American lifestyles, and how LA's Israeli and Jewish ethnic economies provides jobs, survival needs and a social life for a recently arrived sabra, while simultaneously isolating him or her from assimilation-fostering interactions with Americans.

A central feature of migration networks is that they span national borders and often allow elements of communal interconnection – transnational social fields – to develop between discrete nation states (Faist 2000; Portes 2001). By considering the effect of networks – ranging from personal contacts among family members and friends, to "migration channels" (broad patterns of social linkage developed within industries, religious groups, social movements, academic networks and cultural communities) on migration – we can bridge the gap between phenomenological and world systems perspectives (Findlay and Li 1998). While Israeli emigrants travel across geographic space and national borders, many remain within familiar networks. These provide newcomers with resources and a sense of familiarity in otherwise unknown settings. As such, the culture shock associated with moving is moderated. Yes, migrants are in a different national environment. But in coming there, they are able to maintain a way of life – socially, economically, linguistically and even in terms of diet and recreation – that is not so very different from the one they have left behind. Accordingly, their experience of "migration" may be quite distinct from that conjured up in established literature on the topic that assumes geographical movement necessarily yields loss of social ties and social isolation.

Reflecting the power of Israeli networks, Dalia, a London real estate agent, describes her feelings of comfort with what its members call "the Israeli swamp."

INTERVIEWER: Do you feel like an outsider or a minority here?

DALIA: No, because I live in here, among all the Israelis. I feel at home here. I don't feel a minority here. If we lived in a far away village with no Israelis around – I'm sure I would have felt different about this. But here – I feel really comfortable. I feel at home.

A whole series of factors surrounding Israelis makes their movement from the Jewish State to other countries relatively easy. Even prior to migration, Israelis often feel familiar with host societies from popular culture and governmental relations.

America, it might be posited, has become the alter ego of Israel in political, economic and cultural terms . . . The Israeli economy could not sustain the country's present standard of living without massive ingestions of aid from the United States treasury and to a much lesser extent the American Jewish community.

(Sobel 1986: 192–3)

In a recent article, Alejandro Portes (2001: 185–7) describes how transnational migrants use formal border-crossing institutions established by large-scale entities for their own grass-roots goals associated with travel, economic activities, political agendas, communication and the like. Available institutions include "international" resources created by nation states, such as embassies, trade missions and cultural exchanges, and "multinational" structures established by corporations, global religions and the United Nations. Israel and the countries wherein its emigrants settle are characterized by a wide range of such international and multinational organizations, including various government ministries and agencies, religious organizations representing several faiths, and corporate interests involved in manufacturing, consumer goods, agriculture, information technology and defense industries. Accordingly, a wide array of border-crossing ties are readily available for use by emigrants.

In their study of "Migration of Highly Trained Manpower to the United States" Cheng and Yang (1998: 649) demonstrate that the sort of links between Israel and the US are likely to foster Israeli emigration:

Economic and educational interactions between sending and receiving countries are important driving forces of professional migration. As the degree of economic interaction and educational articulation between the sending country and the United States heighten, the level of highly trained migration to the United States rises.

This kind of linkage is not limited to the US. The UK, as the former colonial power that oversaw Palestine, has extensive cultural, economic and historical links with Israel, and many of Israel's political and social institutions reflect British traditions (Goldstein 1995; Shafir 1995). Israel and many Western nations enjoy good political relations and are extensively enmeshed. The US government and American Jewish agencies have developed an active presence in the Jewish State. American firms have branches there and American companies sometimes hire professional and skilled workers directly from Israel. At the same time, Israeli government agencies, banks and industrial enterprises have offices in Los Angeles, New York and other American settings. These not only give an Israeli flavor to the American environment, but also provide employment for migrants (Sobel 1986: 196). A similar collection of Israeli institutions can be found in London, Toronto and other points of settlement.

As an example of the highest level of integration, Israeli computer engineers in Silicon Valley or London high-tech firms use telecommunications technology to send jobs to Israel, where coethnic engineers develop hardware and software for a fraction of the cost required to do so in the US, Europe or Japan. Due to the immigration of thousands of Jews from the former Soviet Union, Israel, as of 1995, had 135 scientists and engineers per 10,000 residents, compared to 85 in the US and 80 in Japan. The design specifications for Intel's 286, 386 and MMX Pentium were all devised in Israel, which is now home to major plants for IBM, Intel, Microsoft and DEC (Richtel 1998). These interlinkages between Israel and Western corporations reveal the human and economic integration and networking between nations, regions and labor forces, and suggest the continued flow of technology and people among these settings.

Related to this cooperative climate, travel between places of settlement and Israel is easily arranged. For example, an enterprising Israeli in London provides van service from the Israeli enclave in Golders Green to and from Gatwick, Heathrow and Stansted airports to all El Al flights. Immigrants often report making frequent trips from host societies to Israel and it is not uncommon for children to return to Israel to spend summer vacations with relatives or to fulfill their military obligations. An obstetrician describes the great value he places on his trips back to Israel:

> I was talking to my accountant two days ago – he is also an Israeli – he says "What is going on?" And I said "What can I tell you, we are in a concentration camp." Okay – this is the way you describe it, and it is so true. We are in a concen-

tration camp and we get a relief once a year when we go to Israel for a vacation. This is the bottom line.

At the same time, a variety of Israeli-oriented activities such as schools, day-care centers, synagogues, sports and leisure clubs, publications, restaurants, shops, sightseeing trips and nightspots have been created in major settlement communities so that a semblance of the Israeli life can be lived in the host society (Gold 1992b; Rosen 1993; Uriely 1995; Cohen and Gold 1996). In London, Paris, Chicago, Washington DC and other cities, émigrés can attend social events in a network of embassy-sponsored Israeli Houses that are intended to keep overseas Israelis affiliated with the home country.

Israelis commonly have access to informal networks and coethnic agencies in many countries that can provide a broad variety of resources ranging from job opportunities, to child care, housing and a social life (Korazim 1983; Sabar 1989; Ben-Ami 1992; Gold 1994a; 1994b; 1995). In the following quote, Debbi describes her willingness to assist co-nationals who seek orientation in London:

INTERVIEWER: Do you offer help to Israelis who come here?

DEBBI: Yes, many Israelis who came here and were as lost as we were at the beginning – they called me and I supplied the information they needed: schools, banks, NHS (National Health Service), etc. I help them as much as I can. I remember how miserable I was and I try to help them as much as I can.

Personal networks created among migrants also provide valuable assistance. Regardless of their reasons for emigration, Israelis frequently comment on their access to various networks and connections in places of settlement. As Charles Tilly (1990: 84) asserts in his article on "Transplanted Networks":

By and large, the effective units of migration were (and are) neither individuals nor households but sets of people linked by acquaintance, kinship, and work experience who somehow incorporated American destinations into the mobility alternatives they considered when they reached critical decision points in their individual or collective lives.

Such networks are quite diverse and are based upon personal, familial, religious, ethnic, occupational, lifestyle and other social attributes (Gold 1994b; 1999). The fact that Israelis are involved in chain migration and rely on networks is consistent with the literature on voluntary migration (Lyman 1974; Piore 1979; DeJong and Fawcett 1981; Massey *et al.* 1987). An Israeli obstetrician describes his reasons for coming to the US in view of family connections and economic concerns:

> Everybody has a reason why he came to this country. I tell you something. I had a wonderful lifetime in Israel. I was born in Israel, my father came to Israel when he was 18 in 1922 and I have a picture of my parents with Ben Gurion [Israel's first Prime Minister].
>
> The main reason I came is professional. I found that the country is very small. The possibilities as a physician are very limited and I had an opportunity. My family was here, my aunt, my uncle, my mother. With all of these connections, I said to myself "If I want to do any change, this is the right time. I cannot leave later on."
>
> I did what I did. I am more respected over here. Even though, to tell you the truth, if I did the right thing or not, I don't know. I mean I guess I enjoy it. I definitely have more possibilities to practice medicine in this country because it is a bigger country. I think professionally it is a better opportunity of practicing medicine.

Finally, emigration networks are not unidirectional. Just as they facilitate exit, they also permit émigrés to stay in touch with the country of origin and expedite return. In fact, the network-based opportunity for easy return may be in itself an additional motive for emigration. Because of these many reasons, it would appear that the whole notion of being an Israeli versus a member of the host society is not nearly as clear cut a distinction as the literature on international migration would generally suggest. Instead, such factors as flexible notions of ethnic and national identity, access to and participation in social and occupational networks, family history in several nations, and the ability of people to sustain cultural competence and legal status in more than a single society allow Israelis to maintain meaningful forms of involvement in multiple national settings at one time.

Networks clearly provide Israeli émigrés with a variety of resources. However, given the diverse characteristics of the Israeli emigrant population and the varied locations in which they settle, it is important to note that these networks provide different kinds of resources to their members, reveal disparate criteria for participation and may be more or less exclusive in permitting people to join. Some recent research depicts migrant networks as if they were widely accessible (Nonini and Ong 1997). However, as suggested by Tilly (1990), Waldinger (1996), and Portes *et al.* (1999), migrant networks – like other collectives – are capable of restricting membership and with-holding benefits as well as providing resources. They may bestow new opportunities to some, while limiting the options of others:

> Networks brought into being by immigration serve to create and perpetuate inequality. Lest anyone think that solidarity and mutual aid have nothing but gratifying results, we should recognize two things: (1) members of immigrant groups often exploited one another as they would not have dared to exploit the native-born and, (2) every inclusion also constitutes an exclusion.
>
> (Tilly 1990: 92)

Further, while networks' role in providing immigrants with infor-mation and resources vital for migration is commonly acknowledged, it is equally true, but less frequently asserted that networks and ethnic communities also play a major role in shaping the ideological and cultural aspects of migration – that is the meanings and expectations associated with migration itself and with one's presence in the new setting.

Like other social structures, access to migrant networks (and the resources they deliver) is a contingent process. They vary according to the characteristics of migrants, the nature of the receiving society, conditions in the country of origin and other factors. "Information may be passed on to a potential migrant by one channel, motivation to move may come from another, while yet another mechanism may be the means by which migration is legally effected between one state and another" (Findlay and Li 1998: 686). Accordingly, while networks often shape Israelis' motives for emigration and patterns of adjust-ment, they are not accessible to all, and different networks may offer their members dissimilar resources and outlooks. (Chapters 3 and 5 examine the role of networks in shaping patterns of work and associa-tion within Israeli émigré communities.)

Conclusions

In this chapter, I have argued that in recent years, social science understandings of migrants' motives have become much more complex and sophisticated. While suggestive, micro and macro perspectives are limited in providing us with comprehensive insight into the actions of Israeli émigrés. However, by understanding international migration as a network-based process, we can consider both macro and micro factors and integrate them into the rich fabric of affiliations and links that shape migration. Finally, the network approach emphasizes that migration is embedded in a series of political, ethnic, familial and communal relationships and environments, including some that cross borders. Through it, we see that migrating populations often remain connected to more than one national context. The network model is especially useful for understanding the experience of Israeli emigrants because they regularly have access to transportable skills, border-crossing social ties, and can often obtain resources in multiple locations.

In retrospect, we realize that each approach to emigration suggests the importance of interlocking networks. The micro perspective emphasizes personal ties of family, community and friends; while the macro outlook instructs us to consider links rooted in international capitalism, global culture and geopolitics. However, the network-mediated approach addresses both of levels and is especially attuned to the interlocking complexity of networks. In reviewing the multiple reasons that drive Israeli emigration, it is apparent that manifold motives – coupled with the diverse groups who travel abroad – set the stage for the wide variety of patterns of adaptation, social membership and plans for return that characterize the Israeli diaspora.

3

WORK AND COETHNIC COOPERATION

Introduction

In Western societies, popular and social scientific thinking about economic life is shaped by neo-classical assumptions, wherein exchange is presumed to take place among profit-maximizing, isolated individuals who have equal access to information. However, in recent years, a growing body of scholars and policy makers have embraced an alternative tradition, derived from the work of Max Weber and currently described through concepts such as social capital, ethnic economies, networks, embeddedness, solidarity, segmented labor markets and enclaves – to understand the significance of social collecties – such as ethnic or religious groups, families, neighborhood and genders – in determining economic outcomes (Cohen 1969; Light 1972; Portes and Bach 1985; Bourdieu 1986; Portes 1995a; Waldinger 1996; Light and Gold 2000).

For example, through their collective experience of discrimination, their social isolation or a mismatch between their skills and employment opportunities, certain groups experience economic disadvantage (Massey *et al.* 1993; Wilson 1996). On the other hand, as a consequence of their trust-based sharing of resources (such as capital, labor, information or goods) groups can enhance their earnings, overcome certain labor market disadvantages or control access to jobs (Min 1996; Light and Gold 2000). An additional feature of collective understandings of economic life is that in contrast to individualistic perspectives, they assume that economic and social relations are inextricably wound up together. Rather than being distinct, they are of a piece (Granovetter 1995a).

This chapter examines the collective basis of Israeli emigrants' economic lives. It explores the ways by which Israelis utilize economic resources within and beyond their co-national communities. It also

Plate 3.1 Israeli shopping district, Queens, New York City.

considers their comprehension of the potential benefits and liabilities associated with ethnic economic collaboration. This exercise permits us to perceive the social origins of this group's economic status and further, to gain insight into central patterns of solidarity and differentiation within the Israeli diaspora.

Israeli émigrés are more skilled and educated than the average citizen of both Israel and the host societies where they settle (Cohen and Haberfeld 1997). Like other groups of skilled migrants, they represent a high-quality labor force whose members often seek nonmonetary rewards from work in addition to survival income. These include personal fulfillment, advanced training and the ability to participate in cutting-edge occupational settings (leading universities, centers of technology, finance and cultural production) associated with advanced nations and world cities. In this, Israelis are enacting a pattern of behavior that has been typical of Jews for centuries (Goldscheider and Zuckerman 1984; Pollins 1984; Goldstein 1995; Hyman 1998). Other Israeli emigrants seek economic opportunity they feel is scarce at home, or simply hope to support themselves during their stay abroad.

While Jews' devotion to and success in their occupational lives is often overstated and attributed to inherent tendencies rather than contextual factors, as a group they have achieved a remarkable degree of accomplishment in a variety of endeavors and settings (Steinberg 1989; Lipset 1990; Gold and Phillips 1996b). Jews' dedication to work and its rewards in earnings, satisfaction and prestige has been attributed to their efforts to escape both the insecurity and psychological wounds associated with their marginal status in the diaspora. Anthropologist Fran Markowitz describes work for Jews in a major diaspora community, as

> the be all and end all of the . . . individual search for a social place and well being . . . Jews overcompensated for their stigmatized "national identity" by pouring their energies into academic and professional pursuits. Some, members of the intelligentsia in particular, found in their work a means of escape from the unpleasantness of other aspects of the Soviet system.
>
> (1994: 8)

Similarly, historian Rafael Patai (1971: 161) argued "This tendency to aim at excellence precisely in the focal concerns of the host cultures recurs with such regularity in the Jewish diaspora that it can be taken as a manifestation of yet another trait characterizing Jewish ethnicity." Suffice it to say that Jews often emphasize meaningful and prestigious work as a key element of their lives.

However, when Israelis pursue wealth and fulfilling careers in the diaspora, they challenge a central tenet of early Zionism. Observing the insecure status of Jews as urban entrepreneurs, traders, wage laborers, bankers and scholars in nineteenth-century Europe, the founders of certain forms of Zionism felt that Jews would only be free, secure and self-respecting if they abandoned these typically Jewish occupations in host societies and, instead, settled in Palestine (Zweig 1969; Kotkin 1992; Zerubavel 1995). Here, it was thought the "new Jew" would engage in a full range of work roles, with a stress on ennobling agriculture. Rather than acquiring money from Gentiles, or conforming to the individualistic achievement culture of the West, work would be determined by collective needs and devoted to building a safe and secure homeland for the Jewish people (Almog 2000). This collective outlook towards work was especially well developed in the highly influential Kibbutz movement of rural collectives that was established by leftist emigrants from Europe during the first half of the twentieth century. Naama Sabar, an authority on Kibbutz education, describes the philosophy:

> For many years, kibbutz education, the main tool of kibbutz socialization, was not achievement oriented. Since achievement leads to competition and competition impedes equality

61

> – a major premise of kibbutz ideology – individuals were
> encouraged to be like everyone else rather that to excel in
> school.
>
> (Sabar 2000: 10)

In their study of Israeli emigrants in New York, Marcia Freedman
and Josef Korazim (1986: 144) assert that in the Jewish State, the self-
employed are stigmatized as self-serving and parasitic tax evaders.
Consequently, the "suspect nature of entrepreneurship from a Zionist
perspective" is a significant motive for business-minded Israelis'
emigration.[1] More recently, Israel has deviated from its socialist past
to more fully embrace capitalism. As testament to this change, Nobel
laureate economist Laurence Klein recently labeled Israel, along with
the US, India and Taiwan as "one of four countries in the world
capable of sustained productivity-lead economic growth" (Gardner
2000). High technology industries have been the source of much of
Israel's current performance (Gordon 2001). The *Jerusalem Post*
regularly celebrates the most recent acquisition of an Israeli high-tech
firm by an American or European corporation or even the purchase
of a Western firm by Israeli investors (for example, Gordon 2000;
Hiltzik 2000).

While Israel's economic performance has been relatively strong of
late, until fairly recently, the country's economic context – as a small,
isolated nation, burdened with many new immigrants, a sizable welfare
state, high rates of inflation, huge military expenditures, restricted
access to higher education and embroiled in hostile relations with its
neighbors – limited its financial prospects, and hence the mobility
aspirations of many of its citizens (Sobel 1986; Goldscheider 1996).
Even without ideological opposition, these conditions discouraged a
single-minded orientation towards work and its rewards. Hence, if
and when Jewish Israelis contrast the way of life available to them in
the Jewish State with that beyond, they were often aware of the
diaspora's opportunities, and diaspora Jews' accomplishments –
financial and otherwise – in the world of work. A business journalist
posits Israelis' awareness of economic opportunities abroad as a cause
of their emigration:

> Like other Jewish sojourners, the Israelis come to the United
> States mainly for economic opportunity, often for a chance to
> participate more fully in those activities – from film making
> and finance to garment manufacturing – that have been
> mainstays of the Jewish economy for generations.
>
> (Kotkin 1992: 64)

Plate 3.2 Israeli bakery, NW London.

Studies routinely report that Israeli emigrants do quite well in their careers and economic lives (Shokeid 1988; Cohen 1996; Gold and Phillips 1996a; Schmool and Cohen 1998). Nevertheless, there is always some debate about the real relationship between emigration and achieving work-related goals (Shokeid 1988; Gold and Phillips 1996a; Sabar 2000). Are economic opportunities really better outside of Israel? And even if an Israeli can have a more prestigious or more affluent career abroad, are these rewards enough to compensate the costs – cultural differences, separation from family and friends, having to speak a foreign language and living among Gentiles – associated with life overseas? Israeli academic reports, newspapers and popular discussions are replete with stories addressing both the successes and the failures of émigrés as well as the broader meaning of work and its rewards both within and beyond Israel. For many émigrés, a pivotal tension exists between their desire to pursue careers freely and without the economic and social constraints imposed by Israeli society, on one hand, and their preference for working among familiar, supportive and like-minded co-national associates, on the other.

Economic cooperation among Israelis in the diaspora

After engaging in fieldwork among Israelis in New York City, anthropologist Moshe Shokeid (1988: 53) asserted: "The Israelis have not evolved an economic basis of ethnic solidarity . . . Yordim appear to be nonexistent as a separate and well defined social category." In contrast to Shokeid's finding, nearly every Israeli emigrant that we contacted, regardless of occupation, background, gender, educational level or place of settlement, relied on co-nationals to achieve economic ends. Paradoxically, Israeli emigrants appear to maintain their Jewish and Israeli-based traditions of collectivism and self-help, even as they pursue individualistic goals beyond the Jewish State (Cohen and Gold 1996; Sabar 2000).

Social science theory predicts that labor migrants and entrepreneurial immigrants are likely to use ethnic networks and resources for finding jobs or opening businesses (Portes and Rumbaut 1996; Light and Gold 2000). In contrast, professional immigrants, it is hypothesized, "seldom form tightly knit ethnic communities," largely because their skills and language competence often permit them to find jobs in the mainstream economy of the host society (Portes and Rumbaut 1996: 19–20). Contradicting this trend, even skilled and educated Israelis who work as professionals, often for large corporations, engage in a significant amount of coethnic cooperation oriented towards fellow émigrés, the country of origin and host society Jews.

A consequence of Israeli emigrants' heavy reliance on coethnic ties in their economic lives is their concentration in a limited number of industries. Among these are traditional areas of Jewish economic specialization, such as diamonds, garments, retail trade, Jewish cultural activities and the preparation and sale of and kosher foods. Israelis are also active in real estate, construction, import/export and the professions, including health care, engineering and information technology. Drawing on their military backgrounds (Israel requires universal military service for men and women alike), a fair number provide security services (Kass and Lipset 1982; Sobel 1986; Shokeid 1988; DellaPergola 1994; Cohen 1996; Gold and Phillips 1996a; Cohen and Gold 1996; Sheffer 1998).

Numerous reports as well as our own fieldwork describe Israelis' visibility in particular occupational niches in specific localities. For example, in Los Angeles, Israelis are active in garments, construction, real estate, entertainment and jewelry (Gold 1994a). Our fieldwork and interviews indicate that a sizable number of Israelis in London are involved in high-tech industries, real estate and international shipping and trade. While statistical data record that Israelis in New York include a significant component of professionals, our own interviews and various reports suggest that they also work as car washers, movers, taxi drivers and purveyors of kosher pizza (Freedman and Korazim 1986; Schnall 1987; Ben-Ami 1992). Finally, interviews and reports suggest that Israelis in nations lacking a significant Jewish population such as Japan, and developing countries like Argentina, South Africa and Peru, concentrate in highly mobile ventures, such as selling consumer good (clothes, watches and electronics) at public markets (Sheffer 1998).

Quantitative data further verify Israelis' propensity towards economic cooperation. In their study of Israelis in the New York labor market, Freedman and Korazim (1986: 143) found that over 70 percent relied on the ethnic community (Israelis or American Jews) as employers, partners, colleagues or customers. Similarly, in their analysis of ethnic occupational concentration in Los Angeles, Waldinger and Bozorgmehr (1996: 450) discovered that foreign-born Israelis had the highest index of occupational concentration of fourteen native and foreign-born ethnic groups, including Latinos, Asians, Middle Easterners, and several European groups. Sixty-four percent of Israelis worked in occupations defined as an ethnic niche. For some nationality groups, niche employment is a mobility trap, yielding low wages. This is not the case for foreign-born Israelis in Los Angeles, who had greater earnings than any other foreign-born group, including Iranians and Filipinos, who have more years of education.

Realms of economic cooperation

Anecdotal reports and census analysis reveal that Israelis engage in various forms of economic concentration and cooperation. However, these kinds of evidence tell us little about the nature and functioning of Israeli emigrants' economic collaboration in various locations of settlement. In the section that follows, we draw on fieldwork and interviews to describe some of the ways that Israeli emigrants join together to accomplish work-related economic goals. In so doing, we are able to link abstract notions about ethnic solidarity with migrants' conception of the relationship between work, nationality and community. In addition, rather than simply assuming that cooperation exists among an entire ethnic/emigrant population, we are able to specify some of the social and economic bases around which the most highly developed forms of collaborative economic action actually take place.

Ethnic economic cooperation has been studied in greatest detail in the realm of self-employment (Waldinger *et al.* 1990; Light and Gold 2000). Israeli emigrants, like Jews generally, are noted for their high levels of self-employment. Yoon (1997) analyzed 1990 US Census data and determined that Israelis have the second highest rate of self-employment of any national-origin group. A number of local studies found Israelis' self-employment rate to be even higher.[2] Similarly, analyses of Australian and Canadian census data also found very high rates of self-employment among Israelis: 13 percent in the 1996 Australian Census and 29 percent in the 1996 Canadian Census. Fieldwork in France, England and South Africa further indicates Israelis' involvement in self-employment (Sheffer 1998).

Through coethnic cooperation, Israelis obtain a series of economic benefits. These include access to jobs, workers, customers, investment capital, goods and services, tools and equipment, skill training, information, and communal prestige (Gold 1994a; 1997; Portes 1995a; Light and Gold 2000). Often, these benefits are provided by coethnics under friendly circumstances, at preferable rates, and with valuable advice on how to deploy them. At the same time, the benefits provided by ethnic economic resources are not free. In order to receive them, Israeli emigrants must conform to various group standards involving philanthropy, religious practice, patterns of consumption, ideological orientation, social engagement and other activities.

While self-employed Israelis are immersed in a variety of cooperative networks, those who work for non-coethnic firms, non-profit organizations and government also rely on coethnic connections in their work lives as they count on co-nationals for advice and job referrals and select other Israelis as employees, clients, subcontractors, suppliers and the like. Finally, many Israeli emigrants retain economic links to the country of origin, engaging in trade, providing and consuming business services, organizing cultural exchanges, working for Israeli companies, cooperating with government agencies and non-profit organizations, while relying on Israeli banks and shipping firms and recruiting employees from the Israeli labor force.

As the following discussion reveals, many emigrants find this symbiotic pattern to be satisfactory and even a source of security. Others however, believe that the costs of coethnic collaboration – economic or otherwise – exceed available benefits. Finally, we observe that because Israeli emigrants are a diverse population and settle in various locations, they are involved in various economic networks oriented towards distinct norms, purposes and constituencies. In this way, they cooperate with selected segments of the coethnic community and host society, while distancing themselves from others (Gold 1994a; 2001).

As they orient themselves in host communities, Israelis rely on various social contacts to establish their economic lives. For some – such as specialists recruited directly from Israel to work for overseas companies or universities – these are provided by professional connections. However, many look to the coethnic community for information and resources. Coethnic cooperation most commonly occurs on three levels that represent Israeli émigrés' multiple affiliations with Jewish and Israeli communities. First, because they tend to settle in Jewish neighborhoods and are active in realms of Jewish economic preponderance, Israelis interact with diaspora Jews in places of settlement. In most cases, these are native-born Jews, but Israelis also develop economic ties with Jewish immigrants from other countries – for example, Russians and Iranians in the US, or North Africans in France. Second, while Israelis share commonalties with host society Jews, they have more in common – language, culture, nationality, life-shaping experiences, education and military service – with co-nationals, and hence cooperate with them. Finally, Israelis' most extensive patterns of economic cooperation develop among co-nationals with whom they share strong social ties. Although Israeli emigrants display extensive coethnic cooperation, they also understand that coethnic arrangements can put them at possible risk of exploitation, abuse and free-riding. Accordingly, workers and entrepreneurs sometimes describe ways through which they avoid undesired interactions with coethnics.

Economic connections with host society Jews

Israeli migrants are generally aware of the Jewish ethnic economy of their host community. They live and locate their businesses in established Jewish neighborhoods, sell products and services to Jewish consumers, enter business fields where Jews already play important roles, and engage in a wide range of joint ventures with native Jews (Goren 1980). Yossi, a Los Angeles building contractor, describes his reliance on the native Jewish community in starting his business:

INVESTIGATOR: Were most of your customers Jews or just anyone who needed contracting?

YOSSI: Basically, it had to be a lot of Jews. Fortunately, most of them were helpful. And all kinds of building supply companies are owned by Jewish people. I would obviously go to them. They don't know that you are Israeli, but if you introduce yourself, they tend to work out with you more. More flexibility and they will stretch a little bit more, too. I like that, so that's why I go to them. That's why I'm still with another Jew. I think it's part of Jewish heritage. We are all one loyal group. Somehow, we become loyal to another or help another whether we plan to or not.

Danni, who has run various businesses in the US and England, described how he relied on coethnic knowledge to establish his first enterprise in England:

> I started selling shirts before the Jewish Holidays. I used to go to Stamford Hill (a highly concentrated Orthodox neighborhood of London) and I sold them straight out of the car. I used to bring a whole van full of nice men's shirts for the Holidays, and sell them there on the main street for much more than I paid. The religious people like to have new clothes for the Holidays so I used to sell a whole van and sometimes I had to go at noon and fill the van again with more shirts. The white shirts were the most popular. I used to do all these deals – three for the price of two – and it worked. They have big families there. On some occasions, it took only an hour to empty the van. I would go and get another load.

Drawing on their linguistic skills and knowledge about Judaism and Israel, some men and many women are employed in Jewish communal occupations. A London-based Israeli woman who made a career in Jewish education explains her gravitation towards the coethnic community: "When I moved here, I realized that if I wanted to work, I need to live where the Jewish people live." In a like manner, Dina describes how the Jewish community has supported her teaching in a French high school:

> I teach Hebrew to French Jews who are doing a Baccalaureate in Hebrew outside their normal studies. The Jewish community is very strong on this. The school is non-Jewish, but it has a Jewish department, and all the Jews in the school attend these classes.

Israeli immigrants and ethnic succession

The orientation of Israelis (as well as other Jewish migrants) towards Jewish enclaves creates a pattern of Jewish ethnic succession. In the Jewish neighborhoods of London, New York, Chicago, Paris, Miami, Toronto or Los Angeles, the Israeli presence is made evident in storefronts with Israeli names like Sabra, Golan, Pita, Carmel or Middle East (Ritterband and Zerubavel 1986). Israelis in the food business often sell a range of kosher delicacies unlikely to be found in a typical East European-style delicatessen. Instead of (or in addition to) corn beef, pastrami, rye bread, smoked fish and Manischewitz products,

Plate 3.3 Israeli caterer, South Florida.

one finds falafel, schwarma, various "mezi" salads, Middle Eastern baked goods, nuts, couscous, Turkish coffee and dried and canned foods exported from Israel. Other stores market publications, religious articles and art works. Israeli shops also provide Hebrew newspapers, phone cards for calling Israel and video and audio tapes and CDs of Israeli music. Bulletin boards advertise religious services, cultural celebrations and events that may interest the community. Finally, local Israeli businesses – musicians, taxi services, child care centers, computer specialists, tutors, home remodeling companies – use these display areas to offer their wares.

In addition to providing goods, service and jobs, the presence of recent Jewish migrants permits older Jewish neighborhoods and industries to retain their Jewish orientation in a context of rapidly changing demographics. Native-born Jews in many countries of settlement have largely abandoned small business pursuits in favor of professional employment and suburban lifestyles (Waterman and Kosmin 1986; Waldinger 1996). In the absence of new Jewish migrants, small retail businesses and urban Jewish neighborhoods are often occupied by other ethnic groups (Min 1996; Kershen 1997). However, Jewish immigrants continue to be interested in running these sorts of businesses and residing in cities. Consequently, new arrivals purchase established operations or start new ones, extending the tradition of immigrant Jewish business ownership and urban residence for another generation while also supporting local Jewish community institutions, such as schools, synagogues, clubs and recreational facilities (Goldscheider and Kobrin 1980; Waldinger 1996; Gold 1999a).

Using their common religion and ethnicity to establish trust, some recent arrivals purchase existing businesses from long-established or native-born Jews who are reaching retirement age. Other migrants direct new operations towards these clients. For example, a restaurateur describes a venture located in the English capital:

> I opened a restaurant in partnership with my brother. It was in the city near the jewelry area. There were lots of Jews and Israelis then in that area. It was specifically designed to serve the business area. We opened it only between 9 and 5. It was very successful.

In an interactive process, Israeli and other Jewish immigrants maintain but also transform the nature of the local Jewish community. Just as Israeli immigrants become familiar with the patterns of native Jewish life, established Jews and other immigrants pick up some of the habits, tastes, business practices and outlooks of the recently arrived. Thus, Israeli emigrants often bring new dimensions to the Jewish communities in which they settle (Gold 1992b; 1999a).

Despite their initial gravitation towards host Jews, some Israeli migrants eventually recognized liabilities involved in working with native co-religionists. The costs of serving local Jewish consumers and using coethnic social capital include conformity to religious rules and having to address security concerns in places like London, Paris and Buenos Aires, where terrorists have attacked Jewish targets. For example, a secular Israeli restaurateur in London complained about the social constraints involving Sabbath observance as demanded by the Orthodox Jews who were her primary customers:

> It is very tough to live among the Orthodox Jews. I think of looking for a flat in another area. For me it is difficult because on Saturday, instead of wearing casual clothes and going to the park, I have to be worried that my religious customers will see me with my son on his bicycle. So personally, it is awful.
>
> In fact, the reason that I am closing the shop on Saturday and holidays is also connected to this subject. I will tell you more. In the winter, when Shabbat starts early, the Orthodox are entering and asking "Till when are you open on Friday?" or "Do you know when Shabbat begins?" Yes, I can swear to you, and it happened not once and not twice. The Jewish school would not work with me if they would have seen that I am opening the shop on Saturday.

In 1999, Isaac, the owner of a bookstore/café in Paris, described marketing his business to a multi-ethnic clientele in order to avoid the downside of being a strictly Jewish-focused enterprise:

> I think that I found the formulation of how to "sell" Israel without turning my shop into a ghetto. The uniqueness of this place is that it is not identified with Jews. The problem is that if you are doing something Jewish, you have to start with the security. Then it is so close and tight that no one wants to come. I think that when I call it a Mediterranean place, I can mix together Jewish, Israelis and Arabs. [One night, we had a reading.] So people came from the French Ministry of Culture, and Israelis came and also Arabic. It was very nice.

Community-wide connections among Israelis

Recognizing the liabilities of doing business with host Jews or simply feeling more comfortable with co-nationals, Israelis express their preference for co-national involvement, as well as their desire to assist fellow Israelis. Nora, a London restaurant owner, describes how familiarity and obligation lead her to hire Israelis:

> It was easier to work with them [Israelis] in terms of language and mentality. But also, when I had these young people

coming to look for a job, I just couldn't say no. If I had no vacancy, I helped them look at other places. They would come to me – and they still do – and say "I'm looking for a job. Can you help?" And I refer them to a coffee shop owned by an Israeli or an Israeli restaurant or an Israeli bakery. I'm good friends with the owners. I can't say I had only Israeli workers, I had others, too, but I liked helping the Israelis.

The owner of a Los Angeles construction company explains his loyalty to fellow Israelis and describes his efforts to help them:

I think that it hurts me and it takes away from my power to see another Israeli without work and without any way to make his living and that's why we are helping them. My company now has at least thirty-five to forty "children" and "grandchildren" in various aspects of the business. I had many foremen who decided to go on their own and they even got a job from me as a subcontractor.

Coethnic and outgroup labor

The quotations above reflect Israelis' desire to help their countrymen and women by providing jobs and advice. Loyalty alone, however, is a poor basis for running a business. A deeper look reveals that the issue of coethnic employment is a complex one. Israelis' desire to hire coethnics must be balanced by economic realities involving the costs and accessibility of coethnic workers versus other potential employees that are available in the labor market.

Israelis often describe coethnics as easier to communicate with than out-group members as well as being more resourceful, knowledgeable, predictable and, sometimes, trustworthy. In the following quotation, Ayelet, who owns a business services company with her husband, describes her preference for co-national employees:

INVESTIGATOR: Do you and David work with Israelis?

AYELET: Yes. We just couldn't find the right people [among the native-born]. The issues we deal with are very sensitive, and we need to trust our employees with big amounts of money. So we were happy to work with Israelis because we knew they would be trustworthy, and although we didn't initially look for Israeli workers, we ended up hiring the Israelis who applied.

INVESTIGATOR: How do you explain that?

AYELET: I think there is a problem with the way the English communicate. They don't talk if something bothers them. They bottle it up, and then one day they say "I quit," and that's it – they already have a new job, and there is no room for negotiation. They will not say "It's hard, I'm having difficulties" and such. They just leave. Now our training is very expensive, so it costs us a bundle on this issue. I think in general, David has a problem with his managerial skills that he is unwilling to admit. However, with the Israelis, it is less problematic. Also, the Israelis are more resourceful, more imaginative. They find their way around things when the others give up. When you choose an Israeli, it is easier to tell who the person is. Having the same background is very helpful when selecting employees. It's not that all Israelis are perfect workers. Not at all. But you are more effective in selecting them.

On the other hand, Israeli emigrants also mention the disadvantages associated with hiring co-nationals. As a result of coethnic expectations, Israeli workers must be given privileges (including preferential treatment and higher wages) not extended to out-group members. A shop owner in London describes this:

The problem with Israelis is that you soon become friends – or at least the worker thinks so – and that can get you into trouble. You speak the same language, and he feels you treat him as one of the family. You joke with him and have fun and soon he wants to sit down and have a drink with you and do what you're doing. But, he is after all, a worker. He's being paid. So he has to work. You can't become friends with workers. It messes it all. It becomes more and more difficult at the end. It's fun to talk and work with them, but there is a problem.

A London real-estate broker who formerly ran a restaurant offered a similar story about avoiding Israeli employees:

I had two chefs – one from Thailand and an Israeli woman – and their attitude was completely different. She was always moody, having a long face. I needed to constantly pacify her. On the other hand, with him, I had no problems whatsoever.

Plate 3.4 Israeli building contractor and Latino employee, Los Angeles.

He recognized who is the boss, and complied with my demands. With her, I needed to plan ahead every conversation.

Ultimately, I quit this business. One of the reasons I wanted to quit is because I was fed up with dealing with prima donna chefs.

Another reason for avoiding coethnics is that their skills and aspirations do not match the employer's needs. Middle-class immigrant groups, such as Koreans, Indians, Taiwanese, Israelis or Russian Jews, include few individuals who seek manual labor jobs of the type often created in small ethnic businesses (Ward 1986; Kim 1999). Accordingly, employees are selected from among groups with a proletarian make-up. The following interchange occurred during an interview with a London shop owner who sought coethnic employees, but could not locate any:

INVESTIGATOR: Did you happen to work with Israelis?

YARON: No. Give me an Israeli and I will take him on board!

INVESTIGATOR: Does this mean you think Israelis are better workers than others?

YARON: No. Not necessarily, but it would simply be easier to work with someone who shares your understanding.

Further, immigrants often lack the language ability, skills, knowledge and contacts available from native-born workers (Leba 1985; Trankiem 1986). Andy owns a metal-casting company in Los Angeles that manufactures collectable figurines. While his factory is staffed by Israelis, Asians and Latinos, Andy relies on native-born white workers in the front office to deal with American customers, distributors and retailers:

> The marketing and distribution and the warehousing are much more of an American labor force. Our product has an "all American" appeal, and some of the people who buy it might be rednecks. So they [American employees] deal with the market, they deal with the collectors, the dealers, with the reps.

Finally, coethnic workers are generally more likely than out-group members to use their employment experience as an apprenticeship that provides them with the knowledge, connections and capital needed to start their own businesses at a later date. This practice is very common among ethnic populations like Israelis with high rates of self-employment and can be a source of considerable consternation, since employers realize that they are training today's coethnic employee to be tomorrow's competitor (Raval 1983; Gold 1994d; Light and Gold 2000). Because Israeli émigrés' business resources and strategies have their origins in common communal sources, the potential for coethnic competition is considerable. Accordingly, Israeli emigrant entrepreneurs are generally concerned with competition control.

Business owners who "started from the bottom and worked their way up" described covertly and intentionally learning a trade in order to escape from wage laborer status. Yossi, a Los Angeles building contractor, recounted his rise from worker to owner:

> When I started out, basically I worked for him [another Israeli contractor] and I learned some skill of construction. Putting my curiosity to work, wherever I went, I always tried to see beyond what I was asked to do. So I see it as very simple for me to be able to understand the business.
>
> But while I'm doing that, I start to get to know some prices. How much it cost or how much I can make – so that I

can do it myself. I started thinking that I'm going to do it myself.

So I went to school to get the [contractor's] license. I tried my best and I failed the first time. So I went the second time, three months later. I know how to study, so I studied it and I went and I passed.

While this story may sound idiosyncratic, in fact we heard very similar accounts from other Israeli immigrants with vastly different backgrounds. For example, Moshe, a Beverly Hills goldsmith twice Yossi's age, told us how he learned his trade through covert observation and night-time practice during his youth in Egypt and later in both Israel and Los Angeles. Similarly, Benji, who owned businesses in both London and New York, describes that when he initially arrived in both cities, he sought out Israelis for jobs. Admitting that employers "used him," he nevertheless knew that this work experience would provide a means of survival as well as a valuable introduction to the local economy:

BENJI: At first I worked for an Israeli who had a shwarma and falafel place in Piccadilly. He used me – I have no doubts about that – but I needed that job then and had no other alternatives.

INVESTIGATOR: How did you find your way to him?

BENJI: I looked for Israeli restaurant owners. This one was easy to spot. I asked him if he was looking for a worker and he said he was. I looked for Israelis on purpose. I could not speak English, so I could not get along with an English employer. I had to look for Israelis. Also, because of my language – I could not work at the front of the restaurant – I could not serve people foods or take orders. I had to work at the back stage. It was hard work. As soon as I had a little money of my own I became an entrepreneur. I started buying and selling.

Israelis often assumed that coethnics would behave in the same manner that they did, using low-level jobs as a means of building their own careers – perhaps at the expense of their employers. Many accepted the fact that Israeli employees would ultimately become competitors. Yossi described his experience with coethnic employees. Despite (or perhaps because of) the fact that they acted in the same way he had, he regretfully resolved not to hire Israelis in the future.

INVESTIGATOR: Did you ever have friction with your Israeli employees?

YOSSI: Well you see, Israelis, I find most of them are like me. They took me as an example for them. They want to also become self-employed. I think it's just the nature of the Israeli.

So there were sometimes friction and also they care too much about the details of how I run my company, and I don't like that. I don't want to say that they are spying, but they copy me which is perfectly okay, but only as long as it helps me.

INVESTIGATOR: Yeah. They'll open their own business and then make it harder for you.

YOSSI: Right. But I understand that and I accept that as long as they are not cheating on me that's fine with me. But if I need to be somewhere else for a while and a potential customer comes to the work site and asks for a contractor and they give their card or leave their number – that's cheating. I don't accept. So I need to be careful of Israelis and now I hire Mexican workers more.

A dishonest [Israeli] guy like that, I will eventually get rid of. I will just throw them from the job. Many times it has happened and I have been hurt. I would not hire another Israeli. I'd hire a Mexican instead. That's very unfortunate, but they can't stop me to hire someone that needs the money.

Echoing Yossi's suspicions, Nora, a London entrepreneur, describes that because of their ambition and self-determination, Israeli workers are likely to extend effort only when it suits them:

They are not the best workers. They make the effort when they are desperate but they "do your accounts" to figure out how much you make, what is your profit and then they bill you at the end of the day . . . [laughing]. They don't like work, but when they are in need, they do good work. When they are young, have visa problems, and such – they work well. But when they don't, they turn on you.

Their keen awareness of exploitative, disloyal and conflict-ridden relations between coethnic employees and employers is why small-scale entrepreneurs, who, like Yossi and Nora, operate on a limited profit margin, find the potential disadvantages of hiring other Israelis to be too great. They now prefer non-coethnic workers. On the other hand, large-scale and well-established entrepreneurs enjoy the fact that they can hire Israelis, safe from the fear that they will be driven out of business by former employees. In the following quote, the owner of an established industrial contracting company offers his view of former workers becoming competitors:

> I would say that I'd rather work with Jewish people rather than Gentiles. If I can choose, I'd rather work with Israelis than with Americans. So, no, I am not afraid to see people competing with me. It hurts though. It really hurts to see one of your best men leave you in order to compete with you. But once you realize that this is the good part of him and if he wasn't aggressive enough to leave you when he can open his own business, then he wouldn't be good at what he is doing.
>
> So I just learn to accept it. It is a fact of life. I just give them my blessing and every foreman or supervisor who wants to get out on their own and compete with me is very welcome. They can come here and get some advice and support. I have no problem with it whatsoever.
>
> I believe that due to the size and the financial strength and the infrastructure of this company, we can still compete with them and beat them and be more successful. Yet, they can take their market share on the other ends that I am not interested in.

Finally, taking a philosophical approach, a entrepreneur asserts that it is in his own interest to increase the number of self-employed Israelis to the degree that an Israeli ethnic economy is brought into existence:

> I would say that the first reaction to this process [of former workers becoming competitors] is negative. You say, "Hey, I taught him everything and now he is going to compete with me." But now I'm saying "So what?" I mean, let it be. I like to work with Israelis, and as I said, I would rather compete with somebody I know than an entity which I know nothing about.

Strong ties and cooperation in the Israeli ethnic economy

When Israeli emigrants engage in economic cooperation with the co-national community writ large, with broad communities of native-born Jews or, especially, with a wide range of potential workers, employers and partners in the host society, they are participating in a form of social cooperation based on what economic sociologist Mark Granovetter (1973; 1995a) calls weak ties. Granovetter, along with other social scientists, have argued that weak ties – extensive but shallow relationships with a very broad range of social contacts – are more beneficial than strong ties (deeper social relations) for finding jobs or employees because they provide the widest possible source of information about potential job referrals (Holzer 1987). In contrast, intensive strong-tie relationships are less capable of delivering non-redundant information.

While this model may apply to job finding within a society's mainstream economy, strong ties are often favored in an ethnic economy, where loyalty, predictability and trust are greatly valued. Further, for Israeli emigrants, information about job openings or available workers is not the sole reason for relying on hiring networks. Coethnic networks also deliver detailed information about workers' and employers' characteristics and reputations. Finally, networks also extend leverage and control over a potential boss or worker, because the source of the referral often has some ability to insure that the relationship between worker and employer takes the promised form (Waters 1999: 102; Wilensky and Lawrence 1979). In the Israeli emigrant economy, strong ties often receive more emphasis than weak ties. Without a good degree of certainty about the behavior of a potential employer or worker, coethnicity exposes one to being exploited and, hence, is considered to be a source of risk. In the following quote, Yoav, a Los Angeles film maker, describes that while he is open to working with fellow Israelis, at the same time, coethnic ties alone don't necessarily lend themselves to serious forms of cooperation:

> Like when an Israeli calls me, I am sure that without even noticing, I am answering the calls in a much friendlier and faster way than I would answer to somebody which I don't know completely, because there is something in the background which I know where he comes from. Then, basically, Israel is such a small place where everybody really, most of the people really know each other, even in Israel and especially coming here. So everybody has a friend or relative or somebody he knows that knows you. So it's like mishpocheh [family]. And it makes it very easy to get access to each other. But in terms of real association, real business, hard business, it doesn't work on the same terms.

Émigrés often resolve the tension between their desire to work with co-nationals and their need for trusting business relations by cooperating most extensively with those whom they already share high levels of personal confidence, common purpose and other forms of social capital. By dealing with known and trusted coethnics, they reduce the likelihood of conflicting relations and reinforce norms that encourage mutual benefit. In many cases, ties within these social circles are so close that the notion of exploitation is downplayed and transfer of assets among network members is seen as a form of beneficence: "people view their well-being as having increased as the well-being of others increases" (Chiswick 1991: 8). Fieldwork and interviews reveal that high levels of cooperation exist among members of various subgroups within the Israeli immigrant community. Some networks are based on patterns of solidarity brought from Israel. Others come into being in countries of settlement. Most subgroups are informal in nature. However, in both London and Los Angeles, émigrés have formed formal business associations to facilitate cooperation and reinforce communal ties.

In Los Angeles, we observed high levels of economic cooperation within subgroups of Kibbutzniks and Mizrahi Jews. Members of both of these groups maintain their own contacts and forms of social and economic cooperation in the US. Prior to migration, each maintained a way of life that was in very different ways distinct from that of the Israeli mainstream. Kibbutzniks hail from a series of socialist collectives throughout Israel that maintain a cooperative lifestyle and, at least initially, emphasized agricultural work. Noted for their idealism, many Kibbutzniks trace their families back to European Jewish migrants who arrived in Palestine prior to the 1948 formation of the State of Israel. In this way, Kibbutzniks constitute a kind of social and cultural elite (Sabar 2000). In contrast, Mizrahi Jews come from Iran, Iraq, Yemen, Morocco, Tunisia, Syria, Turkey and other Middle Eastern countries. Some are long established in Israel while others entered with resources of education and capital and have achieved middle-class status. However, as a group, they are more recently arrived, less educated and of lower social standing than the Ashkenazim (Shama and Iris 1977; Uriely 1995; Goldscheider 1996; Yiftachel 1998). Religiously and culturally, their outlook is often traditionalistic and has been influenced by the Islamic nations from which they came. Despite the fact that they account for a sizable fraction of the Israeli population, Mizrahim are less socially, politically and economically powerful than Ashkenazi Jews, whose outlook is institutionalized in much of Israel's culture (Smooha 1978; Mittelberg 1988; Razin 1991).

The dramatic contrasts in experiences and lifestyles between Kibbutzniks and Mizrahi Jews notwithstanding, both groups developed a strong subgroup identity prior to migration. This outlook is often maintained in places of settlement and used as a basis for organizing collective activities. In this way, their development of ethnic networks in host settings would be predicted by "twice migrant" theory, a perspective that assumes that groups who possess a shared identity and collective outlook prior to migration will create organizations in the new setting more rapidly than immigrants who had been members of a society's majority group (Bhachu 1985; Espiritu 1989; Zenner 1991; Nonini and Ong 1997).

In Los Angeles, Kibbutzniks have an active social and economic life. Established émigrés frequently help their friends emigrate to the US, assist their resettlement and find them jobs. "L.A.'s Kibbutzniks have a very effective informal network to provide help to new arrivals . . . They help each other with loans for business ventures and housing, professional advice and connections" (Sabar 1989: 9). Corroborating Sabar's finding, we interviewed a Kibbutznik building contractor who assisted others in the US. Because he ran a large and well-established businesses, he was unconcerned about potential competition from those who he had helped:

> I'll put it this way. I have few circles around me. And of course, the Israeli circle is closer to me than the Jewish circle. And the Jewish circle is closer to me than the Gentile circle, okay. And the human race is closer to me than, I don't know, the planet. I would say it comes about in this kind of degree and people from my own Kibbutz are closer to me than people from Israel in general. So I hire them and I am glad to see them doing well.

Like Kibbutzniks, Mizrahi Israeli immigrants in Los Angeles, South Florida, Chicago, New York, Paris and London appear to maintain several patterns of social life fairly distinct from those of Ashkenazi Israelis and Mizrahi Jews who, prior to migration, assimilated to Ashkenazi social patterns. These Mizrahi Israelis also maintain distinctive economic patterns. While our sampling is not random, in fieldwork we consistently encountered a disproportionate number of Mizrahi Israelis in retail and manufacturing enterprises such as small shops, restaurants, the garment industry, building contractors and diamonds and jewelry. In contrast, a majority of the college-educated and professional Israelis that we interviewed were of European origins. Informants who are knowledgeable about these communities indicate that while this pattern is not universal, it appears to be a strong tendency (Shokeid 1988; Uriely 1995). In the following quotation, a Hebrew-speaking employee of a school that trains workers for the California State Building Contractor's License examination refers to the ethnicity and patterns of cooperation revealed by the Israelis in her classes:

> They are mostly young guys, age 25–32. The big majority are Sephardic or Eastern. I don't know what countries their families came from because they were almost all born in Israel, second or third generation Israeli. I don't ask them because I don't care at all. The whole class is not Hebrew speaking, so whatever their background, they meet each other, and become friends and sit together in class.
>
> They enter contracting because it is the easiest field to work in without knowing English. They don't have to deal with Americans. They get orders from [Israeli] general contractors and that's it. Working with hammers and saws and wood doesn't require any specific language skills.
>
> The weird thing is that they complain about each other but they will always work together. They like each other but will always compete. They like to cooperate because they share the same language and outlook. They all work very hard, they help each other, they work long hours. They cut some deals and cut some corners which they could not do if they worked with American general contractors. They understand each others' approach:

In some cases, subgroup networks provided access to resources beyond the Israeli or native-born Jewish community. For example, according to Nissan (who moved from Iran to Israel as a child), Persian Israelis in Los Angeles cooperate not only with their fellows, but with Jewish, Armenian and Muslim Iranian immigrants as well, many of whom are well endowed with resources of capital, education and business experience:

> For us it is very easy to find out a job only in the downtown. Before I went in the downtown, I tried to look at the ads in the American newspapers, like the *LA Times*. My son was looking with me. But I couldn't get into the business. But the minute I went to downtown LA, there are a lot of Israelis and Persian guys, we contract between each other and start business.

Our data suggest that these patterns of subgroup cooperation are not limited to Kibbutzniks and Persians. Instead, such networks appear to be common among various subgroups within the Israeli community. For example, forms of economic cooperation are also created on the basis of relationships in the host society. In London, we interviewed several men who owned small businesses and had married local women. They cooperated in business ventures and social affairs. Aaron refers to this group:

AARON: My friends, as I said, most of them are Israelis, and most are married to English women – some are Jewish and some are not.

INVESTIGATOR: So which language do you speak when you get together?

AARON: When I am with friends we speak Hebrew while all the women sit together and speak English.

INVESTIGATOR: So all your friends are Israelis married to local women. It would be interesting to know whether all of you are self employed.

AARON: Well, come to think of it – yes! One is a builder, one has a sport shop, one is a gardener and such.

Another type of network is comprised of middle-class Israeli women who exchange information regarding work, children's schooling, and family needs. We noticed these networks in New York, Los Angeles, Paris, and especially in London. They were generally oriented towards jobs in Jewish communal occupations (teachers, communal activists) as well as residential real estate – fields where numerous Israeli women find work. Mari, a London Hebrew teacher, refers to her reliance on such a group:

INVESTIGATOR: You work mainly with Israelis?

MARI: Yes, I prefer to work with them because obviously they teach Hebrew better than the local teachers. The communication between us is also simplified because we all speak the same language. We're also on the same wave length in terms of pedagogy, because we were all trained as teachers in Israel.

While many members of women's networks are oriented towards Jewish communal occupations, the following woman with expertise in accounting and computers also found a position through such a network:

INVESTIGATOR: When did you start working here?

GOLDIE: That was about three years after we came here. An Israeli woman who I knew told me about another Israeli who was looking for a worker to run his exports to Spain and was looking for someone who speaks Spanish. I spoke Spanish, so that is actually why I applied.

INVESTIGATOR: You have a profession which is constantly in demand, so why didn't you just find a job on your own?

GOLDIE: Well, I knew there was a demand, but I was a bit apprehensive and anxious about it all here, to go into an English company, having a family with three kids. I was scared. I did not even try to pursue this option. All I did was search among the Israelis I knew. I made some attempts which were not successful and then this offer came along. I was offered odd jobs such as to work at nights, but I wanted something that would suit my family life too. So when this Israeli looked for a Spanish speaker, I started working there.

I am their in-house IT [information technology] person. I begun by doing their accountancy. But the company grew and developed and their needs in terms of IT grew as well. So I developed the software they use. The software I write is also used in the mother company in Israel as well. Now I work part time – four days a week and only six hours a day. It's close and comfortable.

INVESTIGATOR: The Israeli woman who linked you to your current boss – was she from here?

GOLDIE: Yes, there was a woman here – her name was Ariela, and she was by herself an institution here. She made all the links between people, distributed information, she did matchmaking, supported people, found jobs and workers for people. She was the center of the community.

Through the closeness of their membership, Israeli networks often provided valuable information, support and economic benefits, but this was not always the case. In other instances, their close relations are seen as a disadvantage because they are corrosive to privacy. Ella, who organized a series of cultural and philanthropic activities for Israeli women in London, found her occupation to be stressful precisely because her clients had so much knowledge about her:

> Now there is group of [Israeli emigrant] women who are not working. They are middle class, bored, and what they do all day is go from coffee shop to another. Their lives are empty, so they fill it with gossip. I stay away from them. I don't mingle with many people, but I need all these people to attend my events.
>
> Instead of accepting me – as someone who wants to give and is willing and able to put energy into the community – they get envy about how much I earn. The hell, I need to live off something. Even a charity has workers who are fully paid. So why shouldn't I profit from what I do? People tend to dismiss what I do for the charity because I get a salary. That annoys me. For instance, I brought here a show – a sing along with one of the best [Israeli] singers – because you people said you wanted this culture and you miss this type of events. So I work for two months to get it done – and I'm not allowed to see a profit? Doesn't make much sense does it?
>
> So this is the group of people who have money but no brains. This is their attitude. I work very hard for what I have. This makes me crazy. I can't even sit at the Israeli restaurant because of the gossip that goes on. Maybe I'm paying the price of being a celebrity.

Finally, it should be noted that while subgroup cooperation may limit certain forms of solidarity – for example, encouraging Persian Israelis to collaborate with each other rather than with non-Persian origin countrymen – at the same time, such a pattern opens up other avenues of economic cooperation by allowing Persian Israelis to do business with immigrants from Iran. In this manner, a multi-ethnic division of labor is established, allowing a whole series of groups to cooperate. In the following quote, a Persian-Israeli garment contractor explains how strong ties are used to reduce the risk involved in selecting subcontractors:

> Persians are very, very careful to do business with themselves and not with other people because they are afraid to make business with unknown subcontractors, like Mexicans.

They ask for references. If the Mexican contractors come, we ask other Persian guys "How he did the work for you in terms of quality and in terms of trust, did you trust him?" And then you slowly give him work and if he does good . . . [you give him more].

They do not trust non-Persians because sometimes they can disappear with the money and you can't find them. But the Persian guy, if he disappears tomorrow, you can locate him, you can find him, you can trace him and get the money back.

In sum, cooperation is most extensive among groups of Israeli émigrés who share well-developed and overlapping strong ties based in experience, ideology, religious outlook, language, lifestyle and family. Such ties serve as social capital (Coleman 1988; Portes 1998) that permits members of these communities to share resources and develop collective endeavors to an extent greater than that evident among co-nationals lacking such ties. These collectivities insure high-quality information and reduce the possibility of being misled or exploited by an unknown, and possibly untrustworthy, Israeli. In many cases, networks and social capital can alter the terms of partnership or employment, reducing risks in joint ventures and investments, providing workers with higher wages, security and better working conditions, and helping to insure employees' punctuality, good faith and cooperation. At the same time, these networks are not universally accessible nor is participation free. Such networks often demand contributions, enforce behavioral norms and maintain their own rules about who can and cannot take part (Portes and Sensenbrenner 1993). Accordingly, ethnic social capital provides both benefits and costs. It is a mixed blessing for Israeli émigrés.

Industry and ethnic cooperation

As we have seen, Israeli emigrants often express a preference for working with co-nationals. However, Israelis' economic activities are embedded in larger contexts that both foster and constrain the nature and extent of coethnic cooperation. In other words, patterns of cooperation are not solely the outcome of émigrés' preference. Instead, they are also the result of the structure and organization of the particular field of economic endeavor in question. Certain industries appear to reward ethnic economic integration, while others discourage it.

The diamond business, the real-estate/construction industry, and information technology depend on an extensive division of labor and many cooperative activities. Diamonds and real estate facilitate sharing referrals and the use of commission sales (Coleman 1988). Cooperation is especially well developed in the real estate/construction business. Wages and earnings are traditionally high in these industries, and hiring networks are an important means of allocating jobs, thus allowing Israeli developers and contractors to employ coethnic subcontractors without having adversely competitive relations (Bailey and Waldinger 1991). In the words of a Israeli-born senior manager of one of Southern California's major real estate development firms:

> There is no question that Israelis, there is some kind of a connection and if I've got a good Israeli – and I don't want to sound like I am discriminating against anybody – but probably subconsciously, there is a warm spot for them. No question about it. A lot of my subcontractors are Israelis. I mean, you would sometimes go through one of my developments and you think you're in a Kibbutz somewhere because you hear so much Hebrew spoken.

Another industry that reveals a high level of coethnic cooperation among Israeli emigrants is information technology. Even more so than construction, this industry offers excellent wages. However, it also demands long hours, a high level of technical knowledge and the ability to quickly and clearly communicate complex ideas to superiors, co-workers and clients. In London, Israeli programmers and engineers often own small computer firms, which function as independent contractors. While owners are thus free to hire whoever they please, such firms tend to be sole proprietorships that have relatively few employees. Nevertheless, these emigrant IT professionals frequently exchange information and referrals.

A more extensive pattern of Israeli cooperation is evident within larger English and multinational companies. Although Israelis are not owners, they often influence hiring decisions, making certain departments of these companies "ethnic controlled economies" wherein coethnics help peers find jobs in non-coethnic firms or in the public sector (Light and Gold 2000). In fact, a fairly sizable fraction of Israeli information technology workers in London had come there because they were recruited by co-national associates who they had known in the country of origin. Such is the case for Mimi, a manager in the computer department of an English media company. Mimi originally came to London because Uri, who had known her in Israel, got her a job there. Later, when Uri returned to Israel, he continued to refer programmers to Mimi who happily hired them, "simply because they are good." Mimi explains why her office in London is full of Israeli workers:

INVESTIGATOR: What do you see as the main differences between an Israeli IT person and Englishmen?

MIMI: There is first of all the issue of motivation. The Englishman does not care and has no motivation to get ahead. To him, it's a place of work, where he gets a salary. Israelis are motivated. They want the money obviously, but they are caring and professional. I could not find a project manager for ten months. One day, I got to meet an Israeli who lives here for four years. I interviewed him in a coffee shop for five minutes and had a feeling that he is what we needed. So I took him in. He is doing great. He is an Israeli in every sense – innovative, assertive, his way of thinking, his technical and managerial perspectives – it's incredible how similar we all are! There is no comparing to English managers!

Gal, another Israeli IT worker in London, found his job through a Dan – an Israeli broker, who like Uri, recruited Israeli programmers to fill positions in the UK:

GAL: When I was 16, I developed with a friend of mine an anti-virus software. It was a real hit and a breakthrough in terms of the technologies we used. We sold it to an American company which is one of the leading firms in the area today. Dan knew about this software since he worked in this area. So he contacted me in relation to that software. Since then, we have been in touch from time to time. Before the army, I worked for him doing all sorts of computing jobs – I earned my pocket money through that work.

After the army, Dan, who had moved to London, contacted me because his wife and him developed a new software. Dan suggested that I come here [London] and work in the new company. He suggested that I would take the lead in the development of the new software. That was a very tempting offer.

Now Dan was smart. When he made his offers, it all sounded very temporary. He did not suggest "Why don't you immigrate to London for the rest of your life?" He suggested I come here for two years, and that I do the MS in computers at the same time. He said he would give me a part time job during my studies so that I could support myself financially. The graduate study would give me legal status to stay.

When I look back at it, I think Dan knew how to play the game to get me here. He "dripped-dropped" the idea in little doses. [Over time,] he talked with me about the possibilities in London and his life here. I also came here a few times back then – he paid me to come here to do some work. So I knew the people who worked here and the whole idea of living in London was not strange to me. So by the time the proposal came, I kind of grew into it already. I was ready for it. I agreed.

INVESTIGATOR: Today – do you still work with Israelis?

GAL: I work with Israelis a lot today. And today, half the workers in the company are Israelis. There are about twenty people there.

In contrast to their relatively smooth relations with co-nationals, émigrés often described difficult interactions with natives. These ranged from problems in communication to attempts by natives to take advantage of Israelis' outsider status. For example, Avi, a software designer, told me how, after moving his entire family from Tel Aviv to the British capital at the request of a single firm, he was invited to dinner at a London hotel by a representative of this company. Over an elegant meal, his employer informed him that unless he agreed to sell the rights to the program that he wrote, he would get no additional work. (Avi resisted, retained ownership of his software and went on to work for several clients, including the manipulative dinner host.)

Israelis' network-based involvement in offshore information technology companies exemplifies sociologist Ronald Burt's (1992; 2000) "structural holes" formulation of social capital. Through his study of corporate managers, Burt determined that individuals able to broker beneficial information and resources between distinct, otherwise disconnected networks were especially effective and successful at their jobs:

> People on either side of a structural hole circulate in different flows of information. Structural holes are thus an opportunity to be a broker of information between people, and control the projects that bring people together from opposite sides of the hole.
>
> (Burt 2000: 4)

The information technology economies and associated labor markets of London, on the one hand, and Israel, on the other, are separate. London, as a global city and center of multinational commerce, has extensive demand for skilled IT workers (Sassen 1991). Additionally, it features a high standard of living, generous salaries and outstanding cultural amenities. In contrast, because of Israel's university systems, its well-developed military, and large numbers of highly educated immigrants (from the former USSR and other nations), the Jewish State has the largest fraction of engineers to population of any country in the world (Richtel 1998).

Accordingly, Israel has a large supply of skilled IT workers of just the sort who are needed in London. However, due to issues of distance, language, culture and citizenship, a structural hole exists between England's and Israel's information technology economies. Individuals like Dan and Uri described above, who are familiar with and in possession of knowledge, contacts and other forms of social capital in both settings, play vital broker roles as they bring Israeli IT professionals to jobs in London. The British companies they work for are happy with their new workers, and the Israeli emigrants they hire are satisfied with high salaries, good working conditions and ample cultural amenities. Moreover, the presence of an accessible community of coethnics in London facilitates the adjustment of newly arrived Israeli workers. By bridging the structural hole between these two settings, Dan, Uri and others like them link the global and local, increasing their own power, while satisfying multiple clients. Interestingly, these network-mediated patterns of work and migration followed by highly skilled Israelis working in London's information technology sector are nearly identical to those maintained by Mexican laborers employed in service industries and factories of Southern California (Massey *et al.* 1994).

In contrast to diamonds, construction and the information technology industry, the garment industry – at least in Southern California – is far less conducive to the type of ethnic cooperation that Israelis favor. Requiring a low cost of entry, and based on widely available skills, materials and information, it generates profits largely by keeping wages as low as possible (Bonacich and Appelbaum 2000). Construction, diamonds and information technology industries require a high level of skill and create custom-made products. Thus, producers have the ability to meet and bargain over prices with clients. In contrast, garments are mass-produced and consumed on a global scale, under super-competitive conditions, involving international production. A very broad range of actors ranging from Asian banks and overseas factories to a wide array of ethnic manufacturers and subcontractors in Southern California are involved, making coordination and cooperation extremely difficult (Bonacich 1990; Waldinger 1986). Accordingly, there are relatively few opportunities for the industry's participants to develop mutually beneficial relations. Protecting slim profit margins, Israeli garment entrepreneurs fear that if they are indiscreet, others will "knock off" (copy) their products and steal customers.

Finally, while the construction, diamond and IT industries include Israeli emigrant workers and companies at many levels in a manner that facilitates coethnic vertical integration, nearly all Israelis in the LA garment industry are manufacturers, and hence employ subcontracting firms run by other ethnic groups to sew, process, cut, package, dye and deliver their product. In fact, so individualistic were Israeli garment manufacturers that we had to expend extra efforts just to conduct interviews for this study. This contrasted dramatically with the general accessibility of Israeli entrepreneurs in Los Angeles. An established sportswear manufacturer, one of the few who was active as a communal leader in Los Angeles' Israeli community, describes the lack of ethnic cooperation in the garment industry:

> Israelis have a tendency to be too smart in a negative way. They come here and they try to capture the most they can in a short period of time. So sometimes it's not to advantage, sometimes its dangerous to work with Israelis.
>
> There are a lot of people who know each other through the marketplace, but there is hardly any cooperation like in the film industry or the jewelry business. Here it's totally separate, a lot more competing.

In sum, Israelis' patterns of economic cooperation are not simply the consequence of their desire to work with co-nationals. Rather, an industry's economic structure establishes conditions which either facilitate or discourage ethnic economic collectivism.

Reflections on work in the Israeli diaspora

Statistics tell us that in comparison to other migrant populations, Israeli emigrants are economically successful, earning sizable incomes, running businesses and working as professionals in many points of settlement (Gold and Phillips 1996a; Schmool and Cohen 1998; Sheffer 1998; Cohen 1999). Financial success, however, is not always indicative of satisfaction with earnings, working conditions and one's way of life. In general, Israeli emigrants feel that opportunities, wages and working conditions in countries of settlement are superior to those at home. Yet, at the same time, a fair proportion – including those who are economically successful – have complaints. Because social science theory and research on migration so heavily emphasize the role of economics in motivating action, it is important to consider data suggesting that affluence is not the sole factor in shaping how people reflect upon geographical mobility. Our findings suggest that other issues, such as satisfaction with working conditions and patterns of coethnic interaction, can be crucially important as well.

As noted, most Israeli émigrés find that opportunities and working conditions are satisfactory. In the words of a returned migrant now working for an American company in Israel: "I think the US is a very open society and speaking as a white male, you can, if you work hard, advance very rapidly. If you are smart, you can really do a lot in the States. The opportunities are terrific." A musician living in London acknowledges the increased opportunities he has encountered:

> With the music issue, UK is a world leader. In London were the great bands, I mean, the Beatles, Queen. London is the place. I love London very much. The way of living, the calmness. This is the reason that I am here and not in Israel.

INVESTIGATOR: What do you think from the economical point of view?

> It is very expensive to live here [but] I do live here well. Right now, I do not have a lot of pupils, but when I have, I enjoy it and this is not a physical work. I am doing what I love to do. In Israel, I could not live like that, to be honest. I wouldn't be able to rent a house, and to buy a car like the one I have. I always wanted such a car. I can open here a business. I do not know how my life would have look without the music. I do not know what it would be like if I would have not come to London.

Nissan, a Persian-origin Israeli who owns clothing stores in England and the US applauds the availability of opportunities, the economic scale and the more organized work-life in England:

> I think I could never have done so well in Israel. No. The store I had in Israel was fairly small, and the prospects for growth were not great. I had something much bigger in my

imagination. I felt I had to go somewhere else if I want to fulfill this ambition. I was sure that I will not be able to fulfill my ultimate goals in Israel. I would have had perhaps a good life; maybe even comfortable life. But to get to where I am now, I knew I had to go to a more central place, a wider market, that offered more clients and more opportunities.

INVESTIGATOR: Has your opinion about Israel changed since you came here?

NISSAN: Well, I think the Israelis are a bit . . . how shall I say it – hafifnikim [– not serious, do things hastily, improvise a lot]. An hour is not an hour and nothing is precise. Israel is a land of haltura [improvisation]. I like things to be organized and precise. Once I used to get annoyed about this. Now I can laugh about it.

A woman who returned to Israel from Australia describes her husband's positive evaluation of his employment there:

In terms of my husband's job – it was great and he loved every minute of it. It was a big job and a big responsibility. The payment was good, so we were able to have a very comfortable life in a stunning place. He had to computerize the whole plant and this was a challenge for him and he really enjoyed it.

Several Israelis described other benefits associated with work outside of the Jewish State. These included a less obstructive bureaucracy, lower taxes, easier access to credit, more opportunities to acquire training and degrees and two-day weekends. (The Israeli weekend goes from Friday afternoon until Saturday evening.)

In the following quotation, Bracha, an Israeli academic who had lived in the US for several years, offers a mixed assessment of working in the US. She feels that financial compensation and quality of work life are fine, but that Americans sacrifice family life for career development:

What do I think about American work style? I think I appreciated it a lot. I appreciate the atmosphere of the workplace. There are things that I like very much, but also things that I still resent after seven years in the United States. I still resent the idea that people will break their family in order to keep a

Plate 3.5 Israeli hair salon and sandwich shop, Paris.

job or go climb higher on the career ladder. I would never do anything like that. But other than that, I think we saw America in its very high levels. We were in Wall Street. We saw people that worked very hard and are paid very well. The other thing that we saw was the university, where people work not as hard and get paid not as well, but are very happy with their work. I didn't see the, you know, any underclass. I didn't come near it. So this is what I know. I know that is very high level and it is there are many things that are admirable there.

While these quotations generally offer positive evaluations of work in the diaspora, such feelings were not universal. Those quoted below express frustrations and regrets about their careers. The general implication is that the single-minded pursuit of work in the diaspora, no matter how successful, did not provide émigrés with a degree of fulfillment adequate to compensate the costs associated with being away from home.

Some respondents, such as Rachel, who worked as a software engineer in the US, and Miri, an educator settled in France, were disturbed by the self-interested attitudes of workers in their countries of settlement:

INVESTIGATOR: What is your general opinion of work life?

RACHEL: What surprised me was to realize that people there don't work as hard as people in Israel – in the same occupation. I think that they are more concerned with not having the company take advantage of them. They keep their hours, but they don't put in too much overtime, unless they are well-compensated for it. They feel like an individual and not really part of the company. And in Israel, I don't know what the reason for it, but people work much harder and get compensated much less for it. And I don't know what there is in Israel – it might that they just don't have any choice – but there's definitely a difference in that respect.

MIRI: The French – everything is difficult for them. So they don't do it. My colleague, the Kibbutznik, says they are hopeless. They simply can't move things. You can't imagine how hard I must work if I want to get a party organized. Hard work.

INVESTIGATOR: What do you mean?

MIRI: Well, the school does not organize anything. No celebrations at all. They say "the children don't go to school so they can sing and dance. They come to learn other things." They don't teach them to sing, ever. I wanted to organize a concert so that children would sing. They didn't know how. They could not digest this. They objected. At the end of the day, we had a cassette in the background and the children sang along with it.

Avi, who owned several auto-related businesses and real-estate concerns in England, regretted his decision to develop a career outside of the Jewish State:

AVI: There was a point when I considered going back and opening a garage in Israel. But I think it's crazy to do that in Israel. Very hard life. Nothing like here. I also think I have become too English in my manners, so I will not be able to survive there. My friends tell me "They will eat you alive there!" They are more aggressive in Israel. So I live here, and basically, I have a good life.

INVESTIGATOR: Would you recommend England to Israelis?

AVI: To businessmen? I think not. I think if someone is doing well in one place he better stay put. One can make good money in Israel. If you are in, why go out? Every move is expensive. If I had a business in Israel, I would not have come here at all. Maybe I have a good life here. But Israel is a good place, too. I know some people who have very hard lives here, just like they did in Israel. Once you succeed – don't move!

Sol, a Los Angeles garment manufacturer who returned to Israel following Southern California's recession in the mid-1990s, also expressed remorse about his emigration when I interviewed him during a business trip to Los Angeles in 1996:

INVESTIGATOR: So what would you say if you had a friend back in Israel and he was thinking of going to the States or someplace else? What would you tell him to do?

SOL: Well I would never recommend for anybody to come to the States. When I was young, it was a different story. But I feel all my friends that stayed in Israel and didn't come here, they did just as well in Israel. And economically wise, they own their own homes, businesses, they are all doing well. As a matter of fact, the last few years in Israel nobody is asking about America anymore because of the situation over here. Years ago, they used to ask all the time, everybody was looking. But lately, Israelis been doing great as far as business wise.

So nobody is really asking about here and I wouldn't recommend to any Israeli to come here. I don't see Israelis replacing what they have in Israel anywhere in the world. I mean, I think that California is the best place [in the world] for foreigners, especially Israelis, but I wouldn't recommend coming here to anybody.

Finally, the manufacturer of what, in the US, is a nationally known brand of clothing, nevertheless felt unhappy with his career:

Israelis come here for money and success, but ultimately it's not worth the cost of adjustment, big cost if you fail, and even costly if you succeed. This country is very sad for Israelis. It splits families – broken apart. My brother and sister are still in Israel, but I tell them not to come.

When you come here, you lose your ties and your family – if you don't have success in business, you lose everything. If you are successful in business, you don't lose quite as much. Family here is too loose. You lose out, don't spend time together, no closeness. You are rewarded economically if you are successful, but it's still not worth the cost. So what if you have a million dollar house and you and your wife and kids all drive Mercedes Benz? You still lose.

Business owners were more likely than professionals to lament emigration. However, some professionals also complained. An ambivalent Santa Monica obstetrician, who established a flourishing practice only after struggling to overcome professional exclusion, offered an apologetic reflection:

The main reason I came is professional. Every Jewish mother wants that her son would be a lawyer or a physician. And I found that the country [Israel] is very small. The possibilities as a physician are very limited and I had an opportunity. My family was here, my aunt, my uncle, my mother. So I left, and I'll tell you something. If I had known what the difficulties were, what I would have to go through, definitely I wouldn't have come. You know it's a free country, but professionally, it is a very closed society. People don't let you get in enough and every step was very hard.

But anyway, I did what I did and I am more respected over here. Even though, to tell you the truth, if I did the right thing or not, I don't know.

Transnational work

As a means of addressing their mixed feelings about living and working outside of the Jewish State, a number of Israelis sought to establish border-crossing lifestyles. Such was the hope of Isaac, a bookstore/café owner in Paris:

I hope to be in a situation when I will be working part of the time in Israel and part of the time in here. I want to live there, but to work and have money in here. I will never become again a small independent worker in Israel.

Benni, the proprietor of a shipping firm with branches in London, Paris and Israel, was able to run an enterprise that permitted him to spend a considerable time in Israel while earning a comfortable income abroad. He explained that the expansion of his business from a locally based outfit to one reaching an international clientele was facilitated by advice and contacts provided by the staff of the Israeli Consulate in London. Benni refers to his international way of life:

> The ideal is to earn in here and to live in Israel. Much better. The rental fees in Israel is much cheaper than here. In principal, I don't have to work. I sit comfortably, have flat in here and flat in Israel. I have a nice salary. I am traveling a lot in the world. My base will be in Israel. I hope to be there for two weeks in a month, then one week in here.

Several respondents involved in transnational activities drew upon years of experience with international businesses. Because Israel's economic development policies are, to a large measure, oriented towards the export of goods and agricultural products, the country trains and sends abroad a contingent of functionaries to engage in international economic transactions. Developing skills and contacts in various settings, a fraction of these eventually become independent workers and entrepreneurs in many national settings (Shokeid 1988). Such was the case of a Los Angeles man referred to us by the Israeli Embassy. After acquiring an advanced degree in an agricultural science from an American university, he had worked for several years in the export of Israeli citrus to Japan. At the time we spoke to him, he was involved in a variety of import/export activities spanning the US and Asia.

Transnational entrepreneurs eloquently reflected on both the possibilities and problems involved in international business. For example, in the mid-1990s, Sol, a Los Angeles garment manufacturer, described his ambitious plan to produce clothes in Egypt, and then transport them, via duty-exempt Israel, to be sold in the US:

SOL: The idea that I developed was that you'd be able to bring garments from the Middle East even cheaper than you can bring from countries like China or Hong Kong, because of the quota limitation. The idea was to take advantage of the Israeli-United States trade agreement where there is no duty involved. What I was hoping to do is to incorporate the neighboring cheap labor countries, like Egypt, Jordan. At the same time I would keep my distribution over here [in Los Angeles].

By cooperating between Israel and Egypt, eventually you will be able to bring in the finished product. They will have to be cut in Israel, it will be assembled in Egypt and brought back to Israel and shipped from Israel. I have some Israeli partners here in LA. They pooled some money together. They see the potential.

See the thing is that manufacturers and importers in the United States always went to the Far East. Whenever they want to import electronics, toys or garments, they always went to the Far East. By now, many have become more aware that the Middle East has a great potential, especially in Egypt, where a lot of the basic items are subsidized by the government. They have all the knowledge, all the know how, and the technology over there.

INVESTIGATOR: So did you get some of the ideas about how to organize this from your experience in LA with the Latino workers, and the garments and fabrics coming in from Hong Kong, and things like that?

SOL: Exactly. Actually, the cold peace that Israel has with Egypt has really handicapped a lot of the business opportunities. In other words, Egypt fills its country with a lot of bureaucracy. I'm still working on it. But I attended a couple of major business conferences in Egypt and in Israel. A lot of Egyptian business people attended. It is a big opening for cooperating between the two countries.

Illustrating the challenges involved in transnational entrepreneurship, a film producer who ran companies in both Israel and Los Angeles asserted that while he enjoyed being in Hollywood, he found it very difficult to remain active and involved on two continents:

YOAV: I was producing films in Israel until 1985, when a film I produced was nominated for an Academy Award. So suddenly the world becomes smaller than it used to be for me and I got an offer which I couldn't refuse – to extend my business opportunities here.

And in looking at it as an Israeli, I see nationalism is a very important thing, because I am trying to keep my own nationalism. But still, you have to start to work in terms of the – how you call it – the global village. That's what we are now.

Now I have a film company in Israel and a film company here. When I arrived, I started with an American partner – she is the one that initiated my coming here. And meanwhile, at the same time, my company in Israel was doing productions for different American projects. They were looking for locations for films and they would do it through my company. So that was the kind of business which I was doing back and forth. Basically I did not discontinue my ties with Israel, business wise, I continued my ties with Israel.

INVESTIGATOR: In fact you probably improved them in a sense.

YOAV: Well, I improved them in one sense, and disimproved in another sense. I improved them because they became more global, but disimproved them because I can't be in both places. So my attention is given to the place where I happen to be at the moment and the other is neglected.

Occupation and international access

Some entrepreneurs are able to run businesses and maintain social and family lives on different continents. However, this transnational pattern seems much more common among professionals, especially those who acquired degrees in top Western universities, than it is among the less educated.[3]

Our sub-sample of Israelis who had lived abroad and then returned was obtained through personal referrals. Accordingly, it cannot be considered an accurate representation of all returned migrants. Nevertheless, the great majority of those included were highly educated persons who said that excellent job offers from universities, corporations or information technology firms were a major motive for their re-migration. The accessibility of opportunities, and the relative ease in travel and return these migrants enjoyed is exemplified in the following quote by Dan, a professor of engineering who – like his father before him – resettled in Israel after a period of education and work in the States:

DAN: I wanted to pursue a Ph.D. I was fortunate that my master's thesis was quite good. I got recommendations and everything. I wanted to study a topic not quite developed in Israel. So it was a great opportunity. You see, it's just by chance that I spent three years in the States from age 3 to age 6 when my father also made a Ph.D.

I was very impressed with the opportunities I was given there. Like I would compete for jobs against other Americans and I got jobs that Americans didn't get, so they were very

100

fair. All the rules of the games are very explicit. I was very impressed with the system: how the system works, how efficiently it was.

INVESTIGATOR: Why did you return to Israel?

DAN: I had a job offer here at this university, so we just returned.

In contrast, Israelis lacking a higher education or professional occupation often supported themselves in the West through self-employment or other forms of participation in the Israeli or Jewish ethnic economy. Some become successful entrepreneurs. However, despite their desire to return home, they often confront considerable difficulties in transporting their businesses back to Israel. Their experience was taken as a lesson by co-nationals, who are often reluctant to risk their livelihood. In the following quote, Sol, the owner of a large Los Angeles garment company, describes the contingencies he encountered when he tried to relocate during the middle 1990s:

> I came here eighteen years ago to try to benefit from some of the good stuff that America has to offer and then go back. Eventually, when my kid was about 15 years old, my wife decided if we don't do it now, we'll never do it. We made the decision and we went. The idea was that I'll go back and forth for a while and try to develop something there that will benefit us economically from the years that we've been here.
>
> But due to the economic situation over here, not every-thing went according to the plan. I had to spend more time here saving my business and also, I was hoping that I'll be able to liquidate some of my assets. This didn't really work out, so I had to continue to go back and forth, to try to develop my business. Also, I had two Israeli partners in the company in the US and when I started going back and forth, they didn't like the idea and they made it actually difficult for me.
>
> I'm still working on it. It has been like that for the last two and a half years. My kids are there [in Israel] and I'm going next month. And it is tough. I go back and forth about nine times a year. When I go, I go for a month.

Similar sentiments were expressed by small business owners in several locations. While comfortable in their host societies, they hope to return to Israel for family reasons, but discover they simply cannot afford to do so. The following account is from Hiam, the owner of a London auto repair shop:

> I went back to [visited] Israel and discussed this with friends of mine. I still have quite a few friends there. And they have large businesses in Israel. One of them has a big garage. He offered me a job. But I didn't want to become an employee again. I did not want to consider that. And opening a business there is a real headache. I have the skills and all that, but I would have had to leave all the machinery here and start from scratch. It means coming in with nothing and starting again. Plus there is income tax.

Generous job offers yielding security and a standard of living approximating that which they enjoyed in the West were not forthcoming for Israeli émigrés like Sol and Hiam who run construction companies, restaurants, body shops or garment firms. Hence, their careers are less compatible with international travel.

Finally, highly educated Israelis working for corporations or universities are likely to have legal residency status and permission to work overseas. In contrast, those with lower levels of education more commonly entered the host society on a tourist or student visa that prohibits long stays and employment. For them, visits home are difficult. Some described how they were unable to attend their parents' funerals for fear that they would be unable to return to their jobs and families (Minster 1998). In sum, transnational businesses and remigration – strategies that allowed Israeli émigrés access to economic resources and opportunities abroad while enjoying social and cultural amenities and family ties located in Israel – were often seen as viable solutions to problems associated with emigration. However, such solutions were much more accessible to educated professionals than they were to small business owners and others lacking easily transportable job skills and legal status in settlement countries (Gold 2001).

Conclusions

Israelis frequently emigrate to access opportunities (for both earnings and job satisfaction) associated with working outside of Israel's borders. Émigrés are often successful in their work lives. They achieve high incomes and hold prestigious occupations. Their accomplishments can be accounted for partly by their lofty educational credentials, which they further improve in countries of settlement. An additional determinant of Israel emigrants' economic adaptation is their high level of economic cooperation. While certain scholars contend that Israeli emigrants don't engage in cooperative behaviors, statistical analyses, published research and our own fieldwork and interviews in several locations all suggest that Israeli emigrants do practice frequent and extensive economic cooperation. Moreover, this is the case not only for workers and entrepreneurs – who are noted in the literature for their engagement in economic cooperation – but among professional Israelis as well. This pattern is unexpected, as the migration literature suggests that professional migrants are less oriented towards ethnic economies than are entrepreneurs and laborers.

Israeli emigrants' economic collaboration often takes place informally and on multiple levels – with native-born Jews, among the entire population of co-nationals in the host society, and amid strong-tie based groups where social capital and trust is most highly developed. While many studies in economic sociology emphasize the strength of weak ties, Israeli emigrants, like other ethnics, appear to favor strong ties in their economic interactions because these provide high-quality information as well as leverage that can be applied to alter bosses' or employees' behavior in the case of conflicts.

Israeli émigrés claim that they engage in coethnic cooperation for pragmatic reasons associated with easy communication and access to resources, and also because of their feelings of obligation and co-national loyalty. Despite their expressed preference for coethnic associates, Israelis also realize that coethnics can have liabilities as workers, employers, customers and partners. In some cases, coethnics are avoided altogether, while in other instances, strong-tie networks are used to increase the likelihood of identifying coethnic business associates who will act in a desired manner. Whatever Israeli emigrants believe about coethnic cooperation, the structure of certain industries – such as construction, diamonds and information technology – appears to facilitate coethnic cooperation to a greater extent than that of others – such as garments.

Finally, despite their largely successful careers, Israeli emigrants hold various opinions about their work lives. Some are quite positive, stressing the lack of taxes, the cooperative and fair atmosphere, and the sophisticated cultural, technological and scientific environments that they feel are wanting in the Jewish State. Other emigrants are ambivalent. They value the efficiency and opportunity available overseas, but dislike the lack of loyalty and single-minded pursuit of work that they associate with Western workplaces and would prefer to interact with co-nationals. Faced with conflicting feelings about the host society versus the country of origin, some Israelis develop transnational strategies. A fraction attempt to link resources and opportunities available in various locations abroad with those in the host society. Others hope to bring skills, outlooks and enterprises acquired overseas back to Israel. In general, we found that those with professional skills had an easier time – both legally and economically – in their transporting livelihoods across borders than did more traditional entrepreneurs.

In conclusion, when Israelis move abroad, they often do so to work and earn in an environment unimpeded by the social, cultural and economic limitations of the Jewish State. At the same time, Israelis maintain a strong coethnic focus that directs them to fellow Jews, and especially to other Israeli emigrants. Their orientation towards co-nationals facilitates economic cooperation and, frequently, provides resources that foster economic success. At the same time, however, coethnic ties also link Israelis to the country of origin in ways that may discourage assimilation and settlement into the host society. These émigrés simultaneously feel the pull of work cultures associated with the Jewish diaspora, on the one hand, and Israel and Zionism, on the other. As we see in the following chapters, for many Israeli emigrants, these feelings of ambivalence are not limited to the realm of work, but are encountered in other aspects of their lives as well.

4

FAMILY AND GENDER RELATIONS

Introduction

The last chapter argued that the promise of work and its rewards abroad entice Israelis to leave their homeland. This chapter describes how family and gender issues shape Israeli emigrants' patterns of adjustment to host societies and often provide the impetus for their return. As noted in Chapter 1, most Israelis migrate as parts of nuclear families, many of which include small children (Ritterband 1986; Gold and Phillips 1996a; Cohen 1999). The fact that so many Israeli emigrants are part of married couples – frequently with small children at home – means that issues of family adaptation are an immediate concern to them. Further, because the vast majority of Israeli émigrés are part of nuclear families, gender issues are commonly experienced and understood within nuclear family settings, thus warranting the combined discussion of gender and family.

A heritage of dispersed families

Unlike many other nationalities whose populations originated in a common location, Israeli families are characterized by geographically dispersed origins. Israel is a young nation of immigrants, and many of its citizens are recent arrivals. As of 1999, approximately 40 percent of the country's population was born overseas. Consequently, Israelis have relatives in numerous countries, and a significant fraction possess citizenship or legal residence in countries beyond the Jewish State. Most of their ties to family members abroad can be traced to a time prior to their families' settlement in Israel. However, a fair fraction of sabras have themselves lived abroad due to their own families' overseas travel, study and work.

Since the propensity to migrate is transmitted along family networks, having relatives abroad is often correlated with one's own emigration (Massey *et al.* 1994; Kandel and Massey 1999). Such was the case for Batya. Having spent part of her childhood in Ethiopia (during her father's military service), she currently resides in London with her husband and children. Her parents, now separated, also live overseas, her mother, a block away, and her remarried father in New Zealand. Batya's brother abides with his family in Boston. Riki, who, like Batya, has numerous relatives overseas, describes how she and her husband relied on various family contacts in planning and carrying out their emigration:

RIKI: Zion [my husband] has a relative in New York who is a millionaire. He told us to come, but when we got there, there was nothing waiting for us.

INVESTIGATOR: So what did you do then?

RIKI: We came here. I have an uncle here. He is a plumber. He told me from the beginning that I shouldn't have gone to New York, that I should have come straight to Los Angeles. Slowly we got familiarized with the city, with the language, and now Zion has his own construction business.

According to our interviews, among international families, information and emotional support are more frequently exchanged than financial remittances (Sheffer 1998). When funds are extended, the exchange pattern is bi-directional, with benefactors and recipients located both within and beyond Israel. Similarly, while some Israeli families advocate their relatives' return, others see their emigration in a positive light, encourage them to stay on overseas, and travel abroad themselves to visit or permanently join their kin. Hence, for many Israelis, family unification is associated with departure – in order to reconstitute families in the diaspora – rather than return.

This legacy has left Israelis with contradictory views of family migration. On one hand, having relatives abroad and feeling themselves to be part of a peripatetic tradition suggests to Israelis that emigration is a viable, even normative, option. Such an orientation implies a free-flowing, cosmopolitan conception of family, wherein intimate relationships, abetted by travel and communication, bond dispersed kin who seek their fortunes wherever they please. On the other hand, raised in a society with an ideological commitment to "the ingathering of exiles," and exposed to the cultural and generational difficulties experienced by the olim (recent immigrants to Israel), many Israelis are acutely aware of the human and familial trauma associated with statelessness. Ideologically, Zionism rejects cosmopolitanism as incompatible with self-determination. "He is what he is and has a right to be what he is on his land" (Zweig 1969: 6). Instead, it emphasizes the rooting of families in the Jewish State and demands immersion in Israel's geography, language, institutions, culture, climate, people and way of life as essential prerequisites for an honest and meaningful existence. While these two images of the grounding of families in space may appear mutually exclusive, both cosmopolitanism and rootedness are important themes in Jewish and Israeli history.

In sum, given their origins outside of Israel and their many connections to relatives and environments abroad, the relationship between country of origin and location of one's family is often more complex among Israelis than it is among nationality groups that are marked by less diverse derivations and a longer history of settlement.

Reflections on family adjustment

The impact of migration on family relations is an abiding concern among Israeli emigrants, one spontaneously brought up during our interviews and fieldwork. In almost every Israeli family we contacted, at least some members expressed a desire to return to the Jewish State, most commonly because they believed Israel to be a superior location for raising children. Beyond that, evaluations of the diaspora as a setting for family life were various and complex. Respondents of all ages admitted that their appraisal of the host society changed over time, in accordance with their degree of adjustment, economic status, and family needs and preferences. While interviewees offered a wide range of interpretations, for convenience our findings and available literature can be sorted into two opposing images of families' adaptation – one positive and one negative. These representations resonate with the yordim and migration studies perspectives summarized in Chapter 1.

The diaspora benefits family life

Émigrés endorsing emigration describe their smooth process of family adaptation, assisted by the many resources and contacts that Israeli emigrants either bring with them or easily acquire in points of settlement. As students of migration instruct, unlike the vast majority of Jewish migrants throughout history, Israelis are not refugees fleeing oppression, but skilled voluntary immigrants, acting to improve their lives (DellaPergola 1992; Goldscheider 1996). Refugees often suffer from trauma and anxiety. In contrast, research has identified voluntary migrants as having excellent mental health (Kimhi 1990; Vega and Rumbaut 1991). Settling in middle-class Jewish communities, with ready access to co-nationals and Israeli-oriented shops and activities, Israeli families – who are already familiar with Western culture – achieve easy economic adaptation.

Émigrés often join an environment that they feel facilitates their children's growth and development. In the words of London resident Or: "I am pleased with the way that we are growing our child in here, as an Israeli and as a Jew. The school is English and Jewish and he can keep his Israeli identity in here." A review of the literature suggests that migrant populations often experience disruptive family role reversals, wherein children's more rapid acquisition of language skills and behavioral norms upsets family hierarchy (Kibria 1993; Gold 1995b; Portes and Rumbaut 1996; Song 1999). We observed little evidence of this pattern among Israelis, most likely due to parents' high educational profiles and host country language competence (Bozrgmehr et al. 1996; Gold and Phillips 1996a; Schmool and Cohen 1998).

Israelis are generally accepted as whites in the societies where they settle and few report encounters with anti-Semitism. As a consequence, they are spared much of the discrimination that non-white migrants typically confront (Basch et al. 1994; Waters 1999). Émigrés often refer to their enjoyment of material and social advantages that are difficult to obtain in Israel, including a higher standard of living, a greater degree of personal autonomy, cordial social relations in public settings, numerous cultural amenities, longer weekends, a wider range of occupational opportunities, easier access to higher education, freedom from military service and a welcome release from the "pressure cooker" atmosphere of the Middle East (Sobel 1986). Exemplifying this position, respondents Irit and Tomer feel that their migration has provided their families with more time together, numerous niceties, and more satisfying work. As a consequence, the move has been beneficial for the entire household:

INVESTIGATOR: How has being here influenced your family life?

IRIT: Very good. First, now that I am working from home it is really fine with the children. Ron [my husband] is coming at about 6 o'clock so we are all together. Then we have Saturday and the Sunday, full of activity trips and museums. It is great not to have all the family duties and not to spend so much time on grandparents, sisters, brothers, etc.

TOMER: Family life is much, much better here. First, I never work here as late as I did in Israel. Miri [my wife] spends much more time at home. She never had so much time in Israel. She worked a full time job in Israel. Here, she has the time to do what she really enjoys – she plays in an orchestra – so she is much happier, and takes care of the kids. Our financial situation is stable. What can I say? It all affected our family life for the better.

Finally, as voluntary immigrants, they have the opportunity to travel in countries of settlement and abroad, to visit or return to Israel and to entertain Israeli family and friends whenever they wish – often several times a year.

Negative evaluations

The contrasting image suggests that Israeli migrant families confront considerable difficulty. The yordim literature asserts that because emigration violates the basic tenets of Zionism, Israeli emigrants' experience is one of alienation, isolation and guilt regarding their presence in the diaspora (Shokeid 1988; Linn and Barkan-Ascher 1996). Seen as deviant both by their countrymen and by host country Jews, émigrés become self-loathing and are incapable of either joining local Jewish communities or creating their own enclaves (Shokeid 1988; Mittelberg and Waters 1992; Uriely 1995). They miss Israel, don't relate to diaspora Jews, and speak of empty plans to return.

Certain scholarly accounts stress these ideological and identity-based matters as the greatest source of emigrants' unhappiness (Shokeid 1988, 1993; Uriely 1995; Sabar 2000). In contrast, problems of child socialization and education were by far the most common negative aspects of emigration mentioned by our respondents. In the diaspora, Israelis become a religious and linguistic minority group, a status that is seen in the country of origin as incompatible with a virtuous and self-defined existence. As sociologist Steven Cohen observes, in Israel it is widely believed that "Diaspora Jews are plagued by a 'galut' (exilic) mentality that precludes them from freely expressing themselves as proud, self-confident and self-respecting Jews" (Cohen 1991: 122).

Identity and education

Israeli emigrant parents often fear that their children will lose their Jewish and Israeli identity as a result of living in Christian societies.

Plate 4.1 Tzofim (Israeli Scouts), Jewish Community Centre, Los Angeles. In order to provide their children with some forms of Israeli experience, Tzofim chapters have been established in several communities of settlement. Here children practice Hebrew, and learn Israeli stories, geography and folk-dancing. Parents often socialize while their children attend Tzofim or Sunday school.

Accordingly, they face a dilemma as they plan for their children's education. If they do nothing, the kids will forsake their Jewish and Israeli heritage. However, if they enroll the youngsters in local Jewish institutions, they will be confronted with another, equally foreign notion of identity – diaspora Judaism. As a consequence, migrant parents must choose between having their children socialized in either of two unfamiliar cultural traditions – those of foreign Gentiles or diaspora Jews. (See Chapter 6 for a more detailed discussion of émigrés' identities.)

Reflecting this dilemma, Tova fears that her son, Gil, may wind up as an outsider in both the country of origin and the place of settlement. At the same time, she worries that means of helping him develop a strong identity – such as becoming an Orthodox Jew in England or serving in the Israeli army – also entail risks:

> It is his feelings of belonging that I was concerned about. I think that Gil is a child of immigrants. Assuming that we will

110

go back someday, he will be an outsider in both worlds [England and Israel] always. Here, in their eyes, we shall always be "bloody foreigners." No matter how many years he will be here, he will graduate the secondary school and still be a foreigner to them, because all his foundation is different from theirs.

This is why it is important to me to go back to Israel. I felt it was important that he had some sense of belonging. It sounds terrible maybe, but I want him to enroll to the army service. As a mother, I am afraid of this like all of us are, but I want him to feel attached to this and [to feel] a deep enough sense of being a part of Israel [so] that he would want to enroll. One of the things that helps me is the Jewish school that he attends. On the other hand, I didn't want an Orthodox Jewish school for him. An Orthodox school would have been off the track for him. For us, as a family, it wouldn't be right. It wouldn't match.

As the following quotes from a group interview of Israeli teenagers in Los Angeles suggest, Israeli children are themselves often critical of diaspora life:

NORIT: My dad came here nine months before us. And I knew one day we're going to come here 'cause of him. I didn't really want to come, you know. I know it was going to be a start again and I was like scared. But I'm here and I have to accept it.

DAN: In the United States it was Yom Kippur. We went to the synagogue and it was so different because we like prayed and then we went home and people were driving by on the street and people were eating in restaurants and it was very hard. It was very different. I felt that I am not in the right place. I shouldn't be here. I told my parents and they said "You are in the United States, you are not in Israel. You should expect that."

AVIVA: I have a little sister. In Israel, we used to go to the park everyday for a walk. To go outside, it was usual. When we came over here, it's like we are stuck in the house. We didn't do anything. One day, my parents had the car, so we went outside for a walk. I took my little sister, and everyone stared at us. It was like what we have done was strange. It's not usual to go outside over here. It's different than you are used to.

These young peoples' statements have paradoxical implications. In expressing their valuation of Israel over the host society, they honor their families' notion of home and reject the pattern of rapid assimilation that is the fate of many migrants' children (Kibria 1993; Portes and Rumbaut 1996). Yet by doing so, they make additional demands on their parents (especially their mothers) to return home or at least maintain an "Israeli environment" in the place of settlement.

Focused on their children's socialization, émigré parents were involved in extensive discussions with co-nationals about available schools and youth programs that could assist them in this endeavor (Shavit nd; Lipner 1987). Despite the numerous Jewish and secular options available in major communities of settlement like London, Paris, New York, Los Angeles, Sydney and Toronto, Israelis remained generally unsatisfied. Their complaints varied according to the settlement's local culture. For example, an Israeli teacher living in Paris explained that the French maintain "a very different approach to teaching, learning, education, childhood. Very different from the Israeli [way]." Israelis in England and Australia described local schools as austere, authoritarian and employing out-dated methods. A father of three characterized the academy his children attended as "the worst combination between the strictness of the English culture and the rigidity of the religious Jewish education." Finally, American public schools were seen as academically inferior and likely to foster children's assimilation to a Christian, American standpoint. A woman who recently returned to Tel Aviv from Los Angeles describes why she sent her children to a private Jewish school in the States:

> I was not willing to compromise on the issue of the quality of their education. I said, "If we cannot afford this, we go back to Israel." The main problem was the violence levels in the state schools. They were simply unsafe. Also, the academic achievements were very poor in the state sector. So we had to go to the private schools. The Americans themselves do not send their kids to these state schools. Only minorities go there.

While generally accepted as the best alternative, Jewish parochial schools were also criticized. They were seen as too expensive, and often, as too religious, such that children who attended them would demand their largely secular parents' conformity to Sabbath observance and dietary laws. Moreover, Israelis feel that Jewish day schools generally provide insufficient training in Israeli culture and spoken Hebrew. For example, during 2000, a Jewish middle and high school popular among London Israelis reduced – and considered eliminating

Plate 4.2 Israeli woman with her son, North London. He attends a long-
established Jewish school, and as such, is growing up in a
context quite different from that of his parents. Israeli women often
expend a great deal of effort to create what they feel is an
appropriate environment for their children in points of settlement.

– its Hebrew program. This upset local Israelis for whom their
children's Hebrew competence is vital both for the family's eventual
return, as well as for the child's ability to attend a university in the
Jewish State.

In the following quotation, a couple emphasizes their children's needs as they explained their reasoning for re-migration to Israel:

INVESTIGATOR: Tell me about the decision to return.

GILDA: The considerations were around the kids entirely. We knew we would be going back to something which has less to offer us from many aspects and we knew we had to do this for the kids' sake.

TEDDI: The kids were part of this decision-making process. Their adjustment was not easy. Actually, it was really difficult. We were absorbed with our own issues and adaptation, and therefore the kids had to deal with it all by themselves. The youngest really wanted to go back all the time.

In addition to their dissatisfaction with schools, Israelis also described their unhappiness with cultural norms regarding child-rearing in host societies. In her study of Israeli women in the US, Israeli-American sociologist Nira Lipner explains their perspective:

Across the board, respondents experience the reality in which their children are growing up as entirely antithetical to the reality they have internalized during their own socialization. Essentially, they see the dominant values of the adult world, competition and individualism, replicated in children's realities. They maintain a highly critical perspective towards the conditions that structure children's realities.

(Lipner 1987: 232)

Nophar echoed Lipner's conclusions as she berated the British attitude about children's appropriate comportment, as well as the means allegedly used for achieving it:

INVESTIGATOR: Do you think it is different to raise children here and in Israel?

NOPHAR: Yes. This is one of the constant pains of being here. There is very little freedom and independence here. You don't find children playing together in the park. There is also the way they raise children. They don't see them the way we do. They are much more authoritarian than we are. Children may be seen and not heard. I think it would be nice to have a pair of tamed children. On the other hand, it doesn't seem normal to me that children should be restricted so much. I hate this oppression. My children often make noise where they are not supposed to and I feel very embarrassed about it. Because of this, I feel I don't belong here.

I remember going to a playgroup one day when a psychologist attended the meeting. All the children sat down and ate quietly and my children ran around like horses. We were embarrassed. So the psychologist said to me "You don't understand what parents are doing to achieve this and you don't want to know, believe me. You wouldn't want to try corporal punishment would you?" She said "Believe me, they will grow up and be OK." I think the discipline they get here and the politeness is good for them. But I wouldn't go that far to do that. It's enough what they get in school.

Another problem cited by émigré parents is that migration has prevented them from sharing a common language, culture and life-shaping experiences with their children. A woman living in London described this:

By the time they went to school, they started talking in a language that is alien to me, singing songs I do not know, experiencing things which are unfamiliar to me. That was difficult for me. I know it sounds selfish, but I want my kids. I want to be part of their lives. I wanted them to have something in common with me. I wanted them to have the same identity as mine.

A Los Angeles-based Israeli psychologist describes the source of the generation gap in the US:

Israelis send their kids to public school and they have this little American running around at home. So where do we meet in the family? On what value system do we meet? There is no value system that Israelis can give to their children as Americans because they don't know it. The children bring home the American culture; their parents don't know it. That's why the breakdown occurs.

An Israeli teenager offered a more dramatic take on generational differences, as he likened an assimilated acquaintance to Frankenstein:

> I am talking about a specific person. Highly, highly assimilated. I couldn't blame him for that because he went to public school. His parents were working. It was their first child, so there was no older brother who teach him what to do. But the parents became more wealthy and they became more successful and he became like the Frankenstein symbol because they saw one day a monster. He is not Israeli anymore. He doesn't know where he is coming from. I suggested to him to come to the Israeli scouts to learn about his home. He looked at me as if I was a crazy man.

Additional problems

In addition to matters of children's education and socialization, another source of concern for Israeli emigrant families involved the economic realties of diaspora life. Since many Israelis went abroad to achieve financial goals, it is not surprising that they have high expectations in this area. Some émigrés were unsatisfied with their earnings:

> We are all living under the American illusion that we can be rich here. It happens when you hit a successful deal. But if you don't, then it's a labor camp and it becomes very difficult to handle the other problems, such as education and culture.

Such complaints were most common during economic downturns of the early 1980s and a decade later, during the early 1990s, when jobs were scarce, interest rates high and loans difficult to pay off.

Economically successful emigrants sometimes lamented that they pay a high price for prosperity. Long hours of work are stressful and leave little quality time for family, friends and religious activities. Émigrés also worried that affluence may be corrupting. While some asserted that Israel has become at least as materialistic as Europe or North America, others contend that its communal and idealistic values endure. As they relaxed at the pool of their San Fernando Valley apartment complex, two Israeli men described how being in the States was corrosive to their families' well-being:

YA'ANKALE: I come home from work between 6 and 7 p.m. My son goes to sleep at 8. So when can I sit with him and teach him? We need some time to talk. So when can I sit with him?

YARON: You want to achieve here something you can't get in Israel. Go to concerts, ski whenever you feel like it, and buy for your children everything you want. If you can't do these things here in America, then what's the point? You stay here only for the materialistic comfort. If you don't have it, then there is nothing to stay for.

Some emigrants told us that they enjoyed a greater abundance of intimate family time together outside of Israel and took pleasure in their freedom from prying grandparents, in-laws and neighbors. Others, however, claimed that they long for the family and friends that they had left behind. A Los Angeles couple exemplified the latter position as they elaborated on their plans to return:

EUGENE: We miss our family. That is one of the terrible things that happens when you are living here.

IDIT: I don't want to raise my children here. My parents are suffering too because I am here. So what the point of bringing up my children here?

Israeli families settling outside of the Jewish State were frequently concerned about the increased probability that their children will marry a non-Jew and as a result, their grandchildren will not be Jewish. This is generally regarded as both a personal loss for the family as well as a collective one for the Jewish people. A Los Angeles émigré describes the risk: "That's how a Jewish boy loses his Jewish identity. He assimilates into the American culture and finally, he'll marry a Gentile girl and will disappear from the Jewish community." The mother of teenage sons told me that she prohibits them from dating non-Jewish women:

> We tell our kids that we would kill them if they don't marry Jewish. It's very clear to them, we do not accept it. And it looks like they are taking the word. However, you never know until they come to you and tell you. But it's a very tough thing. What do you do? What do you do in a case like that? We are living in a mixed society, and we said to them, "don't go out with a non-Jewish girl."

Referring to an alternative strategy, she describes the experience of friends who are arranging the religious conversion of their boy's fiancée:

Where and how do you stop it? These friends of mine, their future daughter-in-law is not Jewish. They sent their son on a trip around the United States when he graduated from high school. He met this girl and he fell in love with her. At first, they wanted nothing to do with her. But then, they realized "We are losing our son. He's going to her parents' house. We never see him anymore. He's always there." So finally, they started getting to know her a little better and all of a sudden, they gained a son. Now they love her and she is excited about converting to Judaism.

A final family problem noted by émigrés is that after years abroad, family members often quarrel about where they would like to live. This is especially vexing because either staying put or returning home inevitably results in someone's unhappiness. Cultural conflicts strain the marriages of Israelis wed to natives, and the divorces that sometimes result are especially traumatic for children whose extended families reside on different continents. A mother who returned to Israel with her adolescent son following a divorce describes such a dispute:

My son did not want to come here at all. He really rejected the whole idea. He still feels more English than Israeli and is still a great fan of the Manchester United football team and is not interested in the Israeli football teams. He still misses his friends in London and [says] that they are still his best friends.

Discussion

The experience of most Israeli emigrant families lies somewhere between problem-free adaptation and the Frankenstein predicament summarized above. In the following quote, Ilana adopts a middle-ground position, agreeing that she misses the level of support that she would have enjoyed in Israel, but claiming her family's emigration has yielded benefits as well:

INVESTIGATOR: Do you feel your life here is different from what you would have experienced if you had lived in Israel?

ILANA: Yes. I think I would have had much more support in Israel, and it would have been much easier with the kids. I think my mother would have helped me with the daily stuff and here I don't have that kind of support. However, life here [in London] is definitely more calm. Less stress and more peaceful. I was able to pay more attention to the kids here, without having money issues to worry about. In Israel, I don't think we would have done so well financially. And also, there are the facilities. There is a lot more here for children: science museum, and things like that. Although in Israel, a lot of the time, children are outdoors.

Regardless of their circumstances, most Israeli emigrants continue to be concerned about their families' well-being. A fair number hope to resolve family problems by eventually returning to Israel. Others, however, maintain a more philosophical approach, admitting that there are costs and benefits for families no matter where they live. Many émigrés contended that Israel itself has changed over the years, becoming both more affluent and less idealistic and unified than it once was. Israel too, they remark, is marked by crime, social conflicts and drug use. Even children raised in Israel sometimes move abroad and marry Gentiles.

For example, Ronni, an Israeli building contractor who lived in South Africa for several years before settling in Los Angeles, asserted that being in Israel offered little insurance against children's involvement in the rebellious youth culture that is so prevalent in California:

> This, there is also in Israel. It was always like that. When we were young, we also listened to the Beatles in Israel and my dad would also get crazy. There's the music, there are the earrings in the nose, all kinds of weird hairstyles, but these aren't important. These small things happen also in Israel. My [Israeli] cousin was here, and he also had his nose pierced, so what can I say?

Hila maintained a similar degree of resignation as she described her husband's outlook following their return to Israeli from the UK: "The only place where he could run away from all the problems is to live alone on an island."

Gendered adjustments

Both Israeli men and women describe the changes that migration imposes upon their families. However, women are most commonly charged with addressing the non-economic dimensions of these. In nearly every study of Israeli emigration, we find that while migration was a "family decision" and the family as a whole enjoys economic benefits as a result of migration, the decision to migrate was made by the men for the expanded educational and occupational opportunities available abroad (Lipner 1987; Rosenthal and Auerbach 1992; Gold 1995b; Sabar 2000; Lev Ari 2000). However, Israeli women's reaction to the decision to migrate has been less clearly documented.

Our interviews indicate that a large fraction of Israeli women (and many children as well) go abroad not of their own volition, but only to accompany their husbands who seek economic and educational advancement. As a result, women have a more difficult time in accepting and adjusting to the new setting and more often seek to return home. This is largely because of the gendered division of labor followed by Israeli families.

The gender patterns of Israeli emigrant families are fairly unique among migrant populations. A sizable literature suggests that among migrant groups, it is women who enhance their income and power through migration, and men who seek to return home (Pessar 1986; Pedraza 1991; Kibria 1993; Hondagneu-Sotelo 1994). Israelis' singular trajectory can be traced to an amalgam of cultural, economic, religious and historical factors far too numerous to describe here. However, a short summary illuminates their experience in host societies. Prior to emigration, Israeli Jewish women were accustomed to working outside of the home for income. Israel has a higher rate of female labor force participation than do many countries of settlement (Simon 1985; Gold 1995b). Further, the Jewish State is marked by gender norms, social patterns and government policies that appear to be at once more liberated *and* more restrictive than those to which most Western women are accustomed (Davis nd). For example, Israel requires mandatory military service for women, and had a powerful woman head of state during the 1970s (Golda Meir). Hanna Senesh, a Nazi-fighting martyr, is celebrated along with many male heroes as a founder of the country. On the other hand, the government-sanctioned Orthodox religious establishment in Israel reinforces "the disadvantaged position of women as decision makers" and discourages the legal incorporation of women's full equality, while privileging men (Goldscheider 1996: 161). These contrasting images of gender can be traced to two traditions – egalitarian, humanitarian political beliefs, on the one hand, and Orthodox Jewish theology, on the other – that are manifested in Israel's national identity, as well as in many of its political, ideological and ethnic conflicts (Azmon and Izraeli 1993).

In Israel, it is generally assumed that women will both work and have a family in order to benefit the larger society. Israel never developed a cult of motherhood that assigns the care of the child exclusively to the mother or views extrafamily partners in this task as harmful. Consequently, there is a general reliance on government-provided daycare and preschool services that are seen as beneficial to children's development. This encourages women's employment, by both caring for children and deflecting the criticism and feelings of guilt experienced by mothers who separate from their small children during paid work (Azmon and Izraeli 1993: 10; Lieblich 1993).

At the same time, because of the society's pervasive familism that emphasizes women's domestic and child-rearing duties, Israeli women are generally discouraged "from investing in high-commitment careers" and rarely hold high-ranking positions (Azmon and Izraeli 1993: 1; Zweig 1969). Many feel that they have few options with regard to basic life decisions concerning marriage, occupation and children (Lieblich 1993: 199). Finally, the relatively small fraction of women who pursue lives without men (those who are unmarried, divorced and single parents) are stigmatized.

These gender patterns shape Israelis' emigration and their reactions to it. Most commonly, Israeli emigrant men are involved in study or work. Men find these activities rewarding, as they provide earnings, a positive sense of self and social contacts. In contrast, Israeli emigrant women who have children are charged with settling the family's domestic affairs. Supported by their husbands' earnings, they remain housebound in suburban communities, faced with the formidable task of recreating a supportive family environment in an unfamiliar cultural and linguistic setting. Consequently, women's encounter with the host society is more difficult than that of co-national men. Two Israeli housewives in Los Angeles described the difference between men's and women's migration experience:

INVESTIGATOR: How would you compare the feelings of the Israeli men versus women who come to America?

MICHAL: Frustration for some women. I am frustrated because I had a career in Israel and I have none here. And do you know what the cost is? The only rewards go to the man – the economic advances. Both spiritually and fulfillment-wise, it is a lot more important for the woman to be in Israel.

MARIUM: Isolation is a big problem. You really go through a down. I have to be busy, to have work. If I am busy, then I am a little bit intense and I really function well. When I have lots of time, even my cooking can take all day. I have too much time and I don't do anything with the time. I get emotionally tired all of the time.

The Israeli couples that we interviewed were generally quite aware of the gender inequalities involved in their decisions about emigration, and the impact that moving would have upon their lifestyles and careers. They had discussed these at length and often engaged in extensive negotiations as they planned their travels. Further, husbands often made special efforts to accommodate wives' needs. They supported their spouses' involvement in education and employment, contributed to housework and child care, settled in neighborhoods that offered communal support, and encouraged family trips back to Israel.[1]

Reflecting this pattern of negotiation, in our interviews with families that had returned to Israel we found that in a fair number of cases, husbands had acquiesced to wives' requests to return home. Malka, an Israeli living in London, describes such a family bargain:

INVESTIGATOR: Are you planning to go back?

MALKA: We have an ultimatum: The ultimatum is that when our son is 12 we'll go back. He's 6 now. I want Etan [husband] to establish his career, and go back home with enough money to be comfortable in Israel. If I didn't put it this way, Etan would not think of going back. He likes it here. He's more engaged in work – and I'm more engaged with life – so it's my decision. If he didn't have a family and friends, he wouldn't go.

Despite their awareness of the unequal rewards associated with the gendered division of labor, many Israeli families maintained this pattern anyway, largely because they believed it would maximize income and benefit children. According to Lilach Lev Ari's (2000: 5) survey of Israeli families in the US, "Generally, a sex division of labor became more distinct by gender *after* immigration to the United States" (emphasis in the original). Dafna describes how moving to London disrupted the egalitarian relationship that she and her husband, Zeev, had maintained in Israel:

Zeev and I were always equals, both in our way of life and our careers, and here that balance changed. Here, his career was more central and more important than mine. So he was the one who determined our future in terms of our stay here. So my career became a job that I did not have to do. I could choose to stay at home or go out to work. It was not an important consideration in our lives.

As Dafna describes, Zeev's greater earnings and job prestige made her career a secondary concern for the family. Following a pattern fairly common among Israeli émigré women, she emphasized raising children in the host society. While this strategy allows women to facilitate their children's smooth adaptation to the host society, it can be limiting and disheartening. In retrospect, Dafna believes that she could have mixed work and family more effectively in Israel than was possible in England:

> When I decided to stay home after my son was born, I thought "I am not only a career woman. I will never forgive myself if I miss out on the experience of motherhood." And in my line of work – had I continued to work as I did before – I would have seen my children only in time to kiss them good night. So I decided to take that time off and stay home with them. I thought, you know, "here is that time in my life where the family comes first." And also, my husband came home, and still does, at very late hours. Never earlier than 8–9 in the evening. Well, that's not very accurate. He comes home earlier when there is a football match . . . [laughs]
>
> He is not going to be at home to take care of the kids. So who will deal with the kids and the house? So to be honest, I do not regret that time, although it was difficult adjusting to that change in my life. What I regret was the results in terms of my career. But I do not live my life today feeling that I missed out on something. I accept life as it is. I know now that there are some decisions that I should have taken when I did not, and one of them is indeed the decision to stay here. If I was then as mature and knowledgeable as I am today, I would have chosen a different path. I would have insisted we went back after two or three years.

Despite women's belief that returning to Israel would provide them with additional options for combining work and family, several Israeli families that did return maintained traditional gender arrangements upon arrival in Israel. Dina, the mother of three children, describes her plan for helping them readjust to life in Israel. "I decided that I will not work at the beginning so I can help them out during the first year. I wanted to stay home so that I can help them with their homework and tests."

As noted, in the majority of emigrant families, men decided to move to enhance their careers, leaving their wives with the task of assisting with family adjustment. This, however, was not always the case. We interviewed several families where wives inspired the travel abroad to work, study or join families. For example, when Gilda was given an overseas assignment by an Israeli company, her husband Teddi put his career on hold and helped the family settle in London. Almost a decade later, he did the same when they returned to Tel Aviv:

GILDA: I think what helped us all and me in particular is the fact that Teddi was there for us so much of the initial period. His support was essential. We could not have done it without this support. For me, that was particularly important because he took all the family and home-making roles that normally I did, and I could devote myself entirely to my work. At the initial stage, he did not work and was simply there for us. Only after a few months he started looking for a job for himself.

TEDDI: Yes, that is true. I spent all the initial period supporting them, supporting her in her job. She had all these new things to do and all these skills to learn – and it was difficult for her.

Exacerbating the gender inequality experienced by Israeli migrants is the nature of their ethnic networks. Many of the most well-developed and visible networks are organized on the basis of male-dominated activities such as occupation or profession, religious affiliation and sports/recreation. In contrast, collectivities capable of providing Israeli women with a social life and aid in fulfilling domestic tasks are fewer in number, less easily accessed, informal, and at an earlier stage of development (Korazim 1983; Sabar 2000; Uriely 1995; Gold 1994c). Sharon describes being isolated and lacking ties during her early stay in England:

Until the my first child was born, I had a very tough period. I didn't know anyone in London and I was very lonely. In Oxford, where we lived at first, we had sort of a social life. Then we came to London and my husband was busy and I didn't know anyone. I was all the time at home, without even speaking to people on the telephone. My son was small, it was cold outside and there was no place to go or to meet people. After he started the [Israeli] kindergarten, I got to know more people, and both me and him were much busier.

Further, while Israeli men can readily participate in Orthodox religious activities, which are especially influential for Mizrahi-origin Israelis, such congregations' traditionalism and gender-based segregation is alienating to many of the Israeli women that we interviewed (Uriely 1995). For example, a Yemeni-origin woman who settled in Los Angeles described her feelings of alienation from the Orthodox synagogue frequented by Yemeni men:

> I was at their Yom Kippur service. I went in and then I left. I could not tolerate the separation of the men and the women. I did not know that was the case before I came. They sat you [in the synagogue] where you can't even see the Rabbi. And I said "no, that's too much for me to handle." So I just left. I went to Temple Emanuel [an American Conservative synagogue, where men and women sit together].

Reflecting the disadvantaged status of the Mizrahim, Lev Ari (2000: 5) found that in comparison to their Ashkenazi co-nationals, Israeli women with family origins in North Africa and the Middle East received fewer educational benefits from their stay in the US, received less assistance from husbands in household chores, were less likely to work outside the home and were "more interested in returning to Israel."

Social capital and gendered adaptation

As noted in Chapter 3, emigration often has the effect of increasing the rewards associated with Israeli workers' social and human capital. This is because at least until Israel's economic transformations of the 1990s, host economies often facilitated and compensated economic initiative to a greater degree than did Israel (DellaPergola 1992). Economic advantages in host societies include lower levels of tax and regulation on business operations, a greater availability of credit and loans, lower inflation, higher salaries, no mandatory military service or reserve duty, greater opportunities for professional advancement, a much larger scale of economic activity, and easier admission to higher education (Elizur 1980; Sobel 1986).[2] The result is that Israeli breadwinners' business skills and resources – such as their occupational knowledge, their ability to import and export goods and their access to benefits provided by ethnic business networks – are often more valuable in points of settlement than in Israel (Sobel 1986; Rivlin 1992; Gold 1994a; Light and Karageorgis 1994).

In addition to the business-relevant skills, training and connections,

Plate 4.3 Israeli bookstore, London. Israeli shops provide religious and cultural materials to co-nationals as well as the larger Jewish population in many points of settlement.

and other ethnic resources that Israelis bring to host societies, emigrants also possess unique cultural competencies. These include knowledge pertaining to the Hebrew language, Israeli history, culture and ceremonial life, and the Jewish religion. All are relatively scarce in the diaspora. Due to the gendered division of labor, Israeli women often become involved in transferring these ethnic resources to their own children, those of local Jews and other consumers (such as Christians seeking to learn Hebrew) (Light and Gold 2000: Ch. 5). However, because there is less demand and little compensation available for providing these services, Israelis involved in child socialization and culture/language training are not generously rewarded for their endeavors.

Hence, both workers' and domestic service purveyors' social, human and cultural capital are essential to Israeli families' adjustment to host societies. However, while the largely male breadwinners' tasks are well compensated and often easier to perform after migration, the typically feminine domestic and cultural duties are poorly compensated, and more difficult in the host society than in the country of origin.

Israeli women encounter difficulties in their domestic and communal tasks because, upon emigrating, they lose the governmental resources and communal networks based upon family, friendship and neighborhood that provided a social life and assistance in raising children. It is telling that in the article wherein sociologist James Coleman first utilized social capital as a tool for sociological analysis, he used precisely this example – the higher quality of family-benefiting communal life in Israel versus the United States – to define the concept:

> In Jerusalem, the normative structure ensures that unattended children will be "looked after" by adults in the vicinity, while no such normative structure exists in most metropolitan areas of the United States. One can say that families have available to them in Jerusalem social capital that does not exist in metropolitan areas of the United States.
> (Coleman 1988: 99–100)

Women generally make up for this lost social capital. The practice of putting women in charge of communal and domestic duties as their main responsibility is common among Israeli immigrants. It is reflected in low rates of labor force participation among Israeli women in various host societies. A survey of naturalized Israelis in New York found that "only 4 percent of the women indicated 'housewife' as their occupation in Israel, while 36 percent did so in the United States" (Rosenthal and Auerbach 1992: 985). According to the 1990 US census, 41 percent of working-age Israeli immigrant women in Los Angeles and 50 percent in New York were not in the labor force.[3] In the UK, a higher rate of male labor force participation was also evident, with 76 percent of Israeli men and 48 percent of Israeli women over age 16 economically active. In addition, 15 percent of Israeli men and 7 percent of Israeli women in Britain were students

(Schmool and Cohen 1998: 30). According to the 1996 Australian census, Israeli men had an 80 percent labor force participation rate, while the rate for Israeli women was 70 percent. Finally, tabulations from the 1996 Canadian census reveal that Israeli men had a 79 percent labor force participation rate, while Israeli women had a 64 percent labor force participation rate.

Because it is relatively scarce in the diaspora, Israeli women's cultural, linguistic and religious knowledge is a prized social resource. There, it is deployed informally to educate their own children, and in communal settings to train both young émigrés and local Jews. However, as is often the case with work performed by women (and sometimes men) to benefit children and families, Israeli women's domestic, cultural and religious contributions are not associated with sizable financial rewards (Hartmann 1989; Blumberg 1991; Milkman and Townsley 1994). In contrast, migration significantly enhances the financial rewards for the efforts and social and human capital of generally male workers. The existence of such gendered inequalities offers a possible explanation for Israeli women's preference for returning home.

Opportunities and choices for Israeli women in the West

It is important to note that many economic advantages of emigration can benefit Israeli women as well as men. According to several respondents, gender-relevant social features of host societies – such as greater economic and educational opportunities, more egalitarian gender roles and a less stigmatized view of single parenthood – offered Israeli women options rare at home (Goldscheider 1996). "The main difference between the American social structure and the Israeli one is that in Israel the structure of opportunities for women is still less egalitarian than in the United States" (Lev Ari 2000: 2). Batia, an Israeli psychologist with many co-national patients, described how Israeli women are empowered by their presence in America:

BATIA: I do see that the Israeli women gain – they are being empowered by coming to this country, which appreciates women more than they do in Israel. And the men lose some of their power.

INVESTIGATOR: How would the increase in power be manifested?

BATIA: The word power in its all meanings – they find jobs easy. They find it very easy to be very sexy and here very easy to go

shop and to buy anything . . . With the same amount of money
you can empower yourself to look better. Women, overall,
they feel much more empowered in the Western countries,
much more than men.

And also, it is easier on the female who's been divorced
here than in Israel. In Israel, it is still a stigma and you are
still being looked at as a disaster for your family or your
parents. And here, you immediately find a single friend. So
it's not such a shame and you continue on with your life.
Maybe life is not scary without a man in United States.

As noted in Chapter 4, many women professionals and entrepreneurs also found enhanced opportunities in points of settlement. An
entrepreneur told us "I think its easier to be self-employed and have
a business in England."

However, not all women émigrés shared this perspective. For
example, because host society employers were often unsupportive
and unwilling to grant time off for child care responsibilities, several
professional women sought to be either self-employed or work for co-
nationals. Women attending universities in the UK also complained
that few accommodations – such as married students' housing – were
made for students with children (Stern 1979: 87).[4] Niri, who moved
to London in the 1980s, describes how sexism prevented her from
finding work in her former occupation:

NIRI: In Israel, my profession was chemical engineer. When I
came here, I didn't go back to my profession because
England is . . . I'll put it this way. Israel looks at the woman as
a professional. A chemical engineer should not be only a
feminine or masculine job. But here it was difficult to find a
position and as they said "We look after our women" which
means you should be home with the kids.

INVESTIGATOR: So it was more sexist here?

NIRI: It's very sexist, its outrageous.

Since that time, she has been self-employed so as to avoid dealing
with these constraining attitudes.

Whether they found extensive or more limited options abroad,
many of the Israeli women we interviewed seemed to emphasize child
rearing, and domestic and communal activities (whether combined
with employment or not) as their highest priority. Many did work and

took advantage of economic and cultural opportunities in host societies. But only to a degree. Often their own goals, including their careers and their chosen place of residence, were treated as secondary to the needs of their husbands and children. A journalist who accompanied her husband to London told us:

> For me the most stressful experience [of migration] was this regression that I experienced into the housewife position. I had no identity of my own, except being "his wife." But I tried my best to function as a mother and wife so that no one could tell how I really felt about the things that happened in my life. I protected my family, my kids, from my own self. I did everything I could so that they will not notice my state.

Women's adaptive strategies

Despite the obstacles they confront in adapting to host societies, Israeli women show a high degree of initiative. Deploying resources from several sources – including their own families, other Israeli immigrant women and the larger Jewish community – they devise a number of strategies that help them cope with the new environment. In so doing, they improve the quality of their own lives. In many cases, their endeavors benefit larger co-national and coethnic communities as well. In the section that follows, I describe several of the schemes that Israeli women use to contend with their family duties and feelings of isolation in points of settlement.

Focus on temporary status

Much of the yordim literature written during the 1970s and 1980s describes Israeli migrants as treating their presence abroad as temporary, even if it is not (Shokeid 1988). In such cases, the clear-cut economic benefits of the stay are seen as justifying the low quality of domestic, communal and religious life. However, because the family asserts that their stay is temporary, relatively little effort is expended in creating a more acceptable environment in the host society. These sojourners feel that such difficulties will be resolved upon their eventual return to Israel.

However, as Shokeid (1988) and others point out, this approach is unrealistic for Israelis who find themselves living abroad for a decade or even more, raising children, taking on citizenship and the like (Linn and Barkan-Ascher 1996). In the following quote, Yael describes her ambivalence. While her heart is in Israel, she is unable to reject

the economic opportunities of life abroad. As a result, she is incapable
of fully committing herself to either setting:

YAEL: I just have no motivation to do anything [in the US] because
we always say we will go back in a few months, maybe in a year.
So why would I start a business? I studied here for eighteen
months. And when I graduated, I was all motivated to start a
business. Then, I went to Israel for two months during the
summer and all the motivation stayed in Israel. Since then, we
say we will go back eventually. Maybe in a year, maybe in a year
and a half. So I say "Why would I work hard and start making
clients and advertisements when I want to go back?"

I know I don't want to succeed here because I am afraid if
I have something going for me, then it will be hard for me to
leave. It's hard for my husband to leave. So I keep myself a
source to push back. If I do well here, it will be real hard for
me to leave, so I just don't want to be successful. In professional language, you call this the fear of success. You are a
failure because of the fear of success. There is the problem.

As Yael suggests, many Israelis realize that focusing upon the temporary nature of their stay does little to solve the problems they face
abroad. In fact, inaction often makes such problems worse. Accordingly,
other emigrant women follow a variety of more concrete strategies to
develop a supportive environment.

Incorporation within the host society

A second approach followed by Israeli women who seek a supportive
community involves social and economic incorporation within the
host society. The women taking this path tend to be highly skilled and
educated, have spent many years in the host society, and often have
close relatives, including spouses, who were born in the hostland.
Michal, a UCLA graduate student who came to the US after receiving
her BA from the Hebrew University of Jerusalem, exemplified such a
position as she recounted her rapid merger into the American Jewish
community:

I came here by myself and I have my cousin who helped me.
I got my job in less than a week – a full-time job, teaching in
Temple Emanuel day school. I was just telling my professor
last week, it was only this summer that I realized that I was an
immigrant – because I did not have a job. I did not have to

struggle at any point of my first five years. Not only that, but I also don't feel an immigrant because when I came here, I did not associate with other Israelis immediately. The pattern of my life in America was much different than the pattern of most people who come here.

As Michal observes, her approach to Western life has limited applicability for many Israelis who cannot find mainstream jobs so readily. As recent immigrants, most have very different social, religious and communal outlooks than host society Jews, and don't feel comfortable communicating in the host society's language. While young single women like Michal may adjust rapidly, more mature women with families told us that it took them far longer – close to a decade in many cases – to feel settled in their new place of residence.

Informal groups and networks

Faced with isolation and the challenges of living in an alien culture, Israeli women created prized networks of support. Danni described the great joy she felt when after three years away from Israel, she finally found a group of friends:

> We used to meet once a week at least, and here I met all the people that later became very important in my life. It became a sort of alternative family for me. We became something very special. There was that sense of being in love with each other and being very intimate. In a flash, I became an adored and loved person. For three years I did not have one person around me that I could appreciate as my own, and now actually there were three. So, I was finally able to open up. I am sorry that I did not get to meet them before that year.

Galit, a woman of Yemeni origins whom I met at an Israeli community event and later visited at her Los Angeles home, relied upon her social network to provide succor and autonomy. Although Galit did not work outside of the home, she was able to mobilize an influential network of older women friends, including other Israelis of Yemenite background and a former landlady of Eastern European Jewish origins. With the moral support and connections provided by this group, Galit was introduced to an Israeli-Yemeni building contractor named Manny, whom she married. On the Sunday when I visited, Manny tended to household chores while treating Galit and her women friends with great deference. In turn, the women teased him

Plate 4.4 Israeli Sunday school, London. Israeli emigrants created this
program because the education provided by local synagogues
places too much emphasis on religion, and offers too little training
in spoken Hebrew and Israeli culture.

for his inability to supervise the couple's children, while crediting
Galit for the redecorating job Manny had done on the couple's home.

Shavit (nd: 19) describes the importance of informal school-seeking
networks as a central force among middle-class Israelis in London.
Upon arrival in the UK, women contact coethnics to obtain information about schools. Accepting their advice, Israeli families settle
within specific neighborhoods and enroll their children in one of the
"network approved" schools. This pattern of settlement opens the
door for further involvement in the local community: "the school's
role is as a 'mag-net,' a meeting point and a channel through which
new members are introduced to the community and gain access to its
networks" (Shavit nd: 19). On a broader level, an Israeli Sunday
school connects Israeli children attending various schools. Social
contacts established here then unite their families. (In Chapter 3, I
described another benefit of women's networks – their ability to
provide family-friendly job referrals.) In this way, having very young
children in the diaspora had mixed impacts on emigrant women. On
one hand, they often tied women to domestic duties. On the other
hand, many networks revolve around child-care activities, so having
kids provided one with access to a social life.

While many emigrant women – notably those with school-aged
children – were encumbered with domestic duties in points of

settlement, others who had enjoyed rich social and occupational lives in Israel simply had to find ways to occupy themselves in the host society while their families pursued their own activities. (In some cases, the women's visas prohibited employment.) In major Israeli settlements, Israeli restaurants, shops, nightclubs, daycare centers and courses provide an accessible setting where Israeli women and men meet and socialize on a regular basis. In the following quote, two women socializing at their favorite Israeli coffee shop discuss the value of their social network:

INVESTIGATOR: So you spend a lot of time with the kids?

SARAH: I don't do anything extra that I didn't do in Israel. They are older now. I devoted much more time in Israel to my children than here.

INVESTIGATOR: What do you do with your time then?

SARAH: I spend a lot of time with my friends. I didn't have as much coffee as I had this year for all my life. When I was a teacher in Israel, on my day off, I would go with girl friends to the coffee shop and have some coffee, have something to eat. But now I have it every day – one long vacation.

CARMELLA: We see each other more than we see the husbands.

SARAH: We see each other a lot. We don't fight. We only fight with our husbands.

While these women's networks provided sociability and support, a fair number of Israeli women find this way of life to be disappointing. Such was the case for Leyat, who had always been employed prior to moving to London:

When I came to the UK, I came to a society that is built around women staying home and drinking tea with each other all the time. After one month, I really had enough of the coffees and teas and mothers! I had enough of the small talk about the weather and about the nappies! [laughs].

Finally, it should be noted that the Israeli emigrant population is a diverse one – in terms of age, ethnic origins, religious outlooks, education, occupation, ideology, tenure in the host society, income and other factors – and that women's networks are segmented according to these social differences. In the following quote, Aviva, the president of the Shalom Lodge – an organization favored by the established elite of Los Angeles Israelis – distinguishes her peers from the members of the Israeli Network Organization – an association oriented towards younger and more recently arrived co-nationals:

INVESTIGATOR: And what about the Israeli Network Organization? Are you involved with them?

AVIVA: The Israeli Network Organization? The Israeli Network Organization is for Israelis only starting [life in the US]. The Israeli Network Organization does everything very, very cheap. You know, there are a lot of Israelis [in Los Angeles] today. I come from a different group. The Shalom Lodge is more established with people that have more money, people who came around '65 or '67 – before the Six Day War.

Creation of formalized activities

Given their feelings of dissatisfaction with life in host settings and their socially isolated status, Israeli migrant women have both the time and the motivation to create communal organizations. In several points of settlement, Israeli women published Hebrew-language newspapers and magazines, ran children's activities and daycare centers, and organized cultural and philanthropic events. (See Chapter 5 for a detailed discussion of communal life among Israeli émigrés.) Many émigré women have social service and pedagogical training, making them well prepared for communal occupations (Sachal-Staeir 1993; Borzorgmehr *et al.* 1996). Often, women's informal groups became formalized as their members met regularly and joined religious and secular associations en masse.

In the following quotation, the director of an Israeli-oriented chapter of an international Jewish women's organization in Los Angeles discusses abandoning her occupation as a nurse in order to become a volunteer community worker:

INVESTIGATOR: Now, more and more women are working full time and going into professions. Would that affect your involvement in the women's organization?

SALLY: Well, I know for sure that if I would work, I wouldn't be doing this. I wouldn't have the time because it is full time. A lot of my members, my board members I am talking about, they are working, – but they are not directors. I worked as a nurse in Israel and here too, for awhile, but I like what I am doing now. It's really interesting.

Motivated by their desire to provide children with some forms of Israeli-style upbringing, a number of émigré women – in consort with Israeli and host society Jewish organizations – developed programs for the community's young people. In Los Angeles, two of the most popular were the AMI (Israeli Hebrew) school and Tzofim (Israeli scouts). (Similar programs exist in Paris, New York, London, Chicago, Miami and Toronto.) In organizing activities and shuttling children to weekly sessions, Israeli mothers found ample opportunities to socialize with their peers. The directors of these two programs describe the rationale behind these institutions:

ISRAELI HEBREW SCHOOL STAFF MEMBER ADI: What does a child that was born to an Israeli family that lives in the United States need to feel comfortable in his community? One thing is Hebrew. They must also know about the culture in which we grew – the poems and the riddles and the rhymes and the stories. We have lessons for the Holy Days and Shabbat. We celebrate the Holy Days the way we would in Israel. They have to know about the geography of Israel to know what's going on political wise. They have to know the history and they should know about the different Jewish heroes from the biblical time to modern history.

TZOFIM ORGANIZER KAREN: What we do basically is give our kids some education. Most of our kids go to public school. Very few get a Jewish education. When people come here, it takes them a while to realize that the kids need more. Basically, what the Israeli Scouts do is give our kids some knowledge . . . first of all the language. So, what we want to do is to keep the language open, keep some of the traditions, stories and holidays, the way we celebrate them. We teach them about Israel.

Israeli emigrants are also involved in non-gender specific community organizations, such as Hebrew-speaking, Israeli-oriented chapters of host society Jewish organizations (Rosen 1993). By linking their activities to those of the local Jewish population, émigré women both benefit from and contribute to the indigenous Jewish communal structure.

Plate 4.5   Fundraising for an after-school Israeli Hebrew program,
Los Angeles.

Transnational family strategies

Recently, a growing body of scholarship has addressed the ways by
which groups have used transnational strategies to cope with the
family-related problems associated with migration. The literature on
this topic suggests that such links and resources can provide useful
benefits – exposing children to diverse environments, allowing them
to know grandparents and cousins, protecting them from hostile and
unsavory places of settlement, maximizing access to health care and
education and freeing parents to work (Gabaccia 1994; Massey *et al.*
1994; Waters 1999; Portes 2001). At the same time, the costs –
psychological and otherwise – for the families involved can be consequential (Hondagenu-Sotelo and Avila 1997; Levitt 2001a).

In our fieldwork and interviews, we found evidence that Israeli
women – and men as well – address their isolation by maintaining
extensive ties with friends and relatives overseas. Some went as far as
keeping multiple households and returning to Israel with children for
extended periods (see Chapter 7). While men were most commonly
involved in transnational business activities, women played pivotal

roles in maintaining transnational family ties. Like other high-status migrants, Israelis deploy the transnational family commuting practices of "astronaut" parents and "parachute" children who reside on different continents in order to access an ideal combination of economic and educational opportunities, while relying on recurrent international air travel to preserve family unity (Ong 1999; Gold 2000). In the following quote, Gilda describes how she travels between London and Israel to care for family members in two countries:

> It is complicated. We came here [London] while our first child was in the army. He was not in a dangerous function so we could come here. A year ago, our daughter who finished the secondary school went to the [Israeli] army. She lives now with her boyfriend in our Moshav [rural collective]. My son is living with my mom [in Israel]. He has a separate floor in her house with a private entrance. Almost every two months, I am traveling there for ten days or so to give them also the feeling that Mom is here.

INVESTIGATOR: Must be very tiring.

GILDA: Yes it is. It also takes a lot of my time. I am organizing things before and after in here, and also there. I take care of all their needs.

Youth programs supported by the Israeli government and various Jewish organizations – including Hetz Vakeshet (summer in Israel), study abroad and military service – also served to keep young emigrants (as well as the children of Israelis) tied to the land, culture, language, religion and people of the Jewish State.

With their close proximity to Israel, London's émigrés appear to be more often immersed in transnational family practices than co-nationals in the US, Canada or Australia. Many of our respondents in London reported visiting Israel four or more times a year, often for weeks at a time. Batya describes a level of on-going contact with Israel that would be rare in North America:

> I managed to maintain the relationships like they were before. I talk with them often, I meet them whenever I come or they visit here. I always meet with everybody when I come. I had organized two meetings of my Kibbutz and my high school mates. These were very exciting. We are still very good friends. We write to each other – mainly e-mail, and we meet.

> Some of my friends visit my parents and sisters regularly, and it's like another family to them.
>
> I want to be together. They are an important part of my life even if I live in London. I still have relationships with the trainees I trained during my army service, and I meet with them as well. I invest a lot in these relationships in order to keep them as they were before. Some of my friends here – their relationships in Israel gradually disintegrated simply because they put very little into the maintenance of these friendships. Mine didn't. I don't forget my life in Israel.

Israelis in the UK may be more transnational in outlook than those in North America because England is less devoted to the assimilation of immigrants than is the States or Canada (Kadish 1998). As countries of immigration, the United States and Canada maintain strong national myths with regard to the inclusion of recent arrivals. Public schools, which are attended by a considerable fraction of Israeli migrant children in the States, have long played a major role in the assimilation of immigrants (Glazer and Moynihan 1963; Gold and Phillips 1996b). Jewish school attendance also promotes the adoption of a US identity (Rosenthal 1989: 149). Further, Toronto's highly organized Jewish community provides Israeli emigrants with many opportunities for involvement (Cohen 1999). In contrast, Israeli migrant children in London often attend multicultural or Jewish schools that include a sizable fraction of Israeli children. This often discourages their acquisition of an English identity.

While Israeli-American parents complain of their kids becoming "totally Americanized," and young Israelis in Toronto increasingly see themselves as Canadian Jews, Israeli parents in England were often concerned about their children's isolation and lack of companionship (Cohen 1999). Many asserted that their kids didn't make friends with British children and would be lonesome if co-nationals weren't located. The mother of a girl attending a Jewish school comments on these national boundaries:

> With the English it is very difficult to have connection. Our daughter brings only Israelis [home as friends]. Once she told me that they have a basketball match at school and it was English Jewish girls against the Israeli girls. I was really shocked. In our house, I don't see English children at all.

Finally, the London Israeli community includes an especially large group of expatriates – Israelis who work overseas for fixed periods of two or three years. These temporary residents participate in the same social circles, schools and neighborhoods as long-term settlers. Accordingly, their returns often encourage settlers – with whom they often socialize – to go home as well.

As émigrés residing in various nations reflected upon their transnational family strategies, they asserted that it solved several problems. It allowed children to develop an Israeli identity, master Hebrew, stay close with relatives; it reduced the chances of marriage to a non-Jew, and allowed kids raised abroad to share common experiences and outlooks with parents. Sol, an entrepreneur who returned from Los Angeles to Israel, hoped that his family's time abroad provided his children with the best of both worlds:

> My son Bar was born in LA and lived here for almost 16 years. Then we moved back. He is graduating high school this year and I told him that he has a choice either to come to go to college here or to go to the army and he decided to go to the army in Israel.
>
> Even though Bar and his brothers they grow up in the United States, they love Israel and follow what's happening. I think for the kids, it was a very good move.
>
> Bar was just in LA and he was able to keep in touch with his friends over here, so when he comes here, he has a lot of friends and he can see a lot of people. So in a way, I feel that my kids have a taste of both worlds and I hope that they'll learn to live in this big village we call the world. Yeah they have a taste of both and I hope it will be for the beneficial.
>
> All of them are bilingual and they speak pretty good English and Hebrew and, when they'll grow, they'll decide what they want to do. But I felt it was my obligation to show them a little bit of Israel. I'm an Israeli and I thought this was the most important thing.

If an enriched life was seen as one of the greatest benefits of a transnational family strategy, disagreements and conflicts were its most troubling outcomes. Such disputes took a number of forms. In some cases, a recently divorced husband or wife would go abroad to escape from a failed relationship in Israel. In other instances, a couple would split up due to discord over where they would like to live (Fish 1984). In the following quotation, Dahlia explains how disagreements about returning to Israel threaten her marriage:

DAHLIA: I do want to see myself as someone who lives in Israel. The problem is that Moshe (my husband) does not feel the same way. Today, I am in a situation where I have to decide if I will have to separate from Moshe.

INTERVIEWER: Are you serious?

DAHLIA: Yes. I did not try it yet, and I am not interested in trying it now. We never had serious discussion about that, but when we talk in a very light way, he always laughs, saying that we [wife and son] would have to go back without him. I am not insulted by that. I think he has to pass [through] the process and then he will be happy to come back. Meanwhile, I am not in a hurry. I am here because of my family- I am happy to live with my husband in a place which is good for him, and personally, I am gaining a lot from my staying here. Maybe in five years I will say "that's enough" – but I really cannot tell when.

Among couples of different nationalities, incompatible expectations as well as unequal access to social knowledge and resources lead to volatile imbroglios. It goes without saying that marital conflicts and divorces are difficult under any circumstances. However, when the families involved are dispersed over different countries, battles are particularly acrimonious. A women who returned to Israel after splitting from her English husband described the impact on her son: "His father and him are very close and love each other very much. But nevertheless, I decided to take him here, knowing that this means taking him away from a person he loves."

Yoni, who married a British woman in Israel and then moved with her to England, described his transnational divorce. As a foreigner forced to deal with the legal system of his wife's home country, he felt victimized, yet refused to abandon his children:

YONI: It took one and a half years to get the divorce and for one and a half years, I could not see my children. This is the usual story of Israelis who are married to English women. They don't let us see the children. They want all your money, the house and all your life.

INVESTIGATOR: Did she criticize you to the children?

YONI: Yes sure. "Your Israeli father, the macho-man. He is rude."

Well, we don't suit them, that's all. She took all my money, and actually she took my life. She wanted to throw me from here without anything. To her sorrow, she tackled someone who was more tough than what she thought. She also didn't know how much I do love my children. Not everyone is like that. I know people who left their children at the same situation, went to Israel, Belgium, South Africa, and built new families. Their old children are with this monster who ruined their lives. I can't make children and then throw them to the bin. So I am here.

An entrepreneur told a similar story about her divorce from an Englishman:

He took everything. I had to walk away with the baby – and nothing else – and he was very rich. He took me to the courts and threatened to take custody of her. I was not allowed to leave the country for more than two weeks – and I had to have his permission to do that. It was a nightmare. He was scared that I would take her to Israel.

In sum, for most Israelis, family transnationalism seemed an awkward compromise – a means of bringing together geographically dispersed economic opportunities, family relationships and cultural contexts. As a consequence, Israeli families tried to adjust as best as they could to the unique possibilities and challenges it produced.

Conclusions

The vast majority of Israelis emigrate within family units. While going abroad provides them with enhanced income, career opportunities, cultural enrichment and intimacy, it also entails considerable costs. These include separation from friends and relatives in Israel, the need to adapt to an alien environment and being forced to live as a religious and linguistic minority. Israeli parents fear that life abroad will have adverse consequences for their children's education and identity as both Jews and Israelis. They also worry that it will be difficult to relate to kids who have grown up outside of Israel.

While husbands and wives alike are concerned with these difficulties, it is the women who are most often responsible for addressing children's social and cultural deficits. In accepting this task, many women sacrifice their own careers and preferred place of residence. Faced with a poor communal climate, but economically supported by their husbands' earnings, they attempt to recreate a congenial environment through informal and formal communal activities and the maintenance of ties with the country of origin. Many Israeli families hope to preserve strong links to the country of origin through frequent visits, such that the Land of Israel and relatives living there will continue to be a part of their identity and experience. Transnational family relations were maintained most extensively by women and seemed more common among Israelis in England than for those in the US, Canada or Australia. These strategies were sometimes effective in allowing family members to sustain relationships and achieve goals associated with multiple locations. At the same time, transnational family arrangements also yielded disputes among family members as genders and generations expressed conflicting ideas about where to live.

In contrast to the optimism with which some scholars view transnational family strategies, Israeli migrants generally believed that permanent remigration would be most beneficial for their families. They often claimed that the only reason for remaining abroad was financial. Further, while many studies suggest that emigration enhances the status of family members lacking power in the country of origin, among Israelis, it was women and children who were seen as losing the most through migration. They often sought to return, while men preferred to stay on.

In conclusion, Israeli families gain economic benefits from emigration. At the same time, living abroad is often seen as corrosive to the quality of family life. Emigrants seek to neutralize these damages through gendered strategies of domestic effort, and communal organization, and by maintaining ties to the country of origin. Unfortunately, as mentioned by a woman who raised her children in London, one's best efforts don't always yield the desired outcome:

> I would like to see the three of them bringing up families in Israel. That's my aim and that's my purpose, because that's what I didn't get to do. But it looks like they will not. And now, I just feel, you know, it's their life. I did what I could. They're all grown now and now it's their life. It's their choice. As long as they are happy . . . . I have got to, how to say, release the reins. I have to let them fly now. Also, they are successful in what they are doing. They are successful in what they are doing and today, it's also important.

5

PATTERNS OF COMMUNAL ORGANIZATION

Perspectives on immigrant communities

One of the most dramatic transformations to occur in both popular and social science thinking on the topic of communal life involves perspectives about ascriptive communities – those based on ethnicity, religion, language, race, family background, nationality and the like. Until the late 1950s, scholars, politicians and pundits ranging from classical sociological theorists like Marx, Weber and Durkheim to progressive era reformers and Chicago School anthropologists felt that ethnic ties and the communities they created were moribund holdovers of an earlier era, mired in irrational superstition and destined to be overtaken by modern, efficient and universalistic social forms (Thomas and Znaniecki 1920; Bonacich and Modell 1980; Gold 1992a).

Since the 1960s, a wide range of studies have shown that immigrant and ethnic communities are not archaic throwbacks. Instead, they have the ability to provide their members with a variety of social, psychological and economic benefits – ranging from business owner-ship and increased earnings, to success in schools, protection from discrimination, moral support and even superior physical and mental health (Sowell 1981; Chiswick 1988; Portes and Rumbaut 1996; Zhou and Bankston 1998). Further, in contrast to "modern" interest and lifestyle-based forms of social orientation that bring together people already sharing commonalties of class, age, lifestyle and ideology, ethnic communities often embrace a socially diverse membership. In *Habits of the Heart*, Bellah *et al.* (1985: 72–3) assert that in contrast to the narcissistic "lifestyle enclaves" that dominate contemporary life, ethnic communities maintain support, mutual responsibility and a genuinely collective outlook. At their best, they constitute "an inclu-sive whole, celebrating the interdependence of public and private life and the different callings of all."

The wide-ranging appeal of this new perspective on ethnic community is evident in the broad array of groups who endorse it, from religious fundamentalists and ethnic nationalist groups such as the Nation of Islam, to business journalists like Joel Kotkin (1992), to third-stream communitarian Amitai Etzioni (1996); to left-leaning supporters of identity politics movements, including bell hooks (1997) and Yossi Dahan, the leader of Israel's Keshet Mizrahi movement (Derfner 2000).

The basis for this new appreciation of ethnic social forms has been partly derived from research on productive and "successful" ethnic communities, including Jews (Cohen 1969; Bhachu 1985; Kotkin 1992; Portes and Rumbaut 1996; Zhou and Bankston 1998; Hyman 1998). Cooperative Jewish communities have provided their own constituents as well as coethnics abroad with education, assistance and social lives; and have played important roles in helping their members resist assimilation into the Christian societies in which they lived (Goldscheider and Zuckerman 1984; Waterman and Kosmin 1986; Gold and Phillips 1996b). Further, such communities have been important sources of financial, political and demographic support for Israel (Waterman and Kosmin 1986; Lipset 1990).

New scholarship on ethnic community has important implications for the cultural outlooks and policy agendas of various institutions, political groups and nations. While these views are not without opponents (Patterson 1977; Gitlin 1994), multiculturalism and community self-determination are increasingly seen as both compatible with contemporary views of human rights and also as practical means of promoting groups' (and societies') social and economic well-being (Baubock 1996; Zhou and Bankston 1998; Light and Gold 2000). This chapter examines patterns of community formation among Israeli emigrants in several points of settlement.

Israeli emigrant communities

Well aware of recent scholarship on the social and economic viability of ethnic communities, students of Israeli emigration – generally those associated with the yordim school of research described in Chapter 1 – were quick to note émigrés' apparent deviation from the general pattern. Studies conducted in New York and elsewhere during the 1970s and 1980s observed a dearth of formal organizations within the emigrant population, few collective ties with host Jews, and awkward relations with the country of origin (Kass and Lipset 1982; Sobel 1986; Shokeid 1988; Rosenthal and Auerbach 1992; Dubb 1994). The lack of organizations is attributed to the fact that Israeli emigrants are stigmatized, occupy a "liminal" (temporary/outsider) status in host societies and as a result, suffer a guilty identity crisis that prevents community unification, integration with host Jews and the development of realistic, long-term plans regarding settlement (Shokeid 1988; 1993; Mittelburg and Waters 1992; Uriely 1995).

Certain scholars make much of Israeli immigrants' frequent mentions of their plans to return home and their refusal to define themselves as members of the host society, suggesting their ambivalence about settlement is unprecedented (Kass and Lipset 1982; Shokeid 1988; Kimhi 1990; Mittelberg and Waters 1992). For example, South African scholar Sally Frankental (1998: 13) asserts "Compared with most migrants, the Israelis appear to be a deviant case" (with regard to forming ethnic organizations), while Israeli anthropologist Moshe Shokeid (1988; 1993) attributes Israeli immigrants' refusal to create immigrant organizations or merge with American coethnics to their stigmatized and self-sustained social status as yordim. He suggests that the case of Israelis is both an interesting and important finding, because it violates a theoretical consensus regarding the behavior of recent migrant populations in the US:

> The Israelis who . . . do not attach themselves to the vast and prestigious network of American Jewish national and communal institutions, and at the same time refrain from expressing a separate ethnic presence, seem to be out of tune with the mainstream of ethnic behavior in America. That phenomenon seems closely related to the Israelis' problem concerning the legitimacy of their emigration, their self-definition and self-esteem.
>
> (Shokeid 1993: 25)

Does the behavior of Israeli emigrants diverge from the communal patterns associated with contemporary communities in general and Jews in particular or are these findings overstated? Alternatively, as the migration studies tradition would contend, do Israeli emigrants reveal patterns of communal behavior that are consistent with broader theorizing about ethnic and immigrant communities (Herman and LaFontaine 1983; Gold 1994c; Goldscheider 1996; Cohen and Gold 1996)? Finally, to what extent does the communal conduct of Israeli emigrants vary in different time periods and locations?

Patterns of communal interaction

During fieldwork, we did find ample evidence of the widely asserted claim regarding Israeli migrants' ambivalence about being outside of

Plate 5.1 Israeli entertainers of Russian and Yemeni origins. Israeli
emigrants (like Israel itself) are characterized by a great ethnic
diversity. While they occasionally get together with all co-nationals,
their strongest social ties exist within subgroups based upon
religious orientation, national origins, and other background
factors.

the Jewish State and their pervasive, if unfulfilled, desire to return
home. Aaron expressed this feeling during an interview conducted in
1991 in a mostly Israeli apartment complex in Southern California:

> An Israeli is torn apart the minute he is leaving Israel [to go
> abroad for an extended period]. It's not like people from
> other countries who come here and settle down, hoping for
> better life. An Israeli is torn apart the minute he leaves Israel
> and that's when he begins to wonder where is it better – here
> or there.
>
> I think that the reason so many Israelis are here is the
> illusion of materialistic comfort they can find here, period. It
> has nothing to do with spiritual, cultural or emotional values
> they are looking for. The issue is materialism. And it doesn't
> fulfill all the needs a human being has. A person needs
> culture and some ideals to believe in. We Israelis continue to
> keep a close contact with Israel as if we left for a short time
> only. We come here and organize our lives as if we are going
> to stay for a short period and our life here is a make-believe.
> The reality is that we live here and at the same time we don't

live here. We are torn apart and that leaves the question for which I don't have an answer – what will happen and where are we? We are in some kind of uncertainty. You miss Israel, your friends, you miss the Israeli culture.

While Aaron's position is commonly held, by no means is it a universal one. Nor is this outlook immune to historical modification. Since the late 1980s, Israeli emigrants' communal lives have been transformed by improved relations with both the Israeli government and local Jews. In turn, these developments have fostered the growth of a wide array of organized activities among Israeli emigrants in many host societies.

The bases of emigrant organizations are numerous. Some – like Los Angeles' Israeli Network Organization, Yemenite minyan, and Summit political club, or London's Israeli Business Club, Sunday school, and various singalong events – are the products of migrants' own initiatives. Other endeavors, like Hetz Vakeshet (youth-oriented summer in Israel program), Israeli Houses and Tzofim (Israeli Scouts), are sponsored by the Israeli government for émigrés in several cities. Still others, such as Israeli migrant programs created by Jewish Community Centers, Young Men's and Women's Hebrew Associations, and Chabad throughout North America, are linked with native Jewish organizations (Schnall 1987: 147). Finally, restaurants, coffee shops, groceries, bookstores, publications, daycare centers, classes and other enterprises that bring community members together are contrived by individual Israelis.

Whatever their basis, these groups reflect migrants' desire to interact and create setting where they can exchange information, share social and economic support and develop common perspectives on life away from Israel. In the past, Israeli emigrants might have privately endured their loneliness and mixed emotions about being outside of the Jewish State. In contrast, today émigrés in many settings now have a greater opportunity to act collectively to fill needs and to express their national, ethnic and religious sentiments.

The community formation activities of Israeli migrants are shaped by an interactive process involving several stakeholders, including the Israeli government, host society Jews and migrants themselves. Migrants' communal behaviors are also partly determined by broader political and economic conditions in both the country of origin and the place of settlement. The discussion that follows considers the communal lives of emigrants in view of these influences. It pays special attention to the transformations that have resulted in the increasing acceptance of and outreach to émigrés by both Israel and

Plate 5.2 Israeli Flying Club booth, Israeli Independence Day celebration, May 1993. Not only have Israeli emigrants created the most basic type of immigrant associations, such as those having to do with religion, politics and economic self-help, they have also initiated leisure associations, such as this.

host communities. To do so, I focus on four realms of communal inter-action: how Israel views émigrés; how host communities view Israeli emigrants; how Israelis view proximal hosts; and how Israeli emigrants view each other.

How Israel views émigrés

Because the State of Israel is grounded upon the in-migration of diaspora Jews, and is engaged in military and demographic conflicts with regional opponents, it is not surprising that it holds a negative view of its citizens' exit (Sobel 1986). Until the 1980s, the Israeli government either ignored or actively condemned emigrants. For example, during the 1970s "one top Israeli government official referred to the émigrés as zevel (garbage) and urged consulates world-wide to have little if anything to do with them" (Cohen 1986: 159). In order to discourage further emigration and impede settle-ment of those abroad, from the early 1970s until the late 1980s, the Israeli Consulate in New York "repeatedly urged the [Jewish] Federation to provide no special services to Israelis" (Cohen 1986:

159). As recently as 1989, an opinion piece in the *Jerusalem Post* described Israeli emigrants as imprinted with "The Mark of Cain." The article went on to condemn "the almost 400 Israeli-born persons" who, during the previous year, had settled in Australia and asserted, "as every yored knows only too well, he has simply deserted, abandoned the defense of his country and the shared responsibility for it" (Zvielli 1989).

In the late 1980s, however, this characterization began to change. Subtly and without grandstanding, the Israeli government encouraged its consular officials to initiate the development of relations between Israeli immigrants and host society Jewish institutions. Yossi Kucik of the Jewish Agency reported that he attended a 1985 meeting wherein "it was agreed that State could no longer afford to ignore these citizens abroad." During a 1989 trip to Los Angeles, Israeli Absorption Minister Yitzhak Peretz claimed that Israel should change its attitude towards émigrés if they cannot be convinced to return. "Israelis," he said, "should be encouraged to be part of the Jewish community and become integrated because it offers them, and particularly their children, some chance of retaining their Jewish identity" (Tugend 1989).

Two years later, in 1991, Prime Minister Yitzhak Rabin recanted his famous condemnation of Israeli émigrés in an interview in the Israeli-American newspaper *Hadashot LA* saying "What I said then doesn't apply today . . . the Israelis living abroad are an integral part of the Jewish community and there is no point in talking about ostracism" (Rosen 1993: 3). Finally, "because of the importance it attaches to the re-emigration of Israelis to Israel" in 1992, the Israeli government offered a package of benefits including cash assistance, low-cost airfares, suspension of import duties, education, assistance in finding jobs and housing, financial aid for school tuition and reduction in military duty for Israelis and their families who return (*For Those Returning Home* 1995).

Of course, these changes did not occur in a vacuum. The new attitude towards emigrants took place in the context of unprecedented demographic and economic growth and significant improvements in Israel's political situation. In 1989 – a relatively recent date for anti-emigrant editorializing – Israel was suffering economic stagnation, had a rate of inflation near 20 percent, an on-going fear of war and an inability to retain many of its best and brightest (Maoz and Temkin 1989). However, a mere decade later, Israel had signed the 1993 Oslo Peace Accords with the Palestinians and seen a relaxation of the Arab economic embargo. In addition, due to the massive Soviet Aliyah, the Jewish State's population had increased by close to

20 percent – almost 1,000,000 persons, many of whom were highly educated. Its inflation rate was below 3 percent, and it had the greatest number of engineers per capita in the world (almost double that of the second ranking United States). Moreover, during the 1980s, Israel's economy was plagued by stagflation and its major export was citrus. By 2000, Israel had become a center of high tech and was seen as among the world's top growth economies (Hiltzik 2000). As such, it could offer its more affluent citizens a standard of material life equal to that of the industrialized West (Trofimov 1995; Hiltzik 2000). These political, economic and demographic developments transformed Israeli society, making it better able to tolerate emigration and ever more in need of a globalized workforce to facilitate the continued growth of its economy (Lipkis 1991). In strictly practical terms, former residents of the Jewish State were determined by the Israeli government to be far more likely to make aliyah (move to Israel) than native-born Jews in affluent Western nations. Hence, the Israeli government recognized the futility involved in denouncing members of the very group in the Jewish diaspora who are most likely to immigrate to Israel (Fishkoff 1994).

Most recently, the economic decline of 2000–1, coupled with the intensifying disruption and violence associated with the Al-Aksa Intifada, has reignited the debate about emigration within Israeli society (Curtius 2001). According to several respondents and newspaper reports, a fraction of the Israeli population is now more tolerant of emigration than ever before. A survey conducted by Israel's *Ha'aretz Magazine* during 2001 found that only 37 percent of respondents had a negative opinion of emigrants. Sixteen percent had a positive reaction while 43 percent were indifferent (Shavit 2001). An Israeli newspaper article contended,

> it is also clear that the Israelis who are leaving the country have liberated themselves from the stigma of being a yored . . . that was once derisively hurled at emigrants. In a world where flights out of the country are available and cheap, and moving from one land to another for employment is a routine matter, leaving is not necessarily forever.
>
> (Shavit 2001)

While some indicators suggest that Israeli Jewish emigration is increasingly tolerated, a recent article in the leading Israeli newspaper *Ha'aretz* reveals that going abroad remains controversial (Shavit 2001). "More than two decades after Yitzhak Rabin disparaged emigrants as 'droppings out of parasites' emigration is still a major taboo in Israeli society. Israelis who are thinking about leaving the country don't usually think out loud." When a 35-year-old tour guide posted his intention to leave Israel with his family on the Internet in June 2001, he was ferociously attacked. One respondent stated "Jewish history is filled with losers and cowards like you, from Josephus all the way to the yordim in Los Angeles who have become car cleaners" (Shavit 2001).

Reflecting the security implications of emigration, the web site for the Israeli newspaper *Yediot Ahronot* reported that during August 2001, the Israeli Defense Forces were preparing recruitment stations in numerous locations in Europe, Asia, North American and Africa to airlift "Israeli reservists sojourning abroad" if their services were required by the Israeli Army. Los Angeles-based Israeli consul for communication and public affairs Meirav Eilon Shahar explained that "Israel, over the years has expressed varying degrees of interest in the mechanics of reaching, recruiting and returning the many battalions of young Israelis who wend their ways around the world." Despite the fact that the standing army now has more recruits than it wants or needs, it still seeks the ability to access these reservists, largely because their experience is of special value (Teitelbaum 2001b: 14).

It would be unreasonable to assume that all diaspora Jewish communities (and émigrés themselves) directly follow Israeli government policies with regard to the treatment of emigrants. However, Israel's changed perspective on emigrants has increased the self-confidence and organizational propensity of exiles and their advocates in many points of settlement.

How host communities view Israeli emigrants

As noted by scholars who emphasize the value of ethnic collectivism, diaspora Jews have a long and often impressive record of assisting their newly arrived landsmen from overseas (Glazer and Moynihan 1963; Sowell 1981). Such cooperative endeavors have been essential in allowing Western diaspora Jewish communities to achieve the enviable record of achievement, security and continuity that they now enjoy (Patai 1971; Goldscheider and Zuckerman 1984; Waterman and Kosmin 1986; Lipset 1990; Gold and Phillips 1996b).

At the same time, the entrance of each new wave of Jewish immigrants has brought with it significant challenges for host and newcomer alike (Goldscheider and Zuckerman 1984). In fact, the organized and cooperative state of being that characterizes contemporary Jewish communities in Western societies has been over a century in the making. These synergetic communities developed only after the resolution of numerous conflicts, and as a consequence of the unifying impacts of the Holocaust and the formation of the State of Israel.[1]

For example, at the end of the nineteenth century, established German-American Jews were confronted by the arrival of hundreds of thousands of Eastern European coethnics. Out of sincere concern for their brethren and wary that the presence of these impecunious relatives – exotic in their dress, Orthodox in their religion, socialistic in their politics and Yiddish-speaking – might arouse anti-Semitism, the German Jewish community sought to aid and Americanize the newcomers (Howe 1976). Resettlement programs were extensive, yet sometimes heavy-handed and condescending. As a result of friction, German and Eastern European Jews feuded, and created parallel community institutions reflecting their different cultures and neighborhoods of settlement (Gold and Phillips 1996b). It wasn't until the mid-1970s that American Jewry "had achieved a high degree of organizational integration" (Wertheimer 1995: 25).

In early twentieth century Britain, Jewish hosts' largess may have been even more restricted. "It is true only in part that the new-comers' passage into British society was facilitated by a pre-existing community with its own institutions" wrote British economic historian Harold Pollins. Rather, there was "much suspicion and hostility" between Yiddish-speaking aliens and the native-born, as "hosts" tried to discourage the settlement of Russian Jews and arranged for their repatriation. As a consequence, "existing institutions were often shunned by newcomers" (Pollins 1984: 82). In France, native Jews aided recent arrivals out of a sense of solidarity, and also because they realized that their own reputation was linked to popular perceptions of immigrants' behavior. Nevertheless, the established Jews shared many of the prejudices of French society toward the immigrants, and as such, hoped to suppress signs of Jewish difference. In 1913, community leader Baron Edmond de Rothschild criticized the new arrivals who "do not understand French customs . . . [who] remain among themselves, retain their primitive language, speak and write in Jargon" (Hyman 1998: 122). For their part, the immigrants – like their cousins in the US – were confident about the superiority of their own Jewish knowledge, culture and vitality. As such, they considered their French hosts' assimilated Judaism to be "moribund" (Hyman 1998: 122; Wirth 1928; Howe 1976).

Finally, as we examine contemporary Israeli policies discouraging emigration, it is worthwhile to recall historical parallels. Throughout the nineteenth and into the twentieth century, the European Jewish elite – including both its rabbinical and intellectual wings – condemned America as a place inappropriate for Jews. Their reason? American

Jews were not concerned with religious traditions, but instead focused only on personal gain. Writing from San Francisco for a journal published in Russia in the 1880s, Hebrew scholar Zvi Falk Widawer asserted "Jews came here only to achieve the purpose which occupied their entire attention in the land of their birth. That purpose was money" (Hertzberg 1989: 156–7). A few years later, a similar report in an Orthodox periodical from Galicia railed that "The younger generation has inherited nothing from their parents except what they need to make their way in this world; every spiritual teaching is foreign to them." In this way, two of the major accusations made against Israelis in the diaspora in the 1970s and 1980s – that they were obsessed with material gain and that their children would lose their Jewish identity – were also leveled at European Jews in the States by their home country elites a full century before. (Similar condemnations were also directed at Jews heading for Palestine. In the 1920s and 1930s, Elazar Shapira, a European Hassidic leader, preached that America's materialism and Jerusalem's secular Zionism were both "gates to hell" [Hertzberg 1989: 158].)

Accordingly, while it is true that modern diaspora Jewish communities have achieved impressive levels of cooperation and coordination, and that Yiddish-speaking Jewish migrants of the early twentieth century created more organizations in New York, London and Paris than did contemporary Israelis, historical evidence suggests that the fabrication of inclusive and effective Jewish communities is a long and difficult process. Thus, it is not so surprising that Israeli emigrants during the late twentieth century encounter difficulties in building communal activities.

As a consequence of the controversies surrounding Israelis in the diaspora, there has been limited organized contact between host Jews and Israeli migrants, much less, for example, than has been devoted to Soviet Jews who entered North America since the 1970s, even though the Soviets' arrival also prompted objections from Israel and its supporters. Israelis' participation in host Jewish institutions has, until quite recently, been limited and relatively little public discussion has been devoted to this new immigrant population (Shokeid 1988; Gold 1992a). Writing in *Contemporary Jewry*, sociologist Steven M. Cohen characterized American Jewry's view of the Israelis in their midst as "part denial and part outrage" – reactions unlikely to foster outreach, incorporation or research. Illustrating this outlook, Netty Chappel Gross, a Jerusalem-based writer who grew up in New York City, describes how her American Jewish neighbors reacted when Israelis began to move to their neighborhood in the late 1960s:

They were not, for some reason, seen in the context of other migratory groups. There was a sense that, although they were merely doing what everyone else on the block had done – pursuing the American Dream – they specifically had betrayed a larger ideal in doing so. They disturbed our equilibrium. That many on the block had never been to Israel didn't mitigate this pious xenophobia.

(Gross 1990)

The number of published reports on Israeli emigrants' communal lives has been small. Moreover, those which exist generally view the newcomers through the yordim perspective – as a threat to the existence of their homeland, rather than as a potential benefit to the host Jewish community or simply as new migrants acting of their own free will. In her 1993 report "The Israeli Corner of the American Jewish Community," Sherry Rosen asserted that the communal response has been to approach Israeli émigrés as "anything but Jewish settlers seeking to build new lives for themselves and their families in the United States." While this declaration is perhaps too strong – in 1983, the Los Angeles Council on Jewish Life published a report stressing "the importance of enabling Israelis to become part of the mainstream of our organized Jewish community" (Task Force on Immigrant Intergration 1986: 8) – its does capture a widely held perspective.

Cultural conflicts and reputation

As both host country Jews and Israeli emigrants admit, conflicts between the two groups are not entirely due to the hosts' concordance with Israel's efforts to discourage emigration. Discord can also be traced to social and cultural differences between the two populations (Schnall 1987; Cohen and Gold 1996). While the Jewish population in countries of settlement generally admires Israelis' chutzpah, idealism and military prowess, they often consider them to be boorish, arrogant, overly aggressive, unwilling to support communal charities and either irreligious or fundamentalist (Shain 2000). For their part, Israelis find diaspora Jews to be rigid, cool and shallow (Shokeid 1988; Mittleburg and Waters 1992). Finally, newspaper articles and rumors describing a few émigrés' involvement with drug smuggling, mob hits and unscrupulous business practices in New York, Los Angeles, Amsterdam, Marseilles and Australia suggest that not all émigrés find employment in such benign callings as Hebrew teachers and software designers (Byron 1992; Warnock 1998; Dudkevitch 2000; Itim 2001).

Suffice it to say that due to policy, reputation and cultural differences, until quite recently Israeli emigrants' communal contacts with host country Jews have been limited, and sometimes tense. In the following quote from a 2000 interview, the director of a New York City Jewish agency that provides services to Israelis describes how the host community initially viewed émigrés:

> I've been at this agency for eighteen years. I wouldn't call it [American Jews' attitude towards migrants] hostility, but I would say that there was a real discomfort. For the Americans, it wasn't an individual thing but a global phenomenon that is, "How could they come here? They belong *there*. I mean, they're beautiful Israeli sabras. Sabras belong in Israel, and you know, we help them and they could fight in the wars." That was the American perception.

According to this informant, while intolerance was the initial reaction of many American Jews, with time, both newcomers and hosts began to accept the permanent presence of an Israeli migrant community:

> [Before the change,] everyone [Israeli] you met would say "I'm going back [to Israeli] next week" or "I'm signing my kid up for summer camp, but I'm not sure if I'll still be here in the summer." It was a very self-conscious thing. These people, they felt awkward. When we wanted to march in the Salute to Israel Parade, none of them would march. They didn't want to be seen marching down Fifth Avenue. They didn't want to admit that they live here and that they're bad yordim.
>
> Somewhere between then and now and it seemed to me to be about . . . eight to ten years ago, it really changed. The changes in Israel made it really okay to be here because now when you're there, you feel like you're here and both places are sort of interchangeable. And all of a sudden, they were saying, "Oh, we bought an apartment." Now, they sign up for camp and they tell me that their kids are at Solomon Schechter [a local Jewish school] and their husband's starting his own business. Then they said to me, "I hope my parents are going to come for Pesach because, now this is our home." (Of course I didn't say, "So, I guess you're not going back.")
>
> And the truth is, as an American Jew, for me, I had already begun to realize "Why can't they live here? They're perfectly entitled to live here." It was funny. My personal thinking was

parallel, to some extent, to what I saw happening around. And now, we have a lot of young Israeli families, some of whom I have been involved with since their little one was in nursery school and now they're in the Israeli Hebrew School and a lot of them started their own businesses and many of them have Green Cards and it's accepted that this is where they want to be.

Reflecting the change in Israeli policy, since the early 1990s major Jewish communities – Paris, London, Toronto, New York, Los Angeles, Chicago, Miami and the San Francisco Bay Area – have supported a series of programs to aid and incorporate Israeli emigrants. These include social activities, the provision of secular, Israeli-style education and the creation of Israeli divisions within philanthropic organizations. Moreover, faced with a shrinking and aging native population, diaspora Jewish communities increasingly understand the communal value of the influx of energetic, family-oriented and Jewishly identified Israelis. The Israeli presence is especially appreciated in older urban neighborhoods, where large numbers of local Jews have recently left for suburban locations or retirement communities.

For example, during an interview in April 2000, American and Israeli-born staff members of a New York City Jewish agency told me how a growing segment of their agency's programming was devoted towards local Israeli families, who, in contrast to American Jews, remained in the neighborhood. They pointed out that since the agency provides recreation and childcare programs for Jews in a minimally religious context, there was an excellent match between this community center and its secular Israeli constituency:

STAN: I think the natural simpatico with the Israeli community as they walk in here, is very clear.

JUDITH: You come here on Purim, on the different holiday celebrations. We were proud 'cause you really saw many diverse communities. You heard Russian and you heard everything but there's always the core base of Hebrew. It's our second language here.

MARTHA: At one point, there was so many Israelis in the day camp that Ozzie [an Israeli counselor] said to me [imitating an Israeli accent], "Martha, there are more Israelis here than in Ramat Gan" [laughs]. Another counselor said: "I have groups with just one poor American child. Since Hebrew is the most common language, I have to say, 'Let's talk in English!' "

In contrast to the cool reception they had initially received from American agency staff, Israelis, who hail from a Westernized society and often have a long tenure in the US, eventually became the preferred clients:

MARTHA: At one time, all the other staff members were upset about it [the many Israeli clients], like, "where are you getting these Israelis from, Martha?" Now with the influx of really a lower, well, a more Eastern Russian community, everyone is much more open, saying, "Let's build up the Israelis." So Leah and I said "Yeah, let's start building." Israelis now take classes in health and fitness. They'll join our activities. And even in the arts programs, we've had some Israeli instructors and we get a lot of Israeli students who are taking painting and ceramics . . .

In a 1991 interview, a staff member from a Los Angeles agency suggested that the local Jewish community had long been interested in welcoming Israelis, having established an Israeli Division in the 1970s. However, more extensive efforts to greet Israelis were restricted in order to comply with Israeli policy. Accordingly, in Los Angeles, Israelis and American Jews alike believed that the former Israeli consul, Ron Ronen, deserved special credit for his early and energetic support of outreach to emigrants:

As you know, there's this whole saga of how the Israelis were not welcomed by the organized Jewish community in North America, or in Los Angeles in particular, because the official policy of the State of Israel in the Foreign Ministry was not to have the North American Jewish community make a welcoming effort to the yordim who are here.

And then roughly seven or eight years ago, a number of leaders here in Los Angeles felt that that wasn't a realistic posture and they began to make feelers to organize some sort of outreach to the Israeli community. At any rate, with his [Ronen's] coming to Los Angeles, there was a change in attitude. So now, at least on the part of the Federation, and I presume continuing to be the case on the part of the consulate, there's no ambivalence. We want to welcome these people and have them as part of our community.

In contrast to the yordim literature's assertion that host country Jews are inhospitable to those who emigrate from Israel, in the following quote a Los Angeles communal professional contends that their stigmatized yordim identity originates in Israel, and serves as an obstacle in furthering the newcomers' incorporation:

> I think that the yored piece is what they bring with them. I think it's a part of their psyche. I mean, I would say that if they feel resentment, that's what they feel. You know, I don't deny that . . . there's a lot of mixed emotions that Israelis have here. I've come in contact with people who live here in LA, and you say "how long have you been here?" and they respond "Twenty-five years, but I'm going back."
>
> So it's a very ambivalent kind of mindset. But then there are others that say "Well, let's face the fact, we came here to make a new life. We are Israelis but we're living here, our children are going to be raised here and we're not going back to Israel." Maybe they are a little bit more realistic. A lot of the younger ones come to make their fortune in real estate or in tile, or in whatever it is that they're doing and then they think that they are going to turn around and go back to Israel; and if they do, fine, if they want to stay here you know, it's up to them.

While host country Jews and Israeli emigrants alike continue to refer to the idea of the stigmatized and marginal Israeli emigrant, by the late 1990s there was considerable evidence to suggest that this stereotype was losing hold. For example, in celebration of the 4th of July (US Independence Day) in 1998, the *Detroit Jewish News* – the leading publication of one of the largest and most vital Jewish communities in the US – ran a full-page article about Nitzana York, an Israel-born employee of the Detroit Area Jewish Family Service, who along with over one thousand other immigrants from many countries, had become a US citizen. Reflecting the close ties between this Israeli-American and her Israeli relatives, the article noted that York's sister and her children had flown to Detroit to witness the event (*Detroit Jewish News,* July 10, 1998: 47). The fact that the *Detroit Jewish News* chose to publicize this Israeli's naturalization even though it could have easily celebrated the granting of citizenship to a Jewish immigrant from the former Soviet Union (whose presence in the US is far less controversial than that of Israelis) shows the extent to which Israelis are accepted as members of the American Jewish community (Gold 1994b). Similarly, in its issue commemorating Israel's 53rd year of existence, the *LA Jewish Journal* published a special section on

Plate 5.3 Israeli Independence Day festival, Los Angeles, May, 1994.

"Israel in LA" that described local Israeli restaurants, shops, synagogues, Hebrew courses and the growing number of Israelis settling in Agoura – one of the newest, most affluent and exurban of Southern California's Jewish communities (Teitelbaum 2001a).

Paradoxically, while only a few years before host country Jewish organizations were reluctant to involve Israelis, by the 1990s leaders and staff sometimes complained about migrants' lack of involvement. This point is revealed in the comments of a Jewish communal leader in a Midwestern US city:

> We have several thousand Israelis and there's minimal involvement. It's very, very, frustrating. They get involved in those things that the community does for them that are Israel-focused – like Israel Independence Day or if we bring an Israeli singer. But we've really outreached and we haven't been very successful.

A Los Angeles communal professional made a similar assertion:

> I've come into contact with many Israelis for years. Some were here for a long time and they didn't want to have anything to do with anybody else. They wanted to have a little Israel you know, a junior Tel Aviv here, a Ramat Gan. And they wanted to associate with nobody else but Israelis and have their kids

hang out with nobody else but Israelis and they didn't want to integrate with the other American Jews.

Trained in social work and marketing, Jewish communal volunteers and staff generally realized the futility of judging Israeli emigrants according to host country standards. Instead, they emphasized outreach services. As an employee of the Los Angeles Jewish Federation explained, it was their duty to welcome Israeli emigrants and help them become familiar with the nature of a diaspora Jewish community, one supported by charitable donations as opposed to government funds:

> We found that . . . the vast majority of Israelis really don't know what Federation is. And don't know, therefore, why they should be involved in the organized Jewish community. So we've slowly, step by step, undertaken some educational efforts and they've begun to bear a little bit of fruit so far.
>
> Because many of them have no concept of an organized Jewish community. Everything that we provide in terms of social services, let alone educational and social activities, was provided by the government in Israel; and they're just not used to a structure that is private, voluntary, non-governmental, and that they might have to pay for it, or that there would be this whole notion of voluntary taxation or contribution.
>
> I know that a lot of Israelis, they are shocked that the synagogue, one way or another, is going to ask for some kind of dues – a monetary contribution. They just don't understand that. So the mindset is so different and the experience is so different, that that's one of the first things that we need to do. We've begun to with some success, mount an advertising campaign in the local Hebrew press here. On a week-by-week basis, we try to put quarter-page ads, under the logo "The Federation" in the Hebrew press, that talk about different institutions and what they do.

By 2000, local Jewish communities began to express satisfaction with their efforts to cooperate with Israeli emigrants. Staff members at a New York City agency have now become so devoted to Israeli clients that they dread their departure:

> In Queens, the Israelis add vibrancy and dynamism to this community and the biggest fear is that they will all do so well

that they'll all want to move to the suburbs. In some ways, we've come a long way but in other ways, it's always going to be the most emotional and controversial issue.

How Israelis view proximal hosts

Israeli migrants often settle in established Jewish neighborhoods, develop personal relations with native-born co-religionists, send their children to Jewish schools and work in areas of Jewish economic preponderance (Herman 1998; Schmool and Cohen 1998; Frankental 1998). Indeed, the Israelis I met during fieldwork in Southern California were so aware of regional Jewish geography that they would spontaneously comment "there are no Jews" in the neighborhood surrounding the college where I taught.

Despite their orientation to coethnics, at the group level, substantial friction exists between Israeli emigrants and local Jews (Goren 1980; Rosen 1993; Cohen and Gold 1996). Such collective conflicts are rooted in the groups' differing cultural, linguistic, ideological and religious outlooks. Further, on a practical level, the social lives and networks of long-established and native-born Jews in host communities generally revolve around very different concerns than those most pressing to recently arrived Israeli migrants. According to Mira Rosenthal's study of Israelis in Brooklyn and Queens, 47 percent had been invited to American Jews' homes less than three times. While 18 percent of these Israeli-Americans reported that their two closest friends were American Jews, 78 percent claimed their best friends were fellow Israelis. Given that most of these émigrés had become US citizens, and therefore had lived in the US at least three to five years and knew English, this appears to be a very low rate of interaction. Similarly, in her study of Israelis in Cape Town, Frankental (1998: 12) found "it appears that the agendas of local [Jewish] communal organizations had no appeal for the majority" of Israeli migrants.

Gaps in communication

On the level of personal interaction, some Israelis described being initially impressed by host Jews' politeness. However, they also felt that American, British, Australian, Canadian or French Jews were less friendly and sincere than Israelis (Lipner 1987). Contrasting cultural styles sometimes led to the transnational divorces described in Chapter 4. For example, Aviva, a young single woman, claimed that when she first dated American men, she was charmed by their smooth and "nice" qualities. However, she later realized that it was these very traits that made her incompatible with them:

> When [single] men come here, sometimes women too, they have this glorified image about Americans. Americans are much more polite than Israelis but they're less honest. And that's the catch. It takes two, three years to see the difference in cultures and stuff, and then they realize, "I have to be with Israelis." I met lots of Israeli men who got married to American women and they found out about the differences and oftentimes that relationship ends up in divorce or if it doesn't, then they say, "We wouldn't do it now, and we wouldn't recommend it."
>
> I met an Israeli guy just recently who married this American woman. She comes from a very rich family and he said they had lots of conflicts because she wanted everything her way and she wouldn't compromise. They're in a divorce right now. Two years married, and they have a baby and it's too bad.

Despite the bravado attributed to Israeli émigrés by diaspora Jews, they are, after all, newcomers and outsiders. Many are sensitive to the negative views of them held by the host Jewish community, and, as the following quotations by emigrants in Los Angeles and London reveal, prefer the comfort of familiar co-nationals:

INVESTIGATOR: In terms of social life, or religious life or friendships, do you mostly hang around with other Israelis?

YOSSI: Well yeah. I hang out with Israelis, actually only with Israelis because unfortunately, Americans are very proud people and Israelis are very proud people and most of the time they communicate poorly. If they cross one another, they cause clash. It's really unfortunate and I wish we can find a channel to communicate and become more of giving and take, more flexible with one another. But I guess it's just the way we grew up. Americans grew up differently than Israelis and we see it as we grew up with different mentality.

INVESTIGATOR: What do you think about the Jews here and the relations between Israelis and [British] Jews?

NORIT: I think that as a community they are rejecting us. I don't really know why. I met quite a few [Israeli] people who had unpleasant encounters with them. They felt rejected and excluded by them. Why? I think they don't like us. Those friends of mine who told me about it – they all live here much longer than me. And they said that they have felt uncomfortable when they visited the synagogue, and at social events.

While Ella was initially put off by British Jews' religiosity, she now feels more comfortable with them. (Like most Israelis, both Ella and her Israeli interviewer call local co-religionists simply "Jews" as opposed to their own group, whom they refer to in national terms, as Israelis.)

INVESTIGATOR: What do you think about the Jews here and the relations between Israelis and Jews?

ELLA: I think they keep to themselves. They are not open to accepting us, and I'm not really sure we want to be part of them. My restaurant was a kosher one, so many of my customers were Jews, but I had to close up on Saturdays. We were in a prison here because we couldn't be seen driving on Shabbat. If I didn't keep this, I would have lost the kosher certificate.

Later, I respected that and at some point, I even enjoyed it and felt I really needed that rest on the weekend. I think the main barrier between Israelis and Jews is religion. If you don't attend the synagogue you can't really become one of them. I have neighbors – we have lived next to each other for 20 years. They have never invited me to their home. Their kids are the same age as mine and they never played together. They are very Orthodox. He put this high fence of trees between us years ago and we never crossed it.

Nira describes the lack of an Israeli or Jewish community in Paris:

INVESTIGATOR: So you say there is no Jewish community in this area, nor an Israeli community in Paris at all.

NIRA: Yes, there is no organization. Things are very disorganized here. I think the Israelis are very impressed with the French people and want to be like them, and maybe I'm talking about myself here, and that's why they do not organize as a community and this is a real loss, eh? There are very few activities for Israelis. There is the Israeli House, but we never went there although they keep sending us information about their activities. The ambassador invites us every year to this annual party on [Israeli] Independence Day, and I was always happy to go and see all these celebrities. There is good food, but the last time it was terrible. The event was in a hotel, and there was a two-kilometer long queue just to get in, so I said that is the last time I come here. And that was it. There are no other events here.

Relations with Jewish agencies

While local Jewish agencies attempted to incorporate Israeli emigrants, relations were often difficult. Resonating with Jewish communal workers' comments about Israelis' lack of familiarity with diaspora Jewish institutions, an Israeli emigrant expresses his desire to avoid involvement with the host community. (Note that the respondent assumes involvement to mean dependency, even though the investigators' queries concern membership and religious practice, not consuming services.)

INVESTIGATOR 1: Do you have any interest in becoming part of the Jewish community here? To be members of a temple, to join the JCC [Jewish Community Center] or to light candles on Friday night or?

ETAN: No. The moment I'll need help from the Jewish community here, I'll go back to Israel.

INVESTIGATOR 2: Why?

ETAN: Because I don't want favors from anyone. As soon as I need to ask for favors from anyone or anything, I am going back to Israel.

An established Israeli living in LA challenges the image of the welcoming host community, as he asserts that services are needed by Israeli emigrants but are not readily accessible or affordable:

I think that if the Jewish community cares and if it has enough funds to send money to Israel in order to build the country, it should realize that it is as important to keep the Jewish and Israeli identity of the Jews in the diaspora. But there is a problem. What I am about to say may sound unfair, but as I see it, the American Jewish community is not willing to give and it keeps itself closed and separated. The Israelis are willing to accept but there is no one to give. I know that many people can't afford a Jewish education for their kids. I think that the Jewish Federation and other Jewish organizations should allocate money for this purpose.

Shoshona, an Israeli woman who organizes activities for her community in American Jewish settings felt that Americans – including communal professionals – often exclude Israeli emigrants because of their negative stereotypes:

> You Americans kind of generalize that all Israelis are like this. And that's what happened in the community center where we were [having events]. There were a few incidents before and they [the American staff] always were reminding us what happened.
>
> A kid wrote something on a picture . . . The American staff claimed that Israeli kids did it, saying, "This is a typical Israeli kid." I said, "How do you know? You didn't see him. I don't know. Maybe it is, maybe it isn't. But how can you say . . . ?" That really bothered me.
>
> And we had an incident at a [Jewish] camp, here in the Simi Valley. The [American] staff, I think probably they had a bad experience with Israelis or something. They kind of didn't want us and they did a lot of things not to bring us there.
>
> I got to a point that I thought that maybe I'm getting, you know, to be kind of paranoid . . . everything that is done against us it seems like because we're Israelis. Maybe I'm overlooking things but, you know there was too many things, one after the other. I know we were trying very hard to erase the image of the Israelis, "the bad Israelis . . . "
>
> Well, there are a lot of Israelis that are pushy, they're dirty, they're a lot of things. But there are nice Israelis too, especially now that it's such a big community. A lot of educated Israelis . . . Finally, it [relations between American Jews and Israelis] got better now. It really got better today.

Joining with local Jews

While many Israeli emigrants felt excluded from Jewish communal agencies, some respondents – especially those who have spent a decade or more in the host society – have become familiar with the norms and customs of local Jews and take part in their activities. For example, Nardit, a leader in the London Israeli community, claimed that with time and effort, émigrés could establish constructive relations with British Jews:

INVESTIGATOR: I've heard a lot of the people say that they're not pleased with their relationship with the British Jews.

NARDIT: I can get along because I live here for such a long time. Having my daughter in an Orthodox school, I found that the relationship is depending on me, and depending on Benni [my husband]. We are different from them [British Jews]. I think we are different but when you live in a society, you have to behave in the society. You can't be an outsider.

Like when my daughter went to Orthodox school. I would not invite her [school] friends for a birthday party on Shabbat. They wouldn't go. You see? It's a relationship between cultures or between people; it needs to be two-sided. If you are here, you can bother to study English. You are not respecting them by going to the synagogue without a hat. You need to respect them to gain respect.

Over ten years ago, I actually formed here a charity for Israelis coming over from Israel who have to get a heart transplant, kidney transplant, if they can't afford it themselves. And I had actually a wonderful response from the Jewish group at my daughter's school. It had been tremendous. They have done so much in the way that they helped. We had a lot of families, Israeli families, they have been really in bad spot because it costs a lot of money being out of Israel, being sick, bringing all the family.

Very few families who came and contributed and helped [the charity] are Israeli. The ones who have come were English-Jewish. They were taking away the burden for paying bills or bringing for Shabbat a chicken or anything else. It's so beautiful in this as Jews that we know how to do that. But when I made a big party to collect money for a ticket for one of the families to go to Israel . . . it was so difficult to collect from the Israelis the money for it. I tried to bring in Israeli women and they did not associate. I made a very big party. I had here maybe over 150 people, but only 20 percent were Israelis.

David – a Los Angeles entrepreneur and communal activist – has, like Nardit, been successful in unifying Israeli emigrants and native-born Jews. He elaborates on his approach to integration:

> The Israelis have to come into the Jewish community. I don't like the fact that some of them want to be independent. I'm not against them organizing, but we should become a part of the mainstream of Jewish-American life because we are not separate. Take for example my own family. I don't see that just because somebody's grandmother left the same village in Poland that my grandmother lived in eighty years ago and came to New York, and my relatives came to Israel, that I'm that different from that person.
>
> So, since we are the same people, we should not have a separate Israeli Federation – for two reasons. The main reason to me is that most Israelis will not admit that most of them will stay here forever. Most of them will end up living here, and 90 percent of their children will end up living here.
>
> I mean, all Israelis somewhere harbor the hope that they will go back to Israel. But the truth is that all of them are here temporarily, and then they die. And that's the reality. I've been here eighteen years, I would like to go back, I don't know if I will. You have your businesses, people have families. You know, they cannot just pick up and leave. And they have gotten used to the way of life here and that's their reality. So these two communities need each other. And I'm not saying the Israelis should assimilate into the Jewish community and become Americans because they won't. Their children prob-ably will, but they won't.
>
> And they can keep their uniqueness, but in total coopera-tion. I think that instead of having their divisive or divided Jewish community, we need to have one strong united commu-nity, because here, you're bringing new Israeli, precious Israeli blood into the Jewish Federation. The Federation will get stronger and I'm going to tell you that some of the nicest people I know work in The Federation and it will do a hell of lot of good for Israelis to meet these people and become one community. Not show the resentment of Americans to Israelis and Israelis see themselves as outsiders. I mean it will take time. This is not a process that will happen overnight, but it will happen.

How Israeli emigrants view each other

While many Israelis feel awkward about being in the diaspora, their ambivalence does not always lead them to avoid interacting with one another, as the authors of the yordim literature often claim (Mittleburg and Waters 1992; Uriely 1995; Shokeid 1993; 1998). On the contrary, our fieldwork suggests that rather than discouraging the maintenance of ethnic ties, feelings of nostalgia, patriotism, guilt and cultural loss can function as an incentive for émigrés to join together. Oded, a teacher at a LA Jewish school who was involved in a variety of Israeli organizations, described his desire to associate with other emigrants:

> You probably know it, when people immigrate somewhere; they tend to get into some ghetto. There is a need to be among those you are comfortable to be with. And I identify more than anybody because my wife is American and I don't speak Hebrew at home so I'm dying for someone to speak Hebrew with. I need an outlet.

In fact, we observed that Israeli emigrants in various points of settlement have developed activities and organizations in order to resolve their ambivalence about being abroad. In the course of our research, we identified some twenty-seven Israeli organizations in Los Angeles alone (Gold 1992b: 18–23; Sachal-Staier 1993: 74–80). These allow émigrés to maintain various Israeli practices and outlooks in the diaspora. Community activities include socializing with other Israelis, living near coethnics (and within Jewish communities), consuming Hebrew-language media (originating in both the host society and Israel), attending Israeli restaurants, nightclubs, social events and celebrations; joining Israeli associations, working in jobs with other Israelis, consuming goods and services provided by Israeli professionals and entrepreneurs, keeping funds in Israeli banks, sending kids to Israeli-oriented religious, language, recreational, day care and cultural/national activities; raising money for Israeli causes, calling Israel on the phone, perusing Israeli web sites, hosting Israeli visitors and making frequent trips to Israel. Reflecting emigrants' high degree of communal organization, their collective endeavors include not just the economic and identity-oriented bodies common to migrant groups, but leisure associations as well, such as an Israeli flying club.

Further evidence of Israelis emigrants' organization is apparent in their political activities. In Spring 1993, Los Angeles mayoral candidate (later mayor) Richard Riordan stumped for votes at the

Plate 5.4 Los Angeles mayoral candidate (later mayor) Richard Riordan stumps for votes at the Israeli Independence Day festival, 1993. Riordan was invited and indorsed by the Summit Club, a group of established Israeli immigrants who lobby the American political system on behalf of Israel. The presence of major American political figures at Israeli community events suggests that Israeli émigrés have obtained US citizenship and are considered to be important players in the local political scene.

community's Yom Ha'atzmaut (Israeli Independence Day) festival as the invited guest of the Summit Club, a pro-Israel lobbying group made up of affluent Southern California Israelis (Gold 1994b). The fact that the mayor of the second largest city in the United States would seek votes at this event demonstrates that Israelis have become American citizens and are political actors of some significance. Most recently, Israeli emigrants demonstrated their confidence as they returned home to participate in the May 1999 and February 2001 elections for Prime Minister. In some cases, their airfares were subsidised by affluent expatriates who hoped to influence the outcome (Broder 1999; Radler 2001).

As these many examples indicate, some Israeli emigrants are quite communal in orientation. In strong contrast to the image of the exile who is too ashamed to make contact with his or her co-nationals, many Israelis abroad asserted a desire to associate with and help one another. A single mother, who has played an important role in linking Israelis with the American Jewish community through affiliation with the Jewish Federation of Los Angeles, describes her experience:

> Along with several Israeli men, we formed what is called the Israeli Business Network in 1986. It was an independent association. And we started meeting once a month and getting a lot of people involved, usually successful business people who are also involved in the community. And we went quite strong for two years.
>
> We Israelis had our own separate organization, so we had to write the newsletter, stick the stamps; you do everything in the night, arguing between ourselves. And on top of it, all of us worked full time, full time – some of us were single parents, working with a family and all these things.
>
> I think Israelis traditionally have this thing [outlook], they say, "I can do it better." I keep saying to them [the members], "We don't need to re-invent the wheel. Do you think we need to create services for Israelis? We already have them in the Jewish Federation. Let's just get our own people in there." So I moved into the Jewish Federation and started the Israeli Division. And I was in charge of the leadership development and I went for a couple of years doing that.
>
> You know, as immigrants, we have a lot of energy. And remember, immigrants go through pain. And when you go through pain, you work it out and become positive. And I tell Israelis – "Come and join us. Look, sure you can come to America and make money and do everything in every part of life. But if you want to be part of the community and you want to preserve something which is important in your life, like your language and the culture, then we need to get together and do some good things." And we become friends.

As a consequence of this sort of mobilization, as well as their geographical concentration and ethnic entrepreneurship, Israeli emigrants in major communities of settlement, along with the many organizations that serve them, approximate what Breton (1964) calls an "institutionally complete" community. Within these collectivities, Israeli immigrants and visitors can obtain nearly all of their needs – ranging from cultural activities to the acquisition of consumer goods, to obtaining health care and legal services – from co-nationals and coethnics without speaking a word of English.

Community organization by locality

While we lack the detailed kind of data that would permit us to systematically evaluate the specific character of Israeli émigré communal activities in various places of settlement, site visits, respondents' comments and perusal of research reports and communal documents (such as ethnic newspaper articles and Hebrew "Yellow Pages"[2]) permit us to make some conclusions.

Settlements in North America, including Los Angeles, New York and Toronto probably have the most extensive array of Israeli emigrant organizations (Schnall 1987; Mittelburg and Waters 1992; Gold 1994b; Cohen 1999). Having already discussed several US organizations, we proceed northward. Canadian scholars Rina Cohen and Gerald Gold (1996: 19) note that "The Israelis living in Toronto constituted in the 1990s a nascent sub-ethnic group, which was developing its own institutions quite distinct from those of the highly-organized Canadian Jews." Their organizations include many shops, Israeli chapters of several international Jewish organizations (WIZO, Naamat, Ort and B'nai Brith), Hebrew radio programs and newspapers, literature clubs, two synagogues, two associations for the elderly, a branch of Israeli Scouts and a disabled veterans' club (Cohen and Gold 1996: 25). Émigrés in London describe their geographically concentrated community as the "Israeli swamp." It features a Sunday school, several child-care programs, a business network association (which has recently affiliated with the native Jewish communal structure), an Israeli House, a magazine (*Alondon*), various Israeli-oriented classes and cultural activities, and an array of guest houses, restaurants, shops, estate agents and coffee houses where community members socialize and exchange information. (I have already described the extensive economic integration that Israelis have developed in the British capital in Chapter 4.) In the following quote, Esther describes the London community:

INVESTIGATOR: When you look at the Israelis here, would you define them as a community?

ESTHER: Yes, I think so. The geographical concentration is important in creating a community. I know many people choose to live in Golders Green because of this. It is very convenient to have some people around who share the same manners – that you can just call and pop in and don't need an appointment two weeks ahead. It's an advantage. Why is it a community? Because they live near each other, because there is all the services around them – the Israeli food, doctors, etc. I think the social life is very much what makes it a community.

According to respondents, Sydney Australia maintains an extensive array of Israeli activities. In her dissertation on Israelis in South Africa, Frankental (1998: Ch. 6) asserts that Cape Town's Israeli networks "indeed generate feelings of community and communality" but that a public dimension of common Israeliness is lacking. Paris features a number of Israeli-oriented shops, restaurants and bookstores, a Modern Hebrew program associated with a Jewish school, and an Israeli House. According to an employee of the Israeli Embassy there, while a large number of former Israelis reside in Paris, relatively few are sabras. Moreover, Parisian Israelis tend to meld into the local Jewish population rather than creating their own activities:

> I would say that the Israelis in Paris are Israelis who went on aliyah [moved to Israel] at some point in their lives, mostly from North Africa, tried to live in Israel for a while and for some reason, things did not go well in Israel for them, and then they came here. I think most of them have integrated into the Jewish community here. Most of them were not born in Israel, and probably did not spend most of their lives in Israel, like the ones in London and New York. So, in fact, there is no Israeli community here. Some have been living here twenty to thirty years and their children barely speak Hebrew. They visit Israel because they have families there, but their ties to Israel are not like those who were born in Israel and grew up there. There are no Israeli organizations at all. However, there are many Jews here, and the Jewish communities here are very organized.

Despite the differences in London's and Paris's communal patterns, the relatively close proximity of these and other European locations to the Jewish State permits Israelis living there to travel home more frequently than is the case for Israelis in distant locations including the Americas, South Africa or Australia.

Extent of ethnic cooperation

In contrast to the assertions of much existing literature, our research suggests that Israeli emigrants do often engage in cooperative behavior. But what is the nature of this cooperation? While Israeli migrants refer to community-wide cooperation, their settlements are clearly stratified by economic competition, ethnicity, class and other forms of social differentiation. Accordingly, as is the case in their economic lives, the most extensive and highly elaborate forms of communal cooperation generally take place within various subgroups based upon factors such as ethnic and national origins, class, religious outlook or tenure in the host society.

Created to provide a homeland to the world's Jews, the State of Israel remains a diverse society, fragmented by ethnicity, class and religious outlook. Recent political and religious controversies in the Jewish State, along with the arrival of almost a million new immigrants from the former USSR, have further segmented Israeli society (Jones 1996; Siegel 1998). These distinctions are often maintained and even enhanced within emigrant communities. An entrepreneur who organizes Israeli cultural events in London, uses sociological terminology to describe communal segmentation:

> The community here, I see it as having four parts. It is a stratified community. There is a clear division between those who are well off, the middle range, and the ones who are not doing so well. There is also a division in terms of culture and quality. There is an enormous hostility between the different groups. There are Mizrahim and Ashkenazim.

Similarly, an accountant in the US describes the stratified Israeli community of Los Angeles:

> There are lots of Israelis here and there are many groups. Everyone finds his own group, and that's how it is, many groups. There are lots of Israelis living in this area of the Valley – Woodland Hills, Tarzana, Encino. My office is in Encino. I meet all kinds of Israelis, my clients. If you are looking for a specific prototype of Israelis here, you won't find it. You will find every aspect of Israelis – for better and for worse. It is demonstrated by their behavior and intellectual levels.

Émigrés are often concerned with their social rank. Those of middle-class standing (persons with college educations and professional jobs) associate together and often distance themselves from working-class co-nationals. They sometimes use the epithet "Chah Chah" to refer to those they feel are below their social position. In both Los Angeles and London, educated Israelis claimed they avoided communal events because a lower-class element would be present. For example, a highly educated Londoner asserted that Israeli House programs are unpopular with her peers because of its proletarian constituency:

> The Israeli house was established about a decade ago as a house for yordim to meet and establish their identity as Israelis, in hope that they will return migrate some day. But as the years went by, the people who attended the lectures and meetings at the house became what we call Chah Chachim – lower working class, mostly divorced or unmarried, and very much detached from the middle-class family community in Golders. As time went by, less middle-class parents attend the House.

Just as the educated middle class seeks to avoid interacting with workers, so too does the well-settled and affluent émigré elite maintain a standard of philanthropy, activism and affluence that excludes the middle class. For example, seated in his Beverly Hills study, a Los Angeles Israeli activist refers to an event that will be attended by his peers:

> I think the top "leaders" of the Israeli community are going now to the policy conference of AIPAC [American Israel Public Affairs Committee, a pro-Israeli political action committee]. A major businessman who is the president of the Summit Club will be there. There is also the publisher of the Israeli Weekly, and two people who are in the leadership of the Israeli Division of the Jewish Federation. There is also a woman who is active in a multitude of Israeli organizations and of course, my good self. We are going to the meeting today. This is really for top people. In addition to AIPAC, they are very active in the [Israel] bonds. Last year at the bonds dinner, they raised over $5,000,000.

In major points of settlement, local Israelis are kept aware of the elite's activities through gossip and ethnic publications. Rank and file émigrés can often point out their homes and businesses. Like prominent members of various ethnic communities, they often pursue philanthropy, donating to both Israeli and local Jewish causes, and sometimes associating with leaders of the native-born Jewish community at high-profile fund-raising events (Light and Gold 2000, Ch. 7).

Among Israelis, class often overlaps with ethnicity. The middle to upper classes are disproportionately of European (Ashkenazi) origins, while many working-class Israelis are of North African or Middle Eastern backgrounds. The ethnic boundary is fairly flexible. Middle-class Israeli circles include mixed and Mizrahi families. Concurrently, a fraction of less educated Israelis is Ashkenazi. Nevertheless, class, along with ethnicity, is a source of division among Israelis at home and in diaspora communities.

Working-class émigrés and those of non-European origins are aware of their disesteemed status among educated, Ashkenazi co-nationals and keep their distance. Avoidance of discrimination is one reason. A Chicago resident interviewed by Natan Uriely reflects upon ethnic divisions among Israelis abroad:

> I am of Kurdish origin, and in Israel, the Polish elite treated us as trash. They acted as if they were better than us. Being Sephardic was associated with being primitive or being Chah-Chah [riff-raff]. When I came to Chicago, I left all of this behind. Nobody treated me as an inferior Sephardic. Here I see Polish people who are lower than me. I see a different reality, and it makes me angry about what I went through in Israel.

> (Uriely 1995: 35)

Similarly, after describing instances of ill treatment and insult suffered by Mizrahim at home, Yariv, whose father was from Morocco, describes ethnic discrimination as among his reasons for staying in England: "I am very worried about Israel's future. There is discrimination against the Sephardim. I always said that it exists, but no one believed me [until now]."

Religious differences also serve to separate émigré subgroups. Middle-class Ashkenazi Israelis are often secular and Western in outlook. In contrast, Mizrahi Jews are more religious and as a consequence, maintain distinct cultural patterns (Derfner 2000). Secular and religious Israelis often eat different foods, have contrary political opinions, believe in dissimilar family values and maintain different tastes in music and attire. Because Israelis of distinct class, ethnic and religious persuasions maintain divergent ways of life, their networks are often mutually exclusive. For example, along Pico Boulvard in West Los Angeles, we visited three synagogues serving distinct Israeli subgroups. These included an independent synagogue lead by a Moroccan-born Rabbi, an Israeli-oriented Chabad synagogue and a minyan for Yemeni-origin Israelis run out of a rented room in a Conservative synagogue. A member describes the Yemeni minyan:

We used to go to Chabad, but now we have our own group. Basically, we want to cherish our tradition and we want to preserve the Yemenite accent, the Yemenite reading, songs, stories. Someone should be educated and have a skill and a lot of, I don't know how to describe it, but good skill and education in our own tradition. I wish every tribe of the Jew would preserve their own tradition.

In addition to their religious activities, the Yemenis – many of who are involved in construction and tile work – maintain a tight and insular community that emphasizes the group's unique cultural, religious and linguistic heritage. It maintains relatively few connections to the larger Israeli community or local American Jews.

Just as Mizrahi Israelis identify with their own religious traditions, an Ashkenazi woman in Paris described how she seeks to maintain her traditions among a population that is largely North African:

I'm disappointed with the religion that does not allow me to say Izkor [prayer for the dead] for the people who died in my life, because they don't do Izkor in an Ashkenazi manner. I need to go very far to an Ashkenazi synagogue. There is a real problem here among the Jews between the Ashkenazim and Mizrahim.

Another dimension of stratification among Israeli emigrants involves distinctions between those who travel abroad temporarily under official auspices, and those who go overseas on their own, often for more extended periods. In London as well as other locations, there is a significant number of schlichim (government staff) and expatriates (employees of Israeli firms). These sanctioned emigrants enjoy a privileged and somewhat controversial status because they are guaranteed employment, receive extensive benefits from their Israeli employers, and especially, because they are able to enjoy the rewards of an overseas life free from the stigma encountered by independent emigrants. (This, despite the fact that schlichim and expatriates also have a propensity to remain overseas for extended periods [Shokeid 1988].)

Early on, as part of its anti-emigration policy, the Israeli government discouraged those on official overseas assignments from interacting with independent emigrants. More recently, relations between the two categories have warmed, and both groups socialize within émigré communities. However, now it is the independent settlers who choose to avoid interactions with the temporaries, because they find the loss of close friends to be emotionally wrenching. A London émigré describes this:

> Well, most of my relations here are schlichim who are supposed to go back in the next two years. I'll be experiencing the dreaded farewell this summer as some of my best friends will be going back. I expect next year will be an unpleasant year. I'm lucky that they are not leaving all together.
>
> I have a few friends who live here many years and they made it a point not to engage with temporary residents. They just don't want to get hurt. They say they just can't stand any more good-byes. Some have really developed a fear of being left behind, a fear of separation. I believe that at some stage I will develop this kind of protection and probably would not want to befriend temporaries.

The continued existence of these patterns of communal segmentation notwithstanding, émigré organizations have become a normal part of Israeli emigrant life in many points of settlement (Fishkoff 1994).[3] As the following excerpt from the Los Angeles Hebrew language newspaper *Hadashot LA* reveals, by 1998, this émigré population was able to support an array of communal events and organizations, including some that the author considers to be "great successes":

> In the last year, and it's saddening, the Israeli organizations in LA continued to decline. On paper, there are 20 organizations but in reality, except several outbreaks of seasonal activities (especially towards the holidays), most of them are paralyzed and are represented in the "Israeli Organizations Council" under Shimon Erem. This is the team who prepares the annual "Yom Ha'atzmaut" festival. The potential is enormous but is wasted on minor intrigues and pettiness, and can decline with the general indifference that characterizes the Israelis here as far as they themselves are concerned.
>
> But everything is not black. In LA, Israeli cultural life is rich and diverse. There are the interview evenings conducted by Dr Yehuda Handelsman 6–7 times a year; the cultural and creative evenings, directed by the sculptor-poet Gadi Efrat every two months; plays in Hebrew by a local amateurs group; singing-in-public evenings led by Shlomo Shafran; an annual Israeli cinema festival bringing the best Israeli cinema and

TV productions (directed by Meir Feningstein); numerous activities that are related to Israel that take place at Skirbol Center, at the University of Judaism, at the big synagogues, and much more. In the educational field, there are also great successes. It's been 10 years now that two schools, Ami and Alonim, operate for Israeli children. There's also a Hebrew high school in the Valley and in the city . . . .

(Shor 1998: 5)

In sum, while the Israeli emigrant community is stratified along many dimensions, it nevertheless maintains a variety of activities, networks and programs. Differences among Israeli subgroups are enduring, and suggest the limited likelihood of unifying the entire population. At the same time however, it is important to remember the population's great internal diversity. Rather than joining together on a inclusive basis, Israeli emigrants reveal a pattern increasingly common among contemporary migrant populations, one stressing communal interaction and organization within an array of subgroups who unite on the basis of common identities, interests, resources and needs (Kim 1981; Gold 1992a; Light *et al.* 1994).

Conclusion: from opposition to accommodation

Early on, Israeli émigrés were generally reluctant to establish formal organizations. They did settle among native-born coethnics and co-operated informally with co-nationals, but created few collective endeavors. Over time, however, Israel's official attitude towards émigrés has changed. While emigration remains an emotionally volatile topic, the role of Israel in the global economy – and the corresponding need for growing numbers of its citizens to travel overseas – is now an accepted fact.

Just a decade ago, scholarly and journalistic reports focused on the lack of organizations among alienated and marginal Israeli emigrants. Today, newspapers, Hebrew yellow pages and web sites publish guides to Israeli-oriented resources, shops and organizations in several points of settlement; Israeli Consulates and local Jews provide cultural programs; and Israeli academics write unselfconsciously about the Israeli diaspora (Sobel 1986; Shokeid 1998; Sheffer 1998). As a consequence of Israel's recent record of economic and demographic growth, Israeli emigration has become much less controversial for the country of origin, proximal hosts and emigrants themselves than it has been in the past.

While Israeli emigrants fail to display the level of organizational propensity revealed by Jewish migrants in diaspora settings early in the twentieth century, they do not appear to be fully at odds with the noted penchant of migrants to create organizations, either. When considering their collective lives, it is important to realize that they are generally well situated and many see their travel abroad as a temporary stay. Accordingly, they have fewer reasons to create organized communities than was the case for the Jewish refugees of a prior epoch or more disadvantaged contemporary populations. Jewish emigrants early this century were impoverished, lacking in host country language skills, subject to harsh anti-Semitism, more numerous than native Jews, and generally unable to return to their points of origin. In contrast, today's Israelis are educated and skilled, often competent in host country languages, unlikely to encounter harsh discrimination, invited to use the extensive organizational resources of native Jews, and able to return home at will. Due to recent changes in the way that both the country of origin and host communities view their presence, Israeli émigrés are now capable of turning their feelings of patriotism, nostalgia and loss into actions on behalf of themselves, their host community and the Jewish State.

A decade ago, Israeli emigrants from all walks of life encountered a common fate – the stigma brought on by their presence outside of the Jewish State. In the current era, it may well be that the identity issues they encounter are more disparate, rooted in aspects of social stratification and differentiation – such as language skills, gender, class, educational level, ethnicity, religiosity, family status and legal standing – that increasingly shape people's life chances and outlooks in the country of origin as well as in the modern world, more generally. The next chapter concerns the nature of Israeli emigrants' identities.

6

NATIONAL, ETHNIC AND RELIGIOUS IDENTITY

Challenges in studying migration and identity

Questions of identity lie at the heart of the study of migration and ethnicity. Social scientists, historians and communal leaders generally believe that when people change their location, they also change their understanding of who they are and how they are linked to others (Glazer and Moynihan 1963; Gordon 1964; Portes and Rumbaut 1996; Appadurai 1996; Min and Kim 1999). In fact, the concepts of identity and identity crisis were developed by immigrant social scientist Erik H. Erikson, and inspired by "the experience of emigration, immigration and Americanization" (Gleason 1981: 31; cited in Rumbaut 1994: 753). Ethnic and national identities are the product of a wide range of factors, including the prevailing legal, racial and economic systems in points of settlement, socially prominent notions about identity and individual migrants' feelings about who they are (Goffman 1963; De Vos and Romanucci-Ross 1982; Soysal 1994; Castles and Miller 1998; Van Hear 1998). In turn, questions of identity affect the viability of social collectivities, ranging from neighborhoods, religious congregations and social movements, to ethnic economies and nation states (Cohen 1969; Calhoun 1994; Warner and Wittner 1998; Light and Gold 2000).

Despite the recent popular and scholarly interest in matters pertaining to identity, many fundamental questions in the study of these issues continue to provoke controversy. Of special concern here is the methodological difficulty involved in specifying the relationship between identity and behavior. While an individual's beliefs about ethnic identity might be strongly held, sentiments alone are difficult to measure, and often change over time and with context (Goffman 1959; Patterson 1975; Waters 1990; Akhtar 1999). A behaviorist solution to this dilemma would be focus on observable behaviors rather than expressed sentiments. However, this strategy is also flawed

181

because of the challenges involved in demonstrating a clear link between a person's behavior and their identity (Gordis and Ben-Horin 1991: ix; Phillips 1991). For example, a person's attendance at a religious ritual might reflect deeply held beliefs and, hence, suggest their strong religious identity. Then again, the ritual observance may be simply the result of habit and conformity, and as such, it may hold no special meaning or indication of identity for the individual in question.

Asserting the difficulties inherent in the study of Jewish identity, David Gordis and Yoav Ben-Horin write:

> Historians, theologians, and sociologists have tried without success to describe Jews by one or another of the conventional sociological categories: religion, nationality or ethnic group ... The difficulty of describing Jews as a group is quite naturally reflected in the parallel difficulty of describing Jewish identity, by and large a personal phenomenon. Everyone seems to sense what Jewish identity is; no satisfactory definition has yet gained wide acceptance.
>
> (1991: vii)

Since we are adding an additional dimension here – the question of nationality – the difficulty of evaluating Israeli emigrants' identities becomes even more complex.

The linking of attitudes and behaviors is a focal concern in studies of Israeli emigration. Researchers have seized upon the apparent contradiction between Israelis' statements of commitment to the Jewish State and their voluntary presence outside of it (Kass and Lipset 1982; Shokeid 1988; Mittelburg and Waters 1992; Uriely 1994). Yordim studies point to this contradiction as indicative of émigrés' confusion. In contrast, migration studies and transnationalist approaches assert that migrants can endure such contradictions, and frequently must do so because personal, financial, political and familial reasons require them to live abroad (Goldscheider 1996).

Differences between Israeli and diaspora Jewish identities

According to several authors, the divergence between Israeli and diaspora-Jewish notions of peoplehood occur because the basic group identities associated with being Israeli, on the one hand, and diaspora-Jewish, on the other, are rooted in particular cultural/national contexts (Herman 1971; Cohen 1991; Zerubavel 1995; Cohen 1997; Shain

2000). Israelis and diaspora Jews speak distinct languages, maintain different cultural norms and practices, eat different kinds of food, have contrasting political outlooks and like different kinds of sports, music and entertainment. Further, in spite of their mutual support of Israel, they have differing national allegiances. Finally, the two groups often express their common religious identification in disparate ways (Liebman and Cohen 1990).

For many Israelis, ethnic identity is secular and nationalistic. While they appreciate Jewish holidays and speak Hebrew, they often connect these behaviors to "Israeliness" rather than Jewishness. They are less accustomed to participating in organized religious activities than is the case among diaspora Jews, and depend on the larger society and public institutions to socialize their children. Thus, there exists "a disparity between the subjective secular, quasi-national Jewish identity of many Israelis, especially of the Ashkenazi elite, and the synagogue-based, ethno-religious identity of diaspora US Jews" (Mittelburg and Waters 1992: 416). And while secular Israelis maintain identities that are distinct from those of diaspora Jews, religious Israelis probably have even less in common with their non-Orthodox co-religionists abroad. The two groups are marked by numerous differences including in their ritual practices, views of gender, cultural traditions, socio-economic characteristics, perspectives on communal life and other matters (Goldscheider 1996; Ben-Rafael 1998; Shain 2000).

Epitomizing the difference between Israelis' national identity and the religious outlook of diaspora Jews is the two groups' distinct reactions to Yom Hazikaron – Israeli Memorial Day. Although religiously involved diaspora Jews typically know about Jewish holidays and many have visited Israel, Israelis realize that diaspora Jews have little knowledge of or reaction to this holiday, which to them, is one of the most profound events of the year – a day which reminds them of the personally felt military sacrifices Israelis have made during their nation's short history. Accordingly, it is during Yom Hazikaron that many Israeli emigrants feel distanced from proximal hosts and close to each other.

In focusing on broad differences between Israelis and diaspora Jews, we may overlook internal differences among emigrants. However, Israeli emigrants *are* a diverse group, with distinct religious and national identities and outlooks, contrasting ideological orientations, varying levels of education and disparate histories in the Jewish State. Moreover, émigrés have different bases of connection to the societies in which they settle. Accordingly, émigrés have variant patterns of adaptation and identification within host societies. No single model of Israeli migrant identity has evolved. Rather, disparate patterns, based on their own characteristics and settlement contexts, are evident (Shokeid 1988; Uriely 1994; 1995; Etzioni-Halevy 1998; Gold 2001). In interviews, Israeli emigrants described how they confront and re-evaluate their identities as Jews and Israelis in the diaspora. As they consider their identities in places of settlement, they cannot help but be aware that their emigration has branded them as yordim and Jewish communal deviants in the eyes of at least some members of those social groups – Israelis and diaspora Jews – with whom they most strongly identify (see Chapter 5). As a consequence, despite the increasing tolerance of Israeli emigration, their considerations of identity are sometimes painful and confusing (Mittelburg and Waters 1992; Uriely 1995; Sheffer 1998; Sabar 2000).

In this chapter, I distill some of the main perspectives about identity that Israeli emigrants described as being meaningful and important in their own lives, while also offering some survey-based findings about emigrant identities and behavior. In our many interviews, we made special efforts to collect information about the groups to which émigrés felt connected. We found that this topic was generally of direct interest to emigrants, who would spontaneously mention their own feelings of social, religious, national and ideological identification. While respondents offered a wide range of answers to our questions about their feelings of connection, three interrelated sources of identification were most common: nation, ethnicity/peoplehood and religion.

Nationality

Nearly every respondent described being an Israeli as their most immediate and powerful base of identity. In specifying the nature of Israeli identity, émigrés emphasized life-shaping experiences, including military service, that they and their families had encountered in the Jewish State. In addition, they referred to the geography and climate of Israel, its language, history, rituals, foods, specific locations, culture, styles of interaction, way of life; and of course, its people. While most emigrants were critical of some aspects of Israeli society, and many had positive things to say about the opportunities and way of life available in countries of settlement, few felt a greater connection to their host society than they did to Israel.

More Israeli than Jewish

In addition to proclaiming the primacy of their Israeliness, many respondents asserted that this national identity was more powerful than their feelings of Jewishness. For example, émigrés universally referred to themselves as "Israelis" while calling local co-religionists "Jews." According to several, being born in Israel makes one immediately and corporally an Israeli, while one must be taught to be a Jew. Moreover, Jews come from many places, but Israelis only come from one place. Offer, the owner of a London cab company, claimed that while his presence in the diaspora has heightened his identity as both an Israeli and a Jew, ultimately, he feels more Israeli:

INVESTIGATOR: Do you feel there was a change in your Jewishness or Israeliness since you came here?

OFFER: I feel a proud Jew and Israeli today. I do not think I felt that in Israel. My car has my name in stickers in Hebrew and I wear this shirt [on which the name of his company is written in Hebrew] and all my drivers wear it, too. I see myself firstly as an Israeli and then as a Jew. I was born in Israel and that is why being an Israeli is much more important to me. I became a Jew only eight days later, when I had the circumcision [laughs].

Amnon, a construction worker who moved with his family to Los Angeles after several years in South Africa, considers Israeliness to be a source of pride and security, but, drawing on the Israeli context (wherein Orthodox religious parties seek to regulate the behavior of all), associates Jewishness with coercion. Consequently, being an Israeli is his primary identity:

INVESTIGATOR: So what is the differentiation for you between being Israeli and being Jewish? Does one come before the other, or do the two intertwine?

AMNON: I was born a Jew. I didn't have a choice in the matter and I don't want to choose any other way. And, as I said, it is a prerogative. It is my right to be a Jew. I don't have to practice Judaism at all to be a Jew. I am a Jew by right, okay. Being an Israeli is having my own country, and [I am] very proud of it. It has to intertwine because Israel belongs to the Jews and therefore only Jews can live in Israel. Jews having their own country don't have to suffer persecution like they suffered in all the generations [in the diaspora]. But if I will have to choose between my country and my religion, I will choose my country first, which is Israel. I identify with my country more than I identify with religion. Now you will ask me why. And it is because of one thing. The religious groups in Israel have made it difficult for me to identify with them.

A London shop owner also asserts the centrality of his Israeli identity:

INVESTIGATOR: Did you change your mind about Israel since you came?

TONY: About Israel? No. Israel always has a place in my life. I always know it's there. It's like the ultimate place for me. I see myself as an Israeli. Even when people ask me "Are you Jewish?" I say "I am an Israeli." So they ask me what is the difference and I explain "An Israeli is someone who lived in Israel. A Jew is from here." I had a star of David that said: I am a Zionist [Ani Zioni]. My friends gave it to me before I left. It says it all.

A returned engineer describes how being outside of Israel heightened his national loyalty and obliged him to become a "little ambassador" for Israel in the US, rather than simply expressing his own personal convictions. However, upon returning to the Jewish State, he resumed the role of a private citizen:

I very quickly realized that my role in the diaspora is as a spokesperson for Israel, even for my non-Jewish friends. So, it did affect my identity. I realized very quickly that I am like a little ambassador. I could not actually expose criticism against the Israeli regime as easily as I was doing here in Israel. My friends wanted to get more explanation on what's going on. So, I changed my role after a year or two and became, like, a little ambassador for Israel, as opposed to just expressing my political opinion, which I switched back to now that we are here in Israel again.

Many studies of Israeli emigration (notably those associated with the yordim tradition) report that migrants – including those who have spent a decade or more in the host society – continue to "sit on their suitcases" and refer to their imminent return. According to this body of research, migrants make such displays in order to emphasize their identity as Israelis, while denying their status as yordim (stigmatized migrants) (Shokeid 1988; Mittelburg and Waters 1992;

Plate 6.1 A representative of the Israeli government addresses Israeli migrants at London's Israeli House. Israeli Houses have been created in several points of settlement to help Israelis retain their connections to the country of origin and its culture.

Uriely 1994). Several of our respondents did just this. Ilan, a London restaurateur, told us "I make a living here – I don't really live here":

INVESTIGATOR: Do you feel any change in your identity? Do you feel more or less Israeli or Jewish since you came here? Do you feel English?

ILAN: No change at all. I'm an Israeli and I will go back to Israel. I do not see myself living here, and we made no such decisions to stay here. We have no plans to emigrate. It's a rolling snowball. We will go back eventually. When I'm 40 years old – I'll go back home.

To sustain the same impression, a Los Angeles restaurant owner, like many emigrants, mentions his ownership of property in the Jewish State as evidence of his determination to return:

Before I retire, I will go back home. Sooner or later I am going to go. You see, I didn't sell my house over there. Still, I have my factory over there. I didn't sell it. I just rented it out. I didn't plan when I came here from the first minute to stay here. If I decided to stay here, I would sell my house and sell

my everything and come here with a little bit more money to
do something. But I didn't plan this.

Another way some émigrés had of reconciling their strong Israeli
identity with their long-term residence overseas was to assert that
their presence abroad was beneficial to the Jewish State. In the words
of a London entrepreneur:

> So this way we contribute to Israel. So if those who are here
> can do that, Israel should encourage them to go abroad and
> contribute in this way. We use El-Al [the Israeli airline]. When
> we come to Israel, we stay in hotels. We buy all sorts of stuff
> Israel exports here. We contribute to the Israeli economy. If
> you look at El-Al flights – 90 percent of the passengers are
> people who live here. I often need to deliver merchandise by
> air. I use El-Al although they are definitely more expensive
> than others. But this is my contribution, I feel. I try to do this
> in other issues as well. I also always travel with El-Al. I can't
> say that their services are better or worse than others. I use
> them because of their Israeliness. No other reason. We do try
> to work with Israel as much as possible.

Repelled by the host society

In addition to declaring their identity as Israelis, many emigrants
also described strong negative reactions to the host society as reinforcing their feelings of connectedness to the Jewish State. Some
respondents described specific interactions or practices that they
found repellent. However, many simply disliked the frailty of their
connections to the country of settlement.

For example, in the following interchange, a professional who had
returned to Israel from the US explains a pattern quite common
among Israelis who had lived in America: in large cities, with many
other migrants present, émigrés did not feel like foreigners. However,
in smaller towns in New England or the Midwest (places where
émigrés often found an otherwise desirable quality of life), constant
questions about their accents made them feel like nonmembers:

INVESTIGATOR: Did you feel like an outsider or minority in the
US?

MORRI: Well, it depends where. In New England, there it tended
to be more homogeneous than, for example, in California, so

from time to time, yes, I was feeling that I was standing out. Especially because my accent is very clearly foreign sounding – you know, it's not an American accent – so after snapping half a sentence, they recognize you are like a recent immigrant or something like that. So they treat you a little differently. I wouldn't say to the worse, but suddenly, they talk slower and they look at you with, like, a strange face, you know. They see you as a stranger. In California, we have the Latino population and many other populations and many recent immigrants. You hardly notice that actually anything changes when they talk to you. So, I would say, in California, we didn't feel as a minority or an outsider. In New England which is more homogenous–from time to time – yes, we did feel it.

Mentioning a similar reaction, several respondents who resided in Canada, France, England and Australia as well as the US asserted that while they were not mistreated, at the same time they didn't enjoy being outsiders. Consequently, they either planned to return home or actually did so. In the words of a returned woman:

I felt that the United States is a society that opened its arms for us. I think we had wonderful opportunities there and we took advantage of them. We had a very good life, but I was still an outsider. I would have remained an outsider and that's why we decided to come back. We didn't want to be outsiders for the rest of our lives.

A former resident of Sydney explained that she felt no ownership of Australian political and cultural life. Realizing that she continued to celebrate Israeli events from afar, she decided to return home:

In Australia, there is a real democracy, but it wasn't mine. It's important for me to be a part of it, to be involved. I hated the fact that I was not a part of it all. It was OK to begin with, but then, I missed the involvement. For me Yom Hazikaron [Israeli Independence Day] is a special day and when Yom Ha'azmaut [Israeli Memorial Day] comes, it is a very special moment for me – I am always choked with tears. I missed that when I was there. I really missed it. I felt sad in these events away from home. I simply felt sad and detached.

I used to organize all these events for Israelis that enabled us to celebrate these events together but it was not the same as it is here. The real thing can only be here. So we lived in

Australia and we lived like Israelis there in a little Israeli social circle. Had we learned to live in Australia like Australians – we could have stayed there. But that did not happen and at the end, that brought us back. Because if we live like Israelis there – we might as well live the real thing here!

A software designer who came back to Israel remembered feeling especially awkward during Christmas:

> Christmas was always very odd. We never knew what to do with ourselves during Christmas time, so, we'd always go away. It seemed like we were the only people outside. It seemed like everybody else was having Christmas dinner or something.

An entrepreneur described her distance from English culture in political terms, condemning its inequality and social isolation:

INVESTIGATOR: What do you think about the English?

DAFNA: I think that they are very different from us. They have some good facets. They are quiet; it is comfortable to deal with them. A queue is a queue; you do not have to be bothered by their behavior. But they are a completely different world. The [economic] classes is very strong. In Israel they exist, but they give a chance to a child from a poor area. I was brought up in a country where everyone has equal opportunities, and is pushed to learn. Here, they do not give a chance. Also, when you look here at the female position, you see that the women here are saying all the time "Sorry," and you see that they are not allowed to be aggressive. And in Israel, a woman is going to the army. She is much more independent.

The worst topic is that they do not have a commitment to friendship. They live as lonely people and die like that. What is a friend? They do not know what that term means. The other thing is that they have to organize everything in advance. The last thing that I cannot stand is the hysterical stinginess. This is really disgusting. I do not have another word for that.

The owner of an auto repair shop describes his confrontation with what, from an Israeli perspective, might be a predictable risk of life in the diaspora – anti-Semitism – encountered in the company of Israeli visitors, no less. Rather than passively accepting the insult, Tony struck back:

INVESTIGATOR: Did you encounter anti-Semitism?

TONY: Yes. But it was years ago. I have an earring with the Star of
David shape. So people ask me "What does this mean?" One
time, a person – he was drunk, mind you – he said to me:
"Fucking Jew." I gave him a punch! And that was it. It was
here, in Camden Town. I went with some family members
who came for a vacation to London. I took them to the
market in Camden Lock. And this salesman opened his big
mouth. He also said "You bloody foreigners." I gave him a
good punch! He was either drunk or doped. Now he has to
speak with a few less teeth in his mouth.

Despite this unpleasant experience, Tony has no plans to return to
Israel. As the owner of a successful small business, his consultations
with similarly employed friends in Israel have convinced him that
going home would result in an intolerable reduction in his family's
standard of living.

Interactions with Arab-Israelis and Palestinians

As noted, about 20 percent of the Israeli population is made up of
non-Jewish Arabs, and a fraction of this group have left the Jewish
State to settle in the same locations as their Jewish co-nationals. In
places like New York, Toronto, London and Los Angeles, Jewish and
Arab Israelis shop at the same food stores, work in common occupations and occasionally employ one another. As immigrants and
minorities coming from the same society, some Jewish Israelis assert
that they feel more comfortable with co-national Arabs than they do
with native-born Jews, and accordingly, cooperate in various economic
endeavors. Members of both populations who sympathize with Israeli
and Palestinian peace movements have developed various informal
and formal efforts to work for peace in the Middle East, and feel that
it is easier to build such activities in the US or France than in Israel.

At the same time, both groups recognize the national and political
conflicts that are at least partly responsible for driving them away
from the Middle East, and see each other as a reminder of the obstacles facing their own groups' nation-building projects. The presence
of "the other," even thousands of miles away in points of settlement,
is thus a signal of hostilities that continue to simmer back in the
Middle East. While a considerable fraction of the Israeli emigrant
population support right wing organizations that are not sympathetic
to Palestinian aspirations, in my many interviews, I did not hear

expressions of personal antipathy towards Arabs (Sheffer 1998). (Paradoxically, slurs were much more likely to be directed at Jewish Israelis who belonged to rival ethnic, political or religious groups.)

Questioning Israeli identity

Most émigrés valued their identity as Israelis, and did not attribute their presence overseas to anger with the Jewish State. However, certain respondents did discuss feelings of frustration with Israeli society and their connections to it. Reflecting their general state of alienation, in many cases, those most critical of Israel also had harsh words for the host society, and for local Jews as well. For example, in an interview conducted during the summer of 1998, George, a London Israeli, described his feeling of separation from both British Jews and Israel. After claiming that London's Orthodox community was intolerant, and that its secular Jews were overly assimilated, he went on to bemoan Israel's political climate in a matter that reflects both his disavowal of Israel ("I do not have a place to come back") and ongoing obsession with it ("I am buying the Israeli paper every week"):

INVESTIGATOR: Did your opinion about Israel changed since you are here?

GEORGE: The Rabin assassination [was a powerful event]. If I had a hope, now I do not have. I do not have a place to come back. I am disappointed. I left for personal reasons, but now . . . I find our country very disappointing. It is not only the fact that Rabin was murdered, it is also that they chose the murderer. [A reference to the election of Benjamin Netanyahu as Prime Minister with the political support of the anti-Rabin faction.]

And now that the country is more Orthodox, it is worse than anything else. The government is completely blocked. I have strong affinity to Israel. I am buying the Israeli newspaper every week. I am very worried about Israel's future.

A similar degree of ambivalence is expressed by a woman who spent several years in Canada. While she didn't feel Canadian, returning to Israel did little to resolve her confusion about belonging:

I never felt that I belonged there [Canada] and that is something that I really missed. I did not belong to the Jewish community. I did not belong to the things that happened in everyday life. The local or national news did not interest me. Life is comfortable in Canada but you're always a stranger. You're always more Jewish or Israeli than you are Canadian. However, my question of identity is still unsolved today [in Israel]. Do I feel Canadian? Israeli? Moroccan? I'm not sure.

Certain respondents described how migration had broadened their worldview, such that they now questioned Israeli ideologies and national myths. For example, some felt that Israelis' national pride was sustained by chauvinism and naivety.

INTERVIEWER: Would you recommend to other Israelis to live here?

NATALI: Yes, abroad in general, not only here. It opens your mind to new things. You learn a lot. You come out of the bubble where you think that Israel is the best place on earth and stuff like that. You become more modest – you learn about and from other cultures. We come to see that we don't know everything. We're very arrogant. When I was young, my parents did not allow me to read the New Testament. But I think it is important that we do read and understand other cultures and religions. We become more modest – we realize that Israel is a province – and not very central [laughing]. Not the center of the world.

Dorit, who returned to Tel Aviv after several years in Australia, offered a similar view:

What really changed in my sense of Israeliness is the arrogance I had with regard to it. I got to our small Australian town thinking that the Israelis are the best. They know everything and they can do everything much better than others. The Jewish mother is the model mother. That arrogance disappeared after a short while. I realized that the myths I held to were not very true and that others can do no less than we can and that Christian mothers can be much better than Jewish mothers. So I had all these myths about ourselves that were shattered quite soon after we left. Actually, my husband constantly complains about the bad work culture in here in comparison to Australia. Every time he comes here he sees the advantages they have in comparison to us. He also hates the Israeli arrogance. There are many lovely things in the

Israeli culture, but we cannot say that we are the only ones who own them.

Disengagement

Several respondents discussed changes internal to Israeli society that occurred while they were abroad – such as its recent political and economic transformations – as altering their identification with the Jewish State. For example, a leftist Kibbutznik living in England described his anger at the increasing Americanization of Israeli culture: "When I go back, I find that the advertising on the radio and the whole scene – the McDonald's and the Toys R Us and the whole shit – it's coming in from America, and I don't like it." A Londoner who returned to Israel following her divorce from an Englishman felt that the country she left no longer existed:

> I am and always was very Israeli in all my being. And although during these years [in London] I felt less and less of that sense of belonging, I still felt I am an Israeli and felt very strong about my identity. However, when I returned, I felt I did not belong here anymore because things have happened here that I was not a part of. I belonged to that country that I left behind years ago. This country does not exist anymore apart from its existence in my memory.

(Despite her complaints, she was determined to remain in order to raise her son as an Israeli.)

Another set of émigrés asserted that their being away from the Jewish State for an extended period – especially during watershed events – made them so "out of touch" that they no longer felt like a part of the country. Nira, a Hebrew teacher who lived in Paris for two decades, explained how her presence in France during the Gulf War caused her to feel disconnected from the Jewish State:

INVESTIGATOR: Do you feel Israeli? French? Both?

NIRA: Look, I feel Israeli although I don't follow the Israeli path. Since the Gulf War, I changed the way I related to Israel. Up until then, I followed Israel and the local politics and during the Gulf War, I stopped. When they [Israelis] sat there with all the fear and hysteria, and I was here, far away from that, and I knew about every Skud before it fell on them, I felt that this is where the real gap between us began to form. I could understand what they were going through. I could understand some of the humor and slang that developed afterwards, but not entirely. I knew this was the first chapter of my outsiderness. I could not link to the existential experience they went through, and this was a significant gap between us. I was very attached up until then, but something happened that left me out of the Israeli scene and collective experiences.

Then the elections took place and Labor lost, but at that point I was already a bit out of it. I could not understand the new jokes about Bibi and Sara [Prime Minister Netanyahu and his wife], and although I understood my friends' and family's stresses and problems, I was not part of it.

World citizenship

As suggested by both the long history of Jews' cosmopolitan outlook as well as more contemporary writing on transnational identity, some Israelis assert their right to live where they wish (Cohen 1997; Patai 1971; Appadurai 1996; Bhabha 1994). While they generally expressed affection for the Jewish State, they do not emphasize living in Israel as a central goal. For example, a journalist involved with Middle Eastern affairs described his notion of national identification:

> There's a host of reasons for my leaving Israel, but even though I live in Los Angeles, obviously, I've never left. I believe that at birth every Jew should be given three passports of three different countries so that they can always have a place to run away to.

Zippi, who has recently returned to Israel after eight years abroad, identifies with Israel. Nevertheless, she feels that with more time, she could have become an Aussie and that her children have already done so. In contrast, her husband, who commutes between Israel and Australia for work, has a bounded sense of Israeli identity and regrets formalizing his ties to Australia:

INVESTIGATOR: What about your Israeli identity? Did it change while you were there?

ZIPPI: No, I still see myself as an Israeli and not as Australian, but I think if I had lived there longer, I would have defined myself as both. I do have an Australian passport. We all do.

Tzvi [my husband] still feels very much as an Israeli although he still works there, but the kids did not see themselves as Israelis really but more like Australians whose parents are Israelis. I remember when we got the passport there was this ceremony and we went out afterwards and Tzvi asked: "How do you feel?" And I felt nothing of it. But he felt as a traitor. He was ashamed of it for a long time.

My kids do not appreciate this now, but I know we have given them a great gift [the Australian passport]. They may never use it – but knowing that if they need to, they can, is a real comfort. They may want to live in another country and do their university degree or whatever. Now they can and not only in Australia but also in other countries. That's a real gift – a gift of freedom. The world is open for them.

Others, however, take a more ideological approach to world citizenship and question the notion of nationalism. A Moroccan-born writer, who lives in Paris and works with various nationalities, claims that he "feels at home everywhere in the world":

INVESTIGATOR: Do you feel like an outsider or do you feel here at home?

I do feel at home. I feel everywhere in the world as if I am at home. I think that everyone should live where it is convenient for him. I don't think that this ground belongs to a certain French or to France at all, as I think that Israel belongs to the people that live there now. I don't think that Israel belongs to the Jews. It belongs to the people that built it after the Holocaust. I don't think that we should be in Israel from historic reasons. We are there because we are there, but the Arabs who lived there should also have a space.

In a like manner, a cook living in London enjoys the possibility of expressing his free will through migration, and condemns those who would stigmatize him for doing so:

INVESTIGATOR: Do you recommend Israelis to live outside the country?

Yes. Everyone that has a passport should try it. Live in another place. I am not calling that yerida [a stigmatized Hebrew term for emigration]. All the time we have definitions: either you are in the army, you are a yored, you are homosexual. Why do they bother to define people all the time?

Jewish identities: ethnic and religious

Finding it difficult to sustain an Israeli identity beyond the Jewish State, and seeking other sources of identification, many Israelis explore their connections with Jewish ethnicity and the Jewish religion. They do this in order to find a base for communal interaction, the celebration of Jewish or Israeli holidays and assistance in child socialization. While many enjoy a feeling of connection with co-religionists, a large number – especially the recently arrived – discover that they have little in common with host Jews. Further, most believe that secular Judaism is not a viable foundation for Jewish identity and community outside of Israel. Accordingly, many turn to religion.

Jewish ethnicity/peoplehood

Israeli émigrés generally see themselves, Jewish migrants from other countries and native-born Jews as members of the same ethnic group. As such, they share "a common past, the observance of the same holidays, rituals and ceremonies, the retelling of the same myths and similar responses to common symbols" (Uriely 1995: 30; Liebman and Cohen 1990). Verifying this propensity, a survey conducted in the early 1990s found that 96 percent of Israelis "felt a connectedness to fellow Jews around the world" (Liebman and Katz 1997: 30). While it is a less pertinent source of identity than Israeli nationality or the Jewish religion, Jewish ethnicity was also seen as a link to potential friends and allies. A returned engineer described local Jews as being "one notch warmer":

> I found the American Jewish person actually one notch warmer and more friendly than just the typical American. Now, there were more things to talk about. So, I was always warming up to them, naturally – so, you know, I just liked them a lot. I think they were especially friendly.

A couple who returned from London to Tel Aviv refer to the inclusive sense of Jewish peoplehood that develops when Jews of all stripes are brought together by their shared minority status:

> GUILDA: We lived in Golders Green, so there were Jews and Israelis around. We always thought that it would have been

nice to have in here [Israel] the same type of relationship that they managed to establish between religious and secular people. There, it's not their country. They are a minority. So they adjust and conform to the culture and all the rest. They would not throw stones at cars driving on Yom Kippur as they do here. Also, the secular there, including the Israelis, are much more respectful and tolerant and actually open-minded towards the religious people. There is no religious coercion – and so they can be more tolerant to the religious people.

AMNON: For instance, we had friends who were totally secular and had religious Jewish neighbors. During the holidays, they did their best not to do anything that would annoy their religious neighbors. They would not act this way here.

Another Londoner agrees, claiming that she too feels more comfortable with Orthodox Jews in England that she did in Israel:

INVESTIGATOR: Has there been any change in your religious-ness or attitudes towards religion since you have lived here?

SARA: No. I did not become more or less observant. But things that annoyed me in Israel do not annoy me here. I even like to see all the Jews walking along Golders Green Road on Shabbat and the holidays, with their nice clothes and children. Sometimes, I even envy them for their family life and routine. They are really a pleasant sight here. I'm really happy I live within them. I prefer to live among them than among other groups. I know that some Israelis really hate them [observant Jews], but I don't. I am secular here as I was in Israel. I don't attend synagogue and I didn't attend in Israel. But in Israel, I felt the religious people try to take over. Here, I don't feel they are doing that and I have no problem with them. Yesterday, I took the kids to see the Purim assembly near Princess Park. It was really lovely.

Taking a contrary position, a long-time resident of London disliked her ethnic-based connection to Orthodox Jews, a group she ignored in Israel:

INVESTIGATOR: Did life in the diaspora influence your Jewish identity?

I have always been a Jew and I will always be. But it is painful to me to say, the Jews that I know from here [England] are very different from the image I had before. I had a good picture of them and now it is much less positive. They are hypocrites, dishonest, and I feel shame to say that I am connected to them. In Israel, you don't live in B'ney Brak and not in Mea Shearim [ultra-Orthodox neighborhoods]. You hear about them but it doesn't touch you as in here.

When I am driving and see two of them talking in the middle of the road and they don't care that a lot of cars are queuing – you think to yourself "Only Jewish will allow that." Disgusting. In our previous houses, there were Jewish families. The neighbors were very nice and invited us to have dinner with them. On the other hand, we had one neighbor that explained to us that because of Jewish people like us, who are driving their car on Friday, we had the Holocaust. So there are people like this and like that.

A woman who obtained an advanced degree in Jewish studies during her stay in the States concluded that it is impossible to maintain a meaningful Jewish identity on the basis of secular ties outside of Israel:

I enjoy the pluralism there. We visited at least fifteen different synagogues there [in the US] and we found at least one or two that we liked. And I could relate to the others. I think the difficult aspect of being a Jew in the United States is something that a student told me the first year we arrived there. He said to me, there is no way of being non-religious Jew in the United States. The only way to be, not just ethnic Jews – but to have some way to express it and to celebrate it and to experience it in your daily life; not to be just as "I'm a Jew and I know it" – is through religion and religious institutions. And I think this is very true. That's a disadvantage. I'm not the religious person, and it was very hard. Well, I had to go to the synagogue to be a Jew, and here I don't have to go to the synagogue. My life is Jewish because of tons of things that are done the Jewish way and through awareness to the Jewish tradition and culture, here without me being formally religious.

Finally, a London shop owner described how diaspora Jews refused to acknowledge their links with Israeli emigrants. In so doing, he suggested the limited potential of Jewish peoplehood as a basis of unification:

INVESTIGATOR: Who are your friends here?

YAAKOV: Mostly Israelis, very few Jews. I think there is a gap between the Israelis and the Jews due to the mentality differences. I think the Jews are to blame actually. They seem to feel we came to "their territory" and we take something from them. I once reminded them that the only difference between us is that they came here one ship earlier than we did. We are Jews just like they are. They may have been born here, but they are not English.

I will give you an example. My son went to a Jewish kindergarten. The kindergarten teacher was married to a British Jew who put his candidacy for the Conservative Party in Scotland. His name was Rosen. As he started his campaign, he changed his name to Ross so that they [Gentiles] do not stigmatize him. And he has the nerve to ask us why we live here and not in Israel. Of course, there is also the religious issue – those who are religious do not like us because, for them, we are worse than the Gentiles.

Religious identity

Finding it difficult to sustain a secular Jewish identity in the diaspora, emigrants look to the Jewish religion. In a fairly large number of cases, emigrants' concern with organized Jewish activities in points of settlement was reactive – a result of their search for a source of identity and community. Most respondents described themselves as being generally secular or even anti-religious prior to going abroad. (Sixty-two percent of Israelis in a 1990s survey described themselves as either "totally non-observant or somewhat observant" [Liebman and Katz 1997: 3].) However, as they confronted their marginality and isolation in the diaspora, and sought a means to preserve a sense of Israeli and Jewish identity among their children, a fair number became involved in religious communities and activities. For example, a woman employed in a Hebrew language media business, who had no pre-migration religious involvement, sent her pre-school child to the ultra Orthodox Chabad (Hassidic) program in Los Angeles to acquire Jewish knowledge.

Israelis from religious backgrounds also practiced Judaism in the host society. Israelis of Sephardic or Mizrahi origins are generally

Plate 6.2 Yemeni minyan (religious group), Los Angeles. Israelis who trace their familial origins to Yemen come together to maintain their unique religious and cultural traditions.

more religious than Ashkenazim (Liebman and Katz 1997). According to Shokeid (1988: Ch. 7), Uriely (1995) and my own fieldwork, they are especially likely to participate in Orthodox synagogues (Gold and Phillips 1996a). Judging by the large number of photographs of the late Lubuvitcher Rebbi Schneerson displayed in Israeli business and other migrant settings, Chabad-Lubavitch – a Brooklyn-based Hassidic movement that emphasizes outreach programs – has made many connections with Israeli emigrants. Like immigrant congregations more broadly, Orthodox programs provide a social life, support and sense of community for isolated newcomers (Thomas and Znaniecki 1920; Warner and Wittner 1998).

As a consequence of their participation in local Jewish activities, a fair number of émigrés described feeling and acting more religious in the diaspora than they ever had in the Jewish State (Uriely 1995). Several claimed that they enjoyed the highly social and gender neutral forms of Judaism that are common in diaspora settings but less popular in Israel. Having become accustomed to this sort of practice while abroad, they hoped to continue it either in the host society or upon returning to the Jewish State. Such is the case for a woman who returned to Israel after several years in Los Angeles:

My kids went there to a Jewish religious school. It was a Conservative school, so they learned a lot about Judaism and practiced much more than we did at home [in Israel]. They did the prayers before and after the food and in the morning and in the evening, and many other things that my kids did not get to see in our home. Even if I wanted to give them that knowledge, I could not, because I did not have it myself. We are both from secular homes, after all. So we actually learned from our kids all about religious practices, and we tried to do some at home so that they would not feel alienated from what the school is teaching them. That is how we ended up going to the synagogue.

We felt our religion in a way much more than in here. We tried harder to do the celebrations properly around the holidays. Here [in Israel] we go to the synagogue on Yom Kippur but we go because everybody does and it's a social event, not a religious one. There – it was also a social event – but we took it much more seriously on the religious side of it. We went there a few times a year and we went into the synagogue and – I don't know how to define it – there we felt much more Jewish than here. Going to the synagogue was an important part of that feeling, and that sense of belonging. So there we would dress nicely, and drive to the synagogue – we drove because the synagogue was not in a walking distance – and we celebrated the holidays with other Israelis and Jews.

As this woman indicates, Israeli emigrants had a very favorable attitude towards Jewish day schools for their children, and often make sacrifices to pay for tuition. While diaspora Jews sometimes have reservations about sending their children to a religious school because of their commitment to pluralist values and experiences, Israelis – who are accustomed to a Jewish majority environment – feel this way less often. Emigrants also chose Jewish schools as a ready alternative to urban public schools that they felt were overcrowded, violent and ineffective. In his 1997 Jewish Population Survey of Los Angeles, Herman (2000) found that 40 percent of children age 5–17 in Israeli households attended Jewish day schools – twice the rate for all Jews in Los Angeles.

While emigrants suggest that it is not possible to be a secular Jew outside of Israel, they also asserted that it is difficult to be moderately religious in Israel. The following respondents enjoyed the forms of practice they encountered in North America. For example, a university professor who has recently returned to Israel after five years in the

US describes his preference for the sort of Judaism followed in American academic communities:

INVESTIGATOR: What do you think about Jewish life in the US?

MAXIM: Well, in the US, the dominant flavor of Judaism is the Reform Judaism and we liked it a lot, because it allowed us to come as a family unit to the synagogue. We are not, you know, religious, observant Jews, but we do come on the High Holidays. For us, it was extremely important to be able to sit together. We also liked the equal role for women in the Jewish practice. For example, you can have a female rabbi and things like that. So, we liked it a lot, actually. We found that Reform Judaism in the US flavor is much more suitable for us. So, in a way, it opened our eyes. We said, "Now, there is some room to practice Judaism and not feel too silly about it."

Here [in Israel], it's back again – the problem [of religious participation] – because the Jewish system here is not to my liking, actually. We really have to search very hard for a synagogue that we like.

Taking a similar perspective, an engineer who returned from Canada found the moderation and flexibility of diaspora Judaism preferable to that commonly practiced in Israel:

NAVA: My family is what we call in Hebrew "masorti" [traditional] but not really religious or observant. We go to the synagogue in holidays. We keep kosher at home. We don't eat non-kosher meat at home, but we do eat it in restaurants.

Canadian Jews are very attracted to religion. They have a close community life. Since we lived in a very Jewish area of Montreal, until I was 18, all my friends were Jewish. Canadian Jews respect the holidays. They have a very strong Jewish identity. I am very aware of my Jewishness.

In Israel you're either a "dati" [religious person], or a "hiloni" [secular]. It's extreme here. There is no middle ground. For me, life in Canada strengthened my Jewish identity over any other identity.

INVESTIGATOR: Are you more religious now that you are back in Israel?

NAVA: Much less than in Canada. I haven't yet found my place in the community. There's almost no Jewish life here. It is obvious here because the majority is Jewish. In Canada, Jewish life was far richer because it was necessary to preserve our Jewish identity and also for social reasons. There, in Canada, Jewish life was richer than what we experience here, paradoxically. Holidays were celebrated better. On the other hand, everything is easy at work when there are Jewish holidays in Israel. In Canada, you had to ask permission to leave work, etc. All is obvious and simple in this regard in Israel.

A small group of respondents became much more religious as a result of their experiences in the diaspora. Many of these had been raised in masorti (traditional) or religious rather than secular homes. In the following interview excerpts, émigrés describe their immersion in religious communities. After straying from the religious environment of their youth, each returned to their faith in the midst of a personal crisis.

Yoni, a London Israeli who went through a traumatic divorce, described how he became religious in England. During the long and painful process, he became involved with local Orthodox Jews who "saved his life" and "were more than family" to him. "Before, when I was in Israel, I didn't practice anything. Now, I am keeping [religious rules]. I am not driving the car [on the Sabbath]. I am eating kosher only. I am traditional. I am not fanatic." In a similar manner, Amnon who had lived in both New York and London, told us how returning to his Jewish faith helped him overcome a moral collapse brought on by his military experience:

INVESTIGATOR: Was there a change in your religiousness since you came?

AMNON: Yes. I think I am more religious here. After the Yom Kippur War, I lost all my faith and felt that all the moral things I believed in had collapsed. When I came back from the USA, I was in a depression. Slowly, I came back to my strength. I felt that through the process of gaining my strength, I begun to retrieve my lost faith in God. I did not convert to religious habits in everyday life. I am still secular. I did not become a Hozer Bitshuva [returned to the faithful]. But when I see or work with religious people, I feel a lot of respect for them.

The most dramatic case of religious rebirth we encountered involved Ayelet, a secular woman who came to London with her son, Yona, on the rebound from a failed marriage. Ayelet explained that when Yona encountered problems in a British school, he was introduced to Stanley, a boy who had recently joined a community of Orthodox British Jews. Through this contact, Yona and Ayelet eventually became Hozer Bitshuva [returned to the faithful] and joined the community as well:

AYELET: The first few weeks [in the school] were OK but then the trouble started that has changed our lives. Yona was very Israeli and very Zionist. So everywhere he went, he started getting into political and religious disputes. Anyway, not long after he started school he was bullied. This school has many minorities – Indian, Pakistanis, and Blacks. Not many white people and not many Jews either. I guess they bullied him because he was different and because he did not know how to behave with them. So he was bullied pretty badly almost every day. As you can imagine, he was pretty miserable at that school.

At that point, we met another woman who helped us – a friend of a friend. She is a [British] Jew – not an Israeli. She said "I have a son who became religious lately, and I want your son to meet with him." I said "OK." That is how Yona was introduced to Stanley.

Stanley offered him some answers at a difficult time, I think. Stanley offered him a new direction. He told him that he became a Hozer Bitshuva and introduced him to a Jewish organization that promotes this and helps the Hozrim Bitshuva. The organization is a charity and many people volunteer to help there. They meet once a week at a synagogue or in private homes in one-on-one sessions, where a tutor teaches the Hozer Bitshuva all they want to know about Judaism. He invited him to one of his tutorial meetings. Yona started to go with Stanley to his tutorial sessions. There, he met three people who are still very central in our lives. They are all very Orthodox religious people living in Stamford Hill.

They paired Yona up with a tutor, Naftoli. Naftoli was like a psychologist to him, a consultant, a friend and a family member. When they met – if Yona had a problem at school or at home – he would share it with his tutor. Everything was easy going and there was never any hint of pressure at any point. His tutor was a real angel. His friendship with Yona was a real gift. So Yona found an interest in this person, who, I think, took his father's place in his life. He was able to talk and discuss everything with this man. Even sex.

It's a very interesting system for religious teaching. It's very different from sitting in a classroom where some students get attention while others are ignored. It's very personal and relates directly to what is going on in your life.

Obviously Yona has told them about me – that I am divorced and came here on my own and the circumstances of our arrival. As soon as he told him about me and our situation, they invited both of us to dine with them on Friday evening. To be honest with you – I did not want to go there. I felt I had nothing in common with these people and felt a bit awkward about the whole invitation. But Yona convinced me. Since then, we were invited almost every Friday!

I started going to these events and really met the most charming and warm-hearted people I have ever known. This is where I started to feel that I gained a family in this way. They treated me and my son so kindly and wrapped us with love and attention and made us feel welcome and comfortable. These people are really great! I made very strong friendships with two families and often stayed for the whole weekend or spend the Chagim [holidays] with them. One of these families has a very large house and they gave my son and me a separate room and treated us like a queen and prince. That is indeed a part of their way of teaching us about religion – to show us what a Jewish home is and what it stands for.

Anyway, what I got from them was a completely different view of religious life. In Israel, as secular people, we would not have meals together. Now things are very different for us. The sense of togetherness that we have is very different. We spend all our weekends and Chagim with the people we know from the Stamford Hill community. It's a great experience.

Then Naftoli suggested its time to transfer Yona to a Jewish school. Since then, Yona went to Hasmonean (a London Jewish academy) and did the impossible – all his grades were A and A+. It was clear that Yona felt much better at Hasmonean and because he was now in a positive environment that supported him, he was doing very well.

INVESTIGATOR: How did your Israeli and non-religious friends from the Israeli community react to this transformation?

AYELET: I will be honest with you. I was very disappointed with the Israelis here. I learned that the Israelis have a big mouth – but when it comes to giving someone a real helping hand –

they were not the ones to help. I got the real help, when I needed it, from the Jewish community – not from the Israelis. I have very few ties left with the Israelis – I got engaged and am about to get married – he [my fiancée] is also a Hozer Bitshuva. He is Jewish and has lived here all his life. So I guess this makes a difference too, but I think the religious issue drove them off.

Most of the friends we had just cut their ties with me. They all see this in a very peculiar way and criticized us for our new life style. No one accepted us as we were. Some treated us as if we were mad and looked at us in a very funny way. Some criticized us and some simply rejected us and wanted nothing to do with us since we became religious. I had a friend who suggested that I take Yona immediately to a psychologist, who may be able to "save him" from this. What nonsense!

Religious involvement as a means to an end

Some Israelis found satisfaction and meaning in diaspora Judaism. Others, however, felt that it was simply a way of retaining a Jewish identity, socializing children and gaining access to a community. Accordingly, they described their religious association as a means to an end. If and when they returned to Israel, they planned to resume their secular lifestyles. In the words of a woman who recently returned to Israel from Australia: "We went to the synagogue there . . . almost once a month, just for the social aspect of it. We understood that this is what the synagogue is for to the local Jews – a social club around the religious issues."

Remaining secular

While a number of secular Israelis became involved in religious activities in the diaspora, others declined to do so. A couple in Los Angeles described their desire to maintain a Jewish identity that is based upon family celebrations rather than rabbi-approved rituals. In so doing, they shunned religious Judaism:

INVESTIGATOR: So how do you practice your Jewishness?

DINA: The mere fact that I believe in Judaism and not in anything else. Lighting candles doesn't mean anything to me. I do it for my daughter. It depends on each person and the way he was brought up. I didn't grow up in a traditional home and I don't understand why you are not supposed to turn on electricity on Shabbat. It doesn't mean anything to me. The rabbis can come now and start explaining to me everything, and still I won't understand a thing. Everything must have logic.

INVESTIGATOR: And what are you doing on holidays?

DINA: We celebrate the holidays because it's fun and nice and we sing songs that remind us of our childhood. That's what unites us. You feel something inside, and that's it.

RONNIE: We believe in the uniqueness of Judaism. We feel that it is superior to everything else. I don't want to raise my nose or something like that, but I feel that we are a people of virtue. And it's really so. We believe in Judaism but we are not Orthodox.

A London woman who planned to attend High Holiday services with her family found the financial costs of diaspora Judaism excessive. As a consequence, she decided not to go:

For us, the idea that one should pay for his religion, or pay to maintain one's identities – the whole idea is bizarre. The idea that it is that costly and that only affluent people can pay that price is ridiculous. Not only that, we have two identities to maintain and the Jewish one is less important that the Israeli one, so why should we choose to spend money on maintaining our less central identity?

When Miri, a Hebrew teacher living in Paris, invited secular friends to celebrate her son's Bar Mitzvah, few showed up. She described her co-nationals as "having an allergy to religion":

The Israelis I know – most are secular. I invited my Israeli friends to attend my son's Bar-Mitzvah at a synagogue, but very few came. I think because of the religious people in Israel, the people here have developed an allergy to religion. So they don't attend the synagogue, not even for an event. I don't know many Israelis who would go to a synagogue. I invited my friends, who I knew are secular, to a Bar-Mitzvah at a Reform synagogue, that has a woman Rabbi, and still no one came. The religious people made us hate the religion.

Religious rejections of diaspora Judaism

Some Israelis who were religious prior to their travel abroad also avoid Jewish involvement in points of settlement. In the following quotations, religious émigrés elaborate on their rejection of what they see as watered-down diaspora Judaism:

DEBORAH: Most of them [American Jews] go by the Reformed stream and I tend to actually like it because it's more modern and it doesn't come to conflict with family life as much as the other streams of Judaism do, but, I think that from a Jewish life perspective, it's really a lot like Christianity. There isn't that much difference.

INVESTIGATOR: What do you think about the Jewish life in the US?

RON: Their Judaism is quite impressive, but it is treated to their needs and so I think they have a very nice sense of community. But for us, it didn't fit us. It is very foreign for us. It is weird, it is bizarre for us, you know, to see the rabbi that was a woman and she was a lesbian and all. And just weird for us. But, I have lots of respect for their community and the way they live and the sense of community that they had.

INVESTIGATOR: What do you think of English Jews?

GILDA: I had contact with Jewish women. It raise me a thought of how will I bring up my children. Will they be like the English? If so, it is terrible. Their identity is based upon all the English manners. Also, I was in shock to see how they do not care about Israel. The older are better, but my generation completely ignores it. I thought that it is really sad. They are only interested in their work and their mortgage. On Yom Kippur [when Jews atone for sins they have committed over the past year] they are going to the synagogue feeling that they have done everything [fine].

CHAIM: I think that when you live in the diaspora, you do need the religion. Otherwise you will be integrated with the others. But I am also against the Reformists. I prefer someone who is not religious at all. To my opinion, they are not Jewish at all.

They are dangerous to the Jewish community. They invented a new religion and I don't believe in this at all.

Second generation identity

While relatively few mature sabras strongly identify with the host society, there is a greater likelihood that younger emigrants, including the 1.5 (those who migrated as small children) and second generation may do so (Portes and Rumbaut 1996; 2001). After all, in comparison to their parents, the children of immigrants grow up in the host society, and hence are more familiar with and competent in its language, culture and way of life. On the other hand, emigrant children did not voluntarily choose to confront the new society in the manner of their parents, nor did they arrive as resourceful adults. As such, they sometimes experience greater problems of adaptation than older emigrants (Gold 1995a). Further, the children of immigrants often experience cultural differences from both their foreign-born parents *and* their native-born peers, making adjustment especially difficult (Rumbaut 1994; Wolf 1997). It is also important to note that as suggested by the theory of segmented assimilation, the children of Israeli emigrants have various possible trajectories for identity formation within the host society (Portes and Rumbaut 2001). They can join the non-ethnic mainstream of the host society, they can merge with the native-born Jewish community, they can retain an Israel-oriented immigrant identity, or even follow another pattern.[1]

Evidence about the national identification of second generation Israelis is mixed. One body of research, as well as the comments of certain respondents, suggests that émigré youngsters – especially those who arrived at an early age or were born abroad – are likely to identify with the host society. Summarizing her fieldwork in Toronto, Rina Cohen argued:

> interviews with students who are the sons and daughters of Israeli migrants indicate that the younger generation is losing both its fluency in Hebrew and its national affiliation with Israel . . . the second generation is converging into the established Jewish community.
>
> (Cohen 1999: 121, 133)

Amit Goren's 1992 film, *'66 Was a Good Year for Tourism* documents the assimilation experience of an Israeli family in New York City. The youngest son, a muscle-bound, motorcycle-riding bartender, appears unconnected to either Israel or Judaism. Mira Rosenthal (1989: 71),

Plate 6.3 Israeli folk-dancing party held on the American holiday of Thanksgiving. This poster at a Los Angeles Jewish Community Centre advertises an event that seeks to unify American and Israeli traditions in such a way as to permit Israeli migrants to celebrate two national cultures at the same time.

in her study of 753 mostly naturalized Israelis in Brooklyn and Queens, found that while 63 percent of the parents identified as Israelis, less than 7 percent of their children identified as Israelis, while 55 percent identified as Americans. Interestingly, the children of Israeli emigrants who attended Jewish schools became much more assimilated (although "with American Jews") than was the case for those attending public schools (Rosenthal 1989: 149). Paradoxically, then, at least within this study, Israeli parents who sought to preserve their children's Jewish identity by sending them to Jewish schools wound up furthering their Americanization in comparison to co-nationals whose children attended public schools.

Revealing Israeli children's assimilation to the UK, a man whose family returned to Israel two years ago (after eight years in London), describes his daughters' enduring identification with England:

> Both of my daughters talk about the possibility of living in London as adults. My older one is thinking about university studies in the UK. My younger daughter is really English in her character and it would suit her well to live there as an adult. She is a sort of quiet and inward person, she does not

need many friends and does not want people to invade her personal space. My older one is a more complex person who combines many Israeli and English features.

In contrast to these findings, another body of data suggest that some children of Israelis retain their Israeli identity in a diaspora setting. Natan Uriely (1995: 34) found that second generation Israelis in Chicago continue to call themselves "Israelis" rather than Americans by a wide margin, while Moshe Shokeid (1988) encountered a similar pattern among Israeli emigrants' children in New York. During fieldwork, we heard numerous stories of young Israeli emigrants who demonstrated their commitment to the Jewish State by returning to perform military service. A *Jerusalem Post* article corroborates this, reporting that 432 Israeli youths whose families lived in the greater Los Angeles area returned for military duty during 1990, even "though most were under no obligation to do so" (Burston 1990).

An interaction I observed among a group of elementary school-aged Israeli children at a Jewish Community Center playground in the San Fernando Valley communicates something of their Jewish and Israeli identification. One boy – whose strong Hebrew accent suggested his short residence in the US – was climbing in a cabin-shaped jungle gym. Entering its chimney, he shouted "Look I'm Santa Claus." In reaction, several playmates yelled back "No, you're *Moshe* Claus." In so doing, they neutralized their friend's reference to the celebration of a Christian holiday by tagging him with a Hebrew first name. The fact that such small children would act out this scenario suggests the emigrant community's high level of awareness of assimilation and identity maintenance, as well as their children's engagement with these issues.

A third pattern of adaptation available to the children of Israelis is synthetic. Young people who travel back and forth between Israel and points of settlement and were not exposed to the anti-emigration climate of the 1970s and 1980s often developed a cosmopolitan outlook. In the words of a second generation Israeli in London: "I feel, I'm a person who wants to fit in everywhere. That's what I want. I don't know how much this can be true, but I want to travel back to see both sides." In fact, émigré parents frequently described how their children went through periods of changing national allegiance, in which they identified with various environments and practices. For example, a woman who had lived in London almost thirty years told how each of her three children – at their own insistence – had been educated in both Jewish and secular schools in England, attended youth programs in Israel and served in the Israeli armed forces. Now grown, one lives in Israel, while the others are attending graduate school in the US and England.

Survey findings

In addition to relying on in-depth interviews and fieldwork to explore Israeli emigrants' identities, another source of data is provided by survey research. Survey data on Israeli emigrants' religious behaviors are available only for those settled in the US. Moreover, most studies have been collected with non-random sampling techniques that over-represent the well-established. These limitations acknowledged, those data which exist verify that émigrés engage in many Jewish behaviors at higher rates than is the case among the native born. For example, Israelis' synagogue membership, at 27 percent in Los Angeles and 35 percent for singles and 60 percent for married couples in New York, exceeds that of native-born Jews (Herman and LaFontaine 1983; Horowitz 1993).[2]

Further, 80 percent of Israeli parents in Los Angeles provide their kids with some form of Jewish education and 40–50 percent of Israeli children in Los Angeles and over 30 percent in Brooklyn and Queens attend day schools. According to Rosenthal's New York survey of Israelis in New York, the main obstacle that discourages their children's attendance is tuition cost. Considering the fact that as residents of Brooklyn and Queens, these Israelis are among the less affluent of Jewish New Yorkers, and that as Israelis, many come from secular backgrounds, their children's rate of attendance in day schools and Yeshivas is quite high (Gold and Phillips 1996a). Another indicator of Israeli emigrants' maintenance of a strong Jewish identity is their low rate of intermarriage to non-Jews in the US. At only 8 percent, it is one-sixth that of native-born Jews (Herman 1988).

Finally, when comparing Israeli migrants' observance of Jewish customs – lighting candles on Shabbat and Chanukah, attending synagogue on the High Holy Days and Shabbat and fasting on Yom Kippur – with their patterns of practice in Israel, we find that among naturalized Israelis in New York and Los Angeles, these practices increased. Another study of Israelis in Los Angeles, that did not draw from a sample of those with US citizenship, noted a slight reduction in these religious practices. However, for most Israelis, rates of observance of Jewish customs exceed those of American Jews both in Israel and in the US (see Table 6.1). Moreover, data collected for the 1997 Los Angeles Jewish Population Survey reveal that house-holds including Israeli-born members are more likely than all Los Angeles Jews to send their children to day school, belong to Jewish

Table 6.1 Israeli immigrants' observance* of Jewish customs in Israel and the US (in percentages)

	In Israel			In the US			All US Jews NJPS 1990
Author	Herman	Rosenthal	Sachal–S.	Herman	Rosenthal	Sachal–S.	
Location of study	LA	NY	LA	LA	NY	LA	US
Practice							
Light Shabbat candle	73	68	67	85	87	61	43
Light Chanmukah candle	95	85	—	100	91	—	83
Attend synagogue on Holy Days	81	78	69	83	87	58	59
Attend synagogue on Shabbat	44	53	55	45	70	55	—
Fast on Yom Kippur	71	66	78	84	79	73	58

Note: *Always, usually or sometimes.

Sources:

Herman: data collected from 40 randomly selected Israelis naturalized between 1976 and 1982 in Los Angleles County (Herman and LaFontaine 1983).

Rosenthal: data collected from 205 Israelis in Brooklyn and Queens, 1984–6, consisting of sub-samples of 155 randomly selected naturalized Israelis and 50 snowball-sampled non-naturalized Israelis. From the 205 questionnaires, data on 870 individuals were collected (Rosenthal 1989).

Sachal–S.: data collected from 100 Israeli immigrants in Los Angeles in 1991–2 (Sachal–Staier 1993).

NJPS: National Jewish Population Survey, 1990.

Table 6.2 Israeli behaviors in Los Angeles, 1997 (in percentages)

	Israeli by birth households	All LA Jews
Children attend Jewish day school	41	20
Belong to Jewish organization	38	20
Donation to United Jewish Fund in the last 4 years	26	24
Orthodox	23	4
Reside in area of 25%+ Jewish density	59	51

Source: Herman 2000.

organizations, give to the United Jewish Federation and live in Jewishly dense areas. The proportion identifying as Orthodox is five times as great as the general Jewish population (Herman 2000; see Table 6.2). These findings suggest that Israeli emigrants retain strong commitment to religious practice and coethnic involvement in the US.

Conclusions

When Israelis move to the diaspora, they often re-evaluate their identities in view of nation, peoplehood and religion. Most respondents indicated that the experience of living overseas – including the unfamiliarity of host societies and their aversion to the outsider role – had the effect of reinforcing their identification with the country of origin.

Emigrants emphasized non-religious forms of Jewish identity as fundamental. However, as they confront life outside of Israel, they find that ethnicity alone provides few opportunities for collective celebrations, building social ties and passing on an identity to their children. Accordingly, a number of Israeli emigrants become more involved in organized Jewish life in diaspora settings than they were in the Jewish State. Some émigrés treat such religious involvement as a pragmatic coping strategy – the only viable means of maintaining a Jewish life in the diaspora – rather than as a religious quest *per se*. Consequently, they may reduce their religious involvement upon returning to Israel, or when their children are grown. A fraction however, especially those from religious backgrounds, find engagement in a diaspora religious community to be deeply meaningful and worth sustaining.

The literature on Israeli emigration often focuses on the apparent contradiction between émigrés' identification with Israel and their presence elsewhere. We found that émigrés are aware of this concern. Some seek to resolve the paradox by referring to the temporary nature of their stay abroad while others contend that their sojourn is to Israel's benefit. However, many seemed able to reconcile their goal-oriented presence overseas and their Israeli identification.

While adult migrants generally identified with the country of origin, evidence about second generation identity is mixed. Some children of Israelis described their feeling of connected to the host society. Others, however, retain cultural, linguistic and identificational ties to the Jewish State, serve in its military, hope to return, and often do so. Young emigrants who are growing up in an environment that both facilitates and tolerates frequent travel between Israel and points of settlement may be especially likely have a bi-national identity.

Writers critical of Israeli emigration contend that that Israeli emigrants are likely to lose their Jewish identity in diaspora settings. However, interviews and US surveys suggest that as a group, they are more religiously involved overseas than they were in Israel. Further, despite the stereotype of the secular Israeli, surveys also reveal that Israeli emigrants engage in many religious practices at a rate that exceeds native-born Jews. Upon reflection, this is not so surprising, since they tend to live in major Jewish settlements, speak Hebrew and associate with other Jews and Israelis in both work and leisure.

Finally, whatever their opinions about emigration, to a very large extent, Israeli migrants' views are shaped by concerns emanating from the Jewish State rather than the host society. For example, in open-ended discussions of their views on religious identity, a great many more referred to the Israeli-based conflict between secular and Orthodox Jews than any diaspora issue. In other words, diaspora settings are infrequently evaluated according to their own merits, but rather, in terms of their being better, worse or different from Israel. In this, we see the centrality of Israel in emigrants' identities.

7

CONCLUSIONS

The experience of return

Israeli emigrants' intention to return has been well documented (Shokeid 1988; Uriely 1995). Moreover, statistical evidence indicates that a considerable number of Israeli emigrants – 12,000 annually during the middle 1990s – do return each year (Chabin 1997). However, few studies have actually investigated the experience of returned Israeli emigrants (Toren 1980). To learn about this aspect of Israeli emigration, we interviewed thirty Israelis who had lived abroad for at least four years and returned to the Jewish State during the late 1980s and 1990s. In the following paragraphs, I summarize some of the most common reactions to return.

As a group, the returnees we interviewed were well educated, often professionally employed and attached to families with school-aged children. We have no way of knowing the extent to which these respondents represent the larger population of returnees. However, this characterization is consistent with both the findings of Toren's (1980) article on returned Israelis, and with Israeli immigration policy that makes special efforts to encourage the return of highly skilled emigrants (Fishkoff 1994; *For Those Returning Home* 1995). In addition, this characterization of returnees is supported by the fact that less educated emigrants generally asserted that regardless of their desire to return to Israel, such a move would entail such a great reduction in their standard of living that they would be unlikely to do so (see Chapter 3).

Emigrants offered a variety of reasons for returning. However, those concerning family – especially parents' desire for children to grow up in Israel – were the most frequently and passionately mentioned. Other reasons for re-migration included the need to care for a sick or aging parents, a job offer and a simple desire to be in Israel (see Chapter 6). In a few cases, family crises, such as a divorce, precipitated emigrants' return.

In the following quotations, three women describe their family-based reasons for returning:

SARAH: I felt that my girls' identities were not secure and this is actually one of the main reasons we decided to go back and live here. Although they felt that they were Israelis, their Hebrew was deteriorating to the point they started speaking English with each other, and they became English in many aspects of their behavior. They said they are Israelis but I felt that they do not know really what this means. So we came back so they could have that part of themselves developed and completed, and it was important for them to come back here as youngsters and not as adults.

ADINA: My husband and I both felt very deeply that a child needs to have an identity. We felt that our children were losing that identity. We felt that if we are not going back, then we are depriving them from that identity and they are helpless in that respect. They would not even understand that they missed out on something. We knew what they would miss out on, though. And that's why we decided to go back.

NARDIT: It was nice to live in London while our parents were young and were able to come and visit us frequently. But as time went by, those visits became really difficult. Then my dad died, and we realized that it is time to go back before the kids have no family to be with. I also felt that after my dad died, my family needed me more to be here. It was the right thing to do from my mother's perspective.

Despite the nearly universal assertion by Israeli emigrants that they missed the country of origin and wished to return, the practical reality of homecoming was a challenging task. Many described it as just as hard as going abroad, and without the financial options available overseas. Admitting that she confronted obstacles, the following woman, who returned from Australia, was gratified to be home again:

When we returned, my husband was in the middle of a big project at work there. He was not able to go back with us. I came back with the kids and without him, and I did on my own all the packing and unpacking that needed to be done. But to be honest, that was not really so bad. It was really easy, in fact. I was so happy with the idea of going back that nothing seemed hard or tiring. I was doing this with much energy and enthusiasm. I was happy because I felt I was going home. This is my home for good and for bad!

A dancer who returned with her husband and son from the Eastern US offered a similarly positive evaluation:

We came back to Israel and the first period was like falling in love again with Israel. I loved the weather, and the people and everything else. It's not like something bothered me there [in Philadelphia] – but I really loved it here. I felt like I was finally at home. Since I came back, I established my own business – a dance club – and that requires a lot of energy, and time and money. Although I studied there and all that – I feel that I have done the most significant promotion in my career since we came here.

While émigrés found fewer economic options upon return, many also retained valuable social ties in the Jewish State. Access to assistance was very important in determining the quality of returned emigrants' reception. Those able to preserve work-related, social, communal and family ties had an easier time coping than those without such forms of social capital. In the following quotations, returned emigrants Dan and Ella (who as a divorcee, felt that she might be treated as an outcast) describe how social contacts eased their resettlement:

DAN: Our friends have accepted us as if we were never away. So in that respect, we experienced no problem at all and actually went right back into the social circle that we left.

ELLA: I was surprised by people's willingness to help me. Many people offered a hand, even people that I did not know beforehand. I got a lot of support from my old friends and a lot of care and love and I think that this is the real thing that I missed all these years [when I was abroad] – the sense of connection and the human warmth. I know that my divorce is discussed by my friends and I feared that it would create a barrier between us – but I feared for nothing. They do not really care if I am alone or not. They are just *my* friends now. I have not lost them and that's the main thing for me. I actually get more than I did before out of those friendships. I was never in a situation where I was not invited [to an event] because I am divorced now.

While Dan's and Ella's re-entry into Israeli society was facilitated by their access to social support, Tali – who returned to assist her aging parents – had fewer resources at her disposal. As a consequence, her adjustment was much more arduous:

> I came back here to fulfill all my familial commitments and it felt very tight and very sad. From having to deal only with my own little family [in Australia], suddenly I was expected to shoulder the responsibility for the larger family and that was difficult because of the tragedy involved [the death of an in-law] and because my parents were not well and needed constant care.
>
> We did not come back to a family that was able to support us; but to a family that needed our support and we had no time to become used to the switch in our minds. I left Israel as a young girl who used to be supported by her parents and came back as a mother of three that needed to support four other adults and three children, and a husband whose work was not satisfactory. It was a terrible year.

The enduring importance of migrant networks in shaping returned emigrants' lives is revealed by the fact that instead of being cast off upon return to Israel, they are often retained and even built on in the Jewish State. For example, when Dina, who was extensively involved in London's Israeli community, returned, she kept her ties with her friends in London and with returnees in Israel, as well. Each year, to celebrate these ties, she organized a large party in a Tel Aviv hotel for former London residents. In so doing, she developed relations with returnees in Israel whom she had not known in England. Because of her enduring reputation as an expert on London, Israelis planning to move to the British capital were referred to her. In this manner, she held on to the community broker role that she invented for herself in London even when she no longer resided there.

While returned migrant adults like Dina made social contacts in Israel on the basis of their former place of residence, so did children. Several parents told us that their children gravitated toward classmates with similar overseas experience and language preference upon return. Such relationships were important sources of support for newly arrived youngsters who were unaccustomed to Israeli social norms. Chaim describes his daughter's friendship with another returned expatriate:

> Our older daughter had less of a social problem in adjustment because on her first week at school, a girl approached

her who came recently from Switzerland. She said: "I heard you just came from England. I just came from Switzerland." She speaks English because she had attended an American school there. They became very good friends from that day on. At the beginning, they were really close. Today, it's less tight – that friendship – although they are still good friends. But that helped her through the initial phase of adaptation, you know, having another friend who shares the same difficulties. She had a very interesting relationship with that friend. The European culture linked between them, and they are both interested in arts, which is not very common among her other friends. They go to concerts together and to art exhibitions and our daughter knows there are no others who will go with her to these activities.

Problems in return: children's adjustment and culture shock

As indicated in Chaim's quotation, in reflecting upon the difficulties of return, the problems Israeli emigrants most commonly mentioned were their children's social and academic adjustment. Several parents complained that because they were Israelis, their children (who were often born overseas) were not provided with resettlement assistance and, consequently, had a hard time fitting into the new setting:[1]

BATYA: The kids went to new schools and their adjustment was not easy. Yarden [my son] started secondary school and during the first year, I had to sit with him every day and the school did not support him in any way. Socially, things were not well at first and it took almost a year before he found his place among his new classmates. Also, he really had a lot of transitions in life and he takes changes very difficult, generally. So at first, he was all angry and anxious here. He was not excluded by his new classmates when we came here but it took a long time before he established real good ties. Its only now that things have improved and he is really a part of a cohesive group.

SHULA: My children deserved to get assistance as olim [new immigrants] at school – after all they were born there [in England] – but I had a real hard time convincing both the secondary school teachers and the kindergarten teacher that they need that help. "What?" they said. "They are not olim! [new immigrants] You are a yoredet [emigrant] and you speak Hebrew at home so your kids do not deserve to have these resources." I was stunned.

While children frequently encountered difficulties in their adjustment to Israel, this was not always the case. Two women who returned to Israel were quite pleased with their children's progress. In contrast to those quoted above, Shoshie found that ample assistance *was* provided by her sons' schools. Irit's daughter, Shula adjusted well without special assistance:

SHOSHIE: The schools were both very helpful. Etan's teacher was in contact with me almost once a week in the evenings, so I was able to discuss the things that bothered me or Etan. She is extremely helpful, kind and supporting. Yuval was also lucky to get such support from his class tutor. The school is organized well and they are used to newcomers such as Yuval. This year, they had children returning from Mexico, Brazil and Australia. They offered him support in Hebrew but he didn't really need that, so he stopped after two meetings.

IRIT: School started and the kids went to school and their adjustment was so easy I could not believe it. Nothing of the difficulties I feared had happened. It was great. Shula went into the first grade and she started everything like everybody else – from scratch. The class was new – to her and to others – so she was just like everybody else. She was used to a school environment and to the discipline of school and she already read in English and could read a bit of Hebrew. From her point of view, it was a real piece of cake. Also, she loves the space she has here and the fact that we have so much outdoor space suits her. She likes the weather and never complains about the heat. She had no problem adjusting academically or socially. We never had any complaints from her about returning.

In addition to mentioning children's experience of adaptation, returned émigrés also described their own culture shock and the adjustments that were required to re-acquaint themselves with the Israeli way of life. Irina and Sharon describe their reactions to Israeli society:

INVESTIGATOR: Was there anything that made it hard for you to re-adjust?

IRINA: Yes. Everything. Particularly the culture. The little things that make our life: the banks; the services; the car wash; the supermarkets; the schools; the cars; the drivers; the queues; the parks. Everything annoyed us and felt bad when we compared it to LA. But my friends – some of which returned from abroad before us – they told me: "In a year, you would not notice all that." And they were right. I don't anymore. I am not bothered by these things. I even like some of the things that annoyed me at first. The fact that everybody knows me and talks to me when I go into the supermarket – I like it. It gives me a sense of belonging. It took me two years, though. The quality of life there is much higher. What you get for your money is a lot more and there is a feeling of comfort there. Everything is much more expensive here. So as long as you continue to compare the two countries, you suffer. It's only when you quit the comparison that you can really enjoy life here. It took me two years to stop comparing. Today, I got used to it all.

INVESTIGATOR: What surprised you when you returned?

SHARON: When I visited [Israel while living in England], I only came to where my family lives, so I did not get to see all that diversity – the Ethiopians, the foreign workers, the Russians. And so many religious people all around. Many more than I remembered. So now I met face to face with that diversity and I was taken by surprise. Some of it I like and some of it disturbs me. For instance, about the Russians. I think most of them can make a positive contribution to this country, but there are others who are really negative. Some are basically criminals. I found that the verbal aggression and impolite language was really bad, especially among those Russians. But generally, the surprise was about the diversity. I remember how surprised I was to hear Russian spoken almost every-where I went. At the bank, the supermarket, the post office, the social security, the national health. Half the doctors and nurses are from Russia, and so forth. It really felt, at first, like Israel was taken over by Russia!

On the other hand, I was positively surprised by the bureau-cracy in Israel. I expected it to be much worse. It wasn't. You know that many Russians work at the home office and I found them very helpful and understanding. Anyway, I found the general service at different offices quite efficient and even friendly.

The street culture did not surprise me but I do not like it and I try to avoid it as much as I can. I choose carefully where I do my shopping and where we go travelling and all that.

I also thought that life here would be less individualistic than in London. I remembered how it was when I grew up and I remembered actually how my sister, who returned from the US a few years ago, felt that people are entering her personal space too often. I expected that. I guess in the positive sense, that really did not happen. I feel that the people I engage with do respect my personal space. On the other hand, each of them – of us – lives, in a sense, in our own bubble. My friends and family are very busy with their families and work, and other issues. We barely meet and the feeling I get is that each of us lives in his own shell. Surprisingly, I get to see my friends here less than I did in London, even though I do not work here.

Work-related adjustments

While problems of children's adjustment and culture shock were acute, as the above quotes suggest, they often were resolved over time. However, economic and job-related issues provided more lasting sources of concern. Some émigrés were pleased to find that the skills and credentials they obtained abroad improved their occupational possibilities in the Jewish State. Such was the case for Natalia, who received her Ph.D. in the UK, but as a foreign woman, never found a good job there:

All the courses I took there and my Ph.D. and the English – they are bringing me new job offers all the time. I can make a good living here; something that I was not able to manage in London.

Also, I think as a woman, my life is much better here. Here, there is much more equality in the work place. In London, I was simply ignored. Here, if I have the qualifications, my gender would not matter; there it would. No one asked me questions here about my kids or who takes care of them. It is more standard to see women working full time here.

Here, I found work much more easily than I did there. Here I knew who I am working with and what they expect of me. There, I simply did not understand that. I have a much clearer understanding of the rules of the game here and it means going to a job interview with strength that I did not have there. There, they did not understand what a working woman can do and what does it mean that I have a strange accent and two kids. Here, we have a mutual conception of these things. There, I went to interviews where I did not understand the questions I was asked and I was not connected to the right people in the field. Here, I can understand the questions and manipulate the conversation when I want to. I can throw in names of well-known people as referees. So that's helpful in getting a job.

For instance, when I went to a job interview [in Israel] with a patent company, the employer said that he was working with someone I knew, so I said I knew him and worked with him years ago. Before I even had time to think, he said: "Come on, let's go and I will show you the work" and I was simply thrown into work. Once he found out that I knew that person, the employer was able to make the connection and the affiliation. There [in London], I was simply a stranger.

While Natalia's experience was positive, it went against the general trend. Most often, return migration was associated with more limited job prospects. Such was the experience of Dafna, who was unable to find suitable work on her own in Israel, and was forced to take a position in her husband's firm:

The thing that surprised me was the difficulties in finding a suitable job. I was not too serious in looking but I realized quite soon that without the credentials, I have nothing to offer. My experience counts for something but it is not enough to get me a job. In that sense, I feel that I am not really engaged with the real life here. Everybody works and I do not, and the feeling I get is that I must rush and study something so that I can compete well and get a job. So far, what I did is to work again with my husband in his office in Tel Aviv. But that is something I didn't really want to do and I feel that I am doing it because there is nothing else and not because I really want to do this.

Echoing Dafna's fate is the experience of a returnee from Australia, as described by his wife:

When he came back, I think he knew that he would not find a job like he had in Australia. I was also anxious that he might not find a job to match the one that he had there. He started working here as a programmer and he did not like it. He felt it was a terrible fall. He suffered at this job but did not really gripe about the fact that we returned. After a while, he started searching for another place. I think deep down, he may have regretted his own return but on the other hand, he accepted that this was something that was done for the kids and it was definitely the right thing for them. That is why he did not really complain about his work but started searching for another position.

International commuting

Retaining their occupational skills and contacts to the country where they previously lived, returned Israelis who confront difficulties in the local job market sometimes commute to overseas jobs. International commuting is an increasingly common strategy among Israeli emigrants, and in the global labor market generally (Gold 2000). It is often associated with high tech occupations, which are in high demand, offer excellent wages and tolerate flexible working conditions, such as telecommuting. Israelis involved in other internationally focused industries – transportation, trade and culture – also engaged in this practice (Gerstenfeld 1991; Findlay 1995; Findlay and Li 1998). Europe – as the closest highly developed region – is the favored location for international commuting. However, we interviewed Israelis who commuted to jobs as far away as Australia.

Returned Israeli emigrants became involved in commuting arrangements for a variety of reasons. Some families returned home for the benefit of children, but retained the overseas employment of one or more wage earner(s) in order to access a high income or to fulfill obligations to employers. Returned emigrants often looked for work abroad if satisfactory positions in the Israeli economy could not be located. Finally, given the increasing internationalization of the Israeli economy, Israeli firms often find it essential to send representatives overseas to develop ties with customers, capital markets, suppliers or contractors (Machlis 2000). Former emigrants, who possess cultural and linguistic skills and contacts abroad, are commonly assigned to these overseas tasks.

International commuters perform their jobs under a variety of arrangements and circumstances. Some are regular employees of distant companies and maintain recurrent schedules. Others work as

consultants on a job-by job basis, engaging in travel only when necessary to complete a particular assignment. A certain fraction of commuting Israelis are partners in overseas firms. For example, one couple
were part owners of a London accounting firm. The husband made
regular trips to England, sometimes bringing tasks back to Israel.
During tax time, the entire family would move to London, where the
husband and wife would both work in the business.

Certain international commuters treated their country of employment as just that and did not bring their families with them. However,
a fair number, especially those whose entire families had previously
lived abroad, maintained households in the workplace setting, and
were often accompanied by families during vacations. Consequently,
the host society was not simply a place for work, but a second home,
as well. Of all the emigrants we contacted for this study, it is these
international commuters who conform most fully with a transnational
way of life – literally living and working in two or more societies simultaneously (Portes *et al.* 1998; Gold 2000).

Surprisingly, a large number of respondents felt that commuting
was not harmful to family intimacy. Instead, they saw it as beneficial.
In the following quotations, Israelis whose families have returned
from England and Australia discuss how their spouses' continued
commuting improved the quality of their families' interactions:

MARY: He [my husband] goes there [London] for a week and
then comes back and stays here for a week. I think the week
he spends here compensates for the rest. It's a week of rest
and leisure for him. We go out a lot. We go to the gym
together, and such, so I think it's a very comfortable life style.
When we are apart, we both work harder. He stays at work
from 7 in the morning until midnight, and I also work
harder when he's away. So when he comes back, we have a
sort of easier week in terms of work. The kids get to be with
him at noon and he is free for them. That also changed their
relationship for the better. We have much more time together
than we did when we all lived there or when we lived here [in
Israel] before we moved to London.

BENJI: I can frankly say that this commuting life style only did
good to our marriage. After all, we've been married for more
than twenty years now, and we do have different styles and
different opinions. So every time she goes away and every time
we meet after that separation, we have more patience for each
other. Obviously you lose your patience the longer that you are

around someone that annoys you. So those ten day separations allow us to recharge our batteries and be more tolerant towards each other for a while longer. I think that the cause of conflict in marriage is the lack of personal space. Traveling make this space for us. So the marriage has less of these conflicts.

YAEL: Every year we spend about three to four months in Australia together – during all the vacations, including the summer vacation. We have the house there, so it is really comfortable. My young child was happy to go back for these visits, especially in the summer because he hates the heat in Israel and summer here is wintertime there. So he was very happy about that. He used to come down from the airplane and say: "Home sweet home!" He would go to meet his mates and I went to see mine and it was a good time.

Despite these respondents' descriptions of international commuting as beneficial to family life, the strategy was not widely celebrated. According to several interviewees, international commuting provided access to earnings and a quality of work beyond that available in the Jewish State. Understandably, however, those involved also found this to be an exhausting way of life, as it required frequent international travel, separation from families, the upkeep of more than one residence and the need to function in multiple cultural and linguistic environments. For many, the reality of this form of transnational life is more analogous to an arduous journey to and from work rather than an emancipatory pilgrimage to an alternative environment. Two Israelis involved in commuting families describe their reactions:

SHARONA [whose husband commutes to Australia from Israel]: I think the one who really experienced difficulties was my husband because that life style was very tiring and the jet lag was not really easy to handle. It takes ten days to recover. Also, every time he went there he was alone, and all his friends around him were in families who went together on weekends and such. In terms of work, he had to complete a three-week gap every time he flew in. That was not easy for him.

SAUL [an accountant who commutes from Israel to London]: I would actually rather work here and quit traveling. I am too old for this traveling about. But I cannot let my business partner down. He is relying on me to help out with certain issues. Some of the work I take here anyway but there are always clients who want to meet with me when I am there, and that is the main reason I travel. Also, at the end of the year, I always stay there longer to prepare annual reports.

Return in retrospect

Returned emigrants often enjoyed their time overseas and acknowledged the broadening experience they had there. They also noted that time overseas made them more aware of the deficiencies of Israeli life. Nevertheless, most felt relatively satisfied with their return. They appreciated the familiar environment, the feeling of ownership and atmosphere of social and familial closeness that was unavailable elsewhere. A man who returned from London to Tel Aviv explains his perspective on return:

> The main question you need to ask yourself is the economic issue. If the economic issue is OK – then life here could be very good to you all, and especially for the children. All the people we know who returned before and after us are doing well both economically and otherwise and they are content here. I think once the job issue is sorted out, the other things simply fall into place. Then the next step is the children and sorting them out at school. This takes time but normally sorts itself out quite quickly. The only thing that you may miss is the quality of life. That is something you do not get here. The quality of life you will feel here is that you have that sense of belonging and that your children feel rooted here. That is something you cannot have there and no matter how many years you live there.

In a like manner, Sarah contrasts the warmth of celebrating Jewish holidays among family in Israel with her solitary existence in London:

> You are part of a nation that celebrates together an event, a holiday, and that is celebrated at school, at everywhere else. Rosh Hashanah, since we came back was always a happy event that we celebrated with the larger family or with friends and there was less of that doubt and questioning of where we should celebrate it. In London, it was sometimes a bit sad – because we had no one to celebrate it with and we did it on our own. But here, that was not a problem anymore.

Finally, in reflecting on their emigration, some returned émigrés suggested that rather than being a means of solving their economic, affiliational and family predicaments, the ever-present possibility of geographic mobility became a problem in itself. After living in both the US and England, a woman in the midst of a difficult readjustment to Israel described migration as a Pandora's Box that she regretted opening:

> I have friends here who have kids in my children's class. They grew up in the UK then went to live in Ethiopia, then South Africa, and then came here, and all the time they ask themselves: "Why here and not there?" Now they intend to go back to England! I think this is extremely difficult, and I find them often unhappy and discontented. The same applies to us. I think we would have been happier if we had not traveled to the US that first time.

Three perspectives on Israeli emigration

Throughout this book, I have referred to three perspectives on Israeli emigration: the yordim perspective that sees Israeli emigration as harmful to the Jewish State and ultimately unsatisfying to most Israelis who cannot tolerate life in the diaspora; the migration studies outlook which views emigration in light of the pursuit of economic betterment, family unification and personal satisfaction beyond the Jewish State. Finally, transnationalism suggests that some forms of Israeli emigration are a means of optimizing freedom and opportunity by retaining links to multiple national settings. In retrospect, each perspective proved to be useful and valid for understanding various elements of the Israeli emigrant experience, but none captured it fully. Accordingly, I contend that an eclectic application of the three models generates the most insight.

Demonstrating the validity of the yordim perspective, Israeli emigrants made frequent comments about their attachment to Israel, and their desire to pass on an Israeli identity to their children. Further justifying this outlook is the fact that unlike most other Jewish immigrants, many Israeli émigrés refuse to fully identify with the host societies that they admit offer them a more secure, peaceful, efficient and affluent life than they could access in their country of origin. It is important to note that for many emigrants, assertions of a wish to return home are not merely lip service. Rather, Israeli Government statistics suggest that a considerable fraction do come home. To cite a *Jerusalem Post* article on the changing meaning of

Israeli emigration, "In essence, very few Israelis should be viewed as having left Israel for good or forever, and those who have made their fortunes abroad and established themselves in other countries may very well invest and establish second homes in Israel" (Weiss 1990).

In the following quote, a man who returned with his family to Israel after enjoying a high quality of life in England refers to his desire to return as "irrational" – at least in economic terms – suggesting that it was based more on sentiment than on a practical evaluation of the costs and benefits of life in London versus Tel Aviv:

> We decided rationally to make an emotional decision with regard to our return. And when your decision is not rational but emotional, then I cannot say I returned because A, B or C. How shall I say it? It did not seem the wise move but it seemed like the right move.

Most Israeli emigrants expressed strong feelings of connection to the Jewish State and a desire to return, thus confirming the basic assertions of the yordim perspective. However, the significant number of emigrants who continue to maintain successful and satisfying lives abroad are accurately described by the migration studies approach. A major contention of migration studies is that Israelis' emigration can be understood in terms of the same theoretical assumptions that are applied to other migrant groups. Consequently, if Israeli emigrants are reluctant to identify with host societies, this tendency is by no means unique. According to Luis Guarnizo (1997: 15) "no matter how settled, migrants still dream that one day they will return to their homeland." In fact, a large body of literature also questions the myth that migrants unproblematically seek to merge with the host society (Castles and Miller 1998). To quote a leading text:

> A perceptive scholar noted recently that the popular notion that immigrants came to the United States ready to assimilate "is a myth. The specter of 'Americanization,' " he continued, "troubled more immigrants than historians have been willing to admit."
>
> (Dinnerstein et al. 1990: 139)

Further supporting the migration studies tradition is the fact that many Israeli emigrants expressed satisfaction with life in host societies and admired the culture and opportunities they found there. Among other features, they appreciated the atmosphere of public civility, the cooperative work culture and the environment of religious tolerance.

Moreover, rather than losing touch with their ethnic and religious traditions in the diaspora, a significant number became more Jewishly involved in points of settlement than they were in Israel. Finally, while a major contention of yordim studies is that Israeli emigrants' misgivings about their migration status prevent them from organizing their communities or proclaiming an Israeli-emigrant identity, a mounting body of evidence suggests that Israeli emigrants *are* forming increasingly organized and institutionally complete communities with a wide range of activities in many points of settlement. Thus, feelings of nostalgia for Israel do not necessarily preclude the creation of viable, organized and successful communities in many host societies.

The third perspective on Israeli emigration – transnationalism – involves emigrants' connections with multiple locations and networks, frequent international travel, dual citizenship and residence in more than one country. Evidence suggest that an increasing number of Israelis carry out this pattern. Such was the case for Yehuda, a psychologist, who, with his family, owns homes in both Israel and London and regularly commutes between the two locations. Yehuda takes a psychoanalytic tack as he describes his family's border-crossing lifestyle:

> Why is it that men do not want to get married? It is because they do not want to lose the options that may be available out there. In the same manner, I do not commit to one place. Now, in many senses, I live in two.
>
> We all travel to London: my wife for work, I go for pleasure and the girls go either with us or on their own [to visit friends]. We all maintain our ties in London. We call our friends beforehand and see as many as we can when we go.

While asserting that transnational migration is a viable means of solving practical problems, relatively few Israelis described this strategy in the laudatory language used by some cultural studies scholars. More often, they characterized it as an exhausting process, albeit one that provided many valuable options – economic, cultural and otherwise – for themselves and their children. Moreover, in examining Israeli emigration in terms of Portes *et al.*'s (1999: 219) definition of transnational migration: "Occupations and activities that require regular and sustained social contacts over time across borders for their implementation," it is clear that only a fraction of all émigrés – and probably a small one, at that – are transnationals. The behavior of other Israeli emigrants is accurately summarized by the established rubric of settler and sojourner (Portes 2001).

That being said, Israelis' ease of emigration, return and social adjustment was clearly facilitated by the extensive transnational social fields created between the Jewish State and major points of settlement by government (both Israel's and the host nations'), corporations, Jewish communal institutions, cultural organizations, media and emigrants' own networks. In this, theories of transnational migration do contribute considerably to our comprehension of the Israeli diaspora.

To summarize, these perspectives – yordim, migration studies and transnationalism – are all useful for understanding the nature of the Israeli diaspora. But no one outlook is capable of fully informing the topic. To be fair, the concerns addressed here, including religious and national identity, the pursuit of economic opportunity, family unification, group loyalty and the promise of starting a new life, are among the most complex, universal and enduring questions confronted by social science. Consequently, it is not surprising that a single perspective would be incapable of providing a conclusive understanding of all the issues involved.

In fact, a central conclusion of this study is that rather than searching for a single perspective as a means of understanding international migration, eclectic approaches and multiple methods, linked with empirical observation, have clear value for investigating the multifaceted, convoluted and unpredictable experience of migrant groups (Portes 2000; Glick Schiller 1994; Foner *et al.* 2000; Faist 2000). To quote a recent article by Alejandro Portes:

> Sociology's chance . . . at century's end does not hinge on the elaboration of grand engineering blueprints, but instead in careful analyses of social processes, awareness of their concealed and unintended manifestations, and sustained efforts to understand the participants' own reactions to their situation. Without this painstaking effort, any organizational blueprint, no matter how well devised, is likely to yield unexpected outcomes, thus following the fate of so many failed interventions of the past.
>
> (Portes 2000: 15)

In conclusion, regardless of emigrants' reactions to life overseas, the number of Israelis who travel, live and work abroad is likely to increase. Israel's growing social, economic and cultural integration with other countries means that national boundaries will impose ever fewer restrictions on connections with external entities. At the same time, with widening cultural, religious, economic and ideological diversity animating both Israel and diaspora Jewish communities, it is conceivable that a burgeoning number of groups – both in Israel and abroad – will be motivated to develop independent contacts with allies within and beyond the borders of the Jewish State (Shain 2000). In turn, these tendencies will be advanced by the enhanced accessibility of low-cost and highly efficient forms of communication and transportation, as well as further reductions in official and informal sanctions on Israeli emigration.

As a consequence, Israeli emigrants (and their associates abroad) are likely to follow multiform lines of action – including settlement, sojourning, commuting, and return – to adapt to the myriad circumstances, opportunities and obstacles that they confront. A probable outcome of these many trends is the continued expansion and ongoing transformation of the Israeli diaspora.

NOTES

Introduction

1 Alfred Dreyfus, a French-Jewish military officer, was accused of spying for Germany. During his show trial, French Jews suffered from an atmosphere of terror and intimidation (Goldstein 1995: 111).

2 Israel was governed by the Likud party from 1977 to 1992 and 1996 to 1999. Orthodox religious parties that were affiliated with Likud sought to remove the legal standing of religious rituals (such as weddings and religious conversions) performed by the Jewish denominations with which large fractions of diaspora Jews affiliate. A significant component of young diaspora Jews found these actions incompatible with their own values (Cohen 1991; Tobin 1992).

3 http://www.cbs.gov.il

4 Both literature and respondents tend to use the terms Mizrahi, Sephardic, Eastern or Oriental more or less interchangeably to describe non-Ashkenazi Jews.

3 Work and coethnic cooperation

1 The popular view suggests that "the self-employed are tax evaders who do not contribute their fair share to the building of the nation. The self-employed therefore have had a double burden of 'parasitism,' deviant both ideologically and practically" (Freedman and Korazim 1986: 144).

2 The following statistics indicate percentages of self-employment among Israeli immigrants in the US found by various studies. Figures vary widely because very different data sets, in different

regions and years and different samples were used. Freedman and Korazim 1986, 63 percent; Ritterband and Cohen 1982, 53 percent; Gold 1994a, 77 percent; Rosenthal 1989, 20 percent; Razin 1990, 28 percent, Herman 2000, 43 percent.

3   As an example of the transnational options available to the Israeli elite, both candidates for Prime Minister in the spring 1999 elections had degrees from top American universities – Benjamin Netanyahu from MIT and Ehud Barak from Stanford. Netanyahu also attended high school in the US and worked for a Boston consulting firm for several years.

4 Family and gender relations

1   Unfortunately, not all men were so supportive. During a visit to London's Israeli House, we met a lonely woman whose husband insisted that they live in a neighborhood far from the Israeli enclave in Golders Green where she could have frequented Israeli shops, consumed coethnic services and perhaps developed a social network.

2   The recent growth of Israeli high technology companies suggests that some economic activities are currently receiving handsome rewards in the Jewish State.

3   Other tabulations of labor force participation by gender are as follows: Korazim (1983: 79) found that while 30 percent of his sample of Israeli migrant women were not in the labor force prior to emigration, in New York, 56 percent were not in the labor force. In a survey of 496 Israelis living in Los Angeles, Philadelphia and Miami, Lev Ari (2000) found that while 96 percent of Israeli men in the US were in the labor force, Israeli women's labor force participation rate was 78 percent. Further, 88 percent of Israeli men in the US work full time, while only 46 percent of Israeli women in the US worked full time (Lev Ari 2000).

4   An Israeli academic who obtained her Ph.D. in England described the lack of arrangements for students with children. "British universities did not expect women students to be married and have a child! They looked at that, from the very beginning, as a very bad bet . . . In fact, I was twice offered a scholarship by the university women, and twice this was on the condition that I would live in their dorm in London. I couldn't accept it, so it took me almost seven years to do my doctorate" (Stern 1979: 87).

5 Patterns of communal organization

1 Further, the good relations that exist among various communities within diaspora Jewish settings are themselves showing significant signs of wear and even disintegration (Freedman 2000).

2 Some of these directories are quite impressive. For example, in 2000, Dapey Assaf published the twentieth edition of the *Jewish Israeli Yellow Pages of New York*. Printed in Israel, the volume is over 1,500 pages in length, bilingual (in Hebrew and English) and features an on-line edition at www.jewishyellow.com. In the mid-1990s, *Hadashot LA* published a similar volume, the *LA Jewish Yellow Pages*. Approximately 300 pages in length and bilingual, it includes a variety of transnationally focused community information, including "a detailed list of Jewish schools and synagogues, all Israeli organizations and Jewish Federation Council agencies, a full listing of Israeli communal events and Jewish holidays" as well as a Hebrew language section that offers information such as "how to behave during an earthquake, . . . how to immigrate to the US (this includes the 100 possible questions asked on your US citizenship exam, and , of course your answers)" as well as "the list of privileges available to returning residents to Israel" (Toshav Hozer) (*LA Jewish Yellow Pages*, 1993–4, p. 1E).

3 Hamakom.com "The Website for Israelis in the US" lists a number of resources for Israeli emigrants.

6 National, ethnic and religious identity

1 For example, we interviewed the son of Persian Israelis who often associated with Iranian Jews in Los Angeles.

2 According to Rosenthal, Israeli immigrants in the US were 13 percent Orthodox, 7 percent Conservative, 3 percent Reform, 32 percent traditional, 42 percent secular and 3.9 had percent no affiliation (Rosenthal 1989: 81). The affiliation figures for the American Jewish population are 6.8 percent Orthodox, 40.4 percent Conservative, 41.4 Reform, 1.6 Reconstructionist, 3.2 percent traditional, 5.2 percent "Just Jewish" and 1.4 percent other (NJPS 1990: Table 25).

7 Conclusions

1 As a nation with many recent immigrants, Israel offers various programs for migrant integration.

REFERENCES

Akhtar, Salman (1999) *Immigration and Identity: Turmoil, Treatment and Trans-formation*. Northvale, NJ: Jason Aronson, Inc.

Alarcón, Rafael (1999) "Recruitment Processes Among Foreign-Born Engineers and Scientists in Silicon Valley." *American Behavioral Scientist* 42(9): 1381–97.

Allan, Kenneth and Jonathan H. Turner (2000) "A Formalization of Post-modern Theory." *Sociological Perspectives* 43(3): 363–85.

Almog, Oz (2000) The Sabra: *The Creation of the New Jew*. Berkeley: University of California Press.

Anderson, Margo J. and Stephen Fienberg (1999) *Who Counts? The Politics of Census-Taking in Contemporary America*. New York: Russell Sage Foundation.

Appadurai, Arjun (1996) *Modernity at Large: Cultural Dimensions of Globali-zation*. Minneapolis: University of Minnesota Press.

Australian Bureau of Statistics (2000) Unpublished 1996 Census of Popula-tion and Housing Data. Custom Tabulation.

Azmon, Yael and Dafna Izraeli (1993) "Introduction: Women in Israel – A Sociological Overview," pp. 1–21 in Yael Azmon and Dafna Izraeli (eds) *Women in Israel*. New Brunswick, NJ: Transaction Publishers.

Azria, Régine (1998) "The Diaspora-Community-Tradition Paradigms of Jewish Identity: A Reappraisal," pp. 21–32 in Ernest Krausz and Gitta Tulea *Jewish Survival: The Identity Problem at the Close of the Twentieth Century*. New Brunswick, NJ: Transaction Publishers.

Bailey, Thomas and Roger Waldinger (1991) "Primary, Secondary and Enclave Labor Markets: A Training Systems Approach." *American Socio-logical Review* 56(4): 432–45.

Basch, Linda, Nina Glick Schiller and Cristina Blanc-Szanton (1994) *Nations Unbound: Transnational Projects, Postcolonial Predicaments, and Deterritorialized Nation States*. Basel, Switzerland: Gordon and Breach Publishers.

Bates, Timothy (1997) *Race, Self-Employment and Upward Mobility: An Illusive American Dream*. Baltimore: Johns Hopkins University Press.

Bauböck, Ranier (1996) "Cultural Minority Rights for Immigrants" *International Migration Review* 30(1): 203–50.

Becker, Howard Paul (1956) *Man in Reciprocity*. New York: Praeger: 225–37.

Bedford, Richard D. (1975) "The Questions to be Asked of Migrants" in Robin J. Pryor (ed.) *The Motivations of Migration*. Canberra: Australian National University.

Bellah, Robert, Richard Madsen, William M. Sullivan, Ann Swidler and Steven M. Tipton (1985) *Habits of the Heart: Individualism and Commitment in American Life*. Berkeley: University of California Press.

Ben-Ami, Ilan (1992) "Schlepers and Car Washers: Young Israelis in the New York Labor Market." *Migration World* 20(1):18–20.

Ben-Rafael, Eliezer (1998) "Quasi-Sectarian Religiosity, Cultural Ethnicity and National Identity: Convergence and Divergence among Hahamei Yisrael," pp. 33–64 in Ernest Krausz and Gitta Tulea *Jewish Survival: The Identity Problem at the Close of the Twentieth Century*. New Brunswick, NJ: Transaction Publishers.

Ben Gurion, David (1964) *The Eternity of Israel*. Tel Aviv: Aynot [Hebrew].

Bershtel, Sara and Allen Graubard (1992) *Saving Remnants: Feeling Jewish in America*. Berkeley: University of California Press.

Bhabha, Homi (interviewed by Paul Thompson) (1994) "Between Identities," pp. 183–99 in Rina Benmayor and Andor Skotnes (eds) *Migration and Identity: International Yearbook of Oral History and Life Stories*, Volume III. Oxford: Oxford University Press.

Bhachu, Parminder (1985) *Twice Migrants: East African Sikh Settlers in Britain*. London: Tavistock.

Blumberg, Rae L. (1991) "Introduction: The Triple Overlap of Gender Stratification, Economy, and the Family," pp. 7–32 in *Gender, Family, and Economy: The Triple Overlap* (Rae L. Blumberg, ed.). Newbury Park: Sage.

Blumer, Herbert (1958) "Race Relations as a Sense of Group Position." *Pacific Sociological Review* 1 (Spring): 3–6.

—— (1969) *Symbolic Interactionism: Perspective and Method*. Englewood Cliffs, NJ: Prentice Hall.

Bonacich, Edna (1973) "A Theory of Middleman Minorities." *American Sociological Review* 37 (October): 547–59.

—— (1990) "Asian and Latino Immigrants in the Los Angeles Garment Industry: An Exploration of the relationship between Capitalism and Racial Oppression." University of California, Los Angeles, *Institute for Social Science Research Working Papers in the Social Sciences* 1989–90 Vol. 5, No. 13.

Bonacich, Edna and Richard P. Appelbaum (2000) *Behind The Label: Inequality in the Los Angeles Apparel Industry*. Berkeley: University of California Press.

Bonacich, Edna and John Modell (1980) *The Economic Basis of Ethnic Solidarity: Small Business in the Japanese-American Community*. Berkeley: University of California Press.

Borjas, George J. (1990) *Friends or Strangers*. New York: Basic Books.

—— (1996) "The New Economics of Immigration: Affluent Americans Gain; Poor Americans Lose." *Atlantic Monthly* (November): 72–80.

Bourdieu, Pierre (1986) "The Forms of Capital," pp. 241–58 in John G.

Richardson (ed.) *Handbook of Theory and Research for the Sociology of Education*. New York: Greenwood.

Boyarin, Daniel and Jonathan Boyarin (1993) "Diaspora: Generation and the Ground of Jewish Identity." *Critical Inquiry* 19: 693–725.

Bozorgmehr, Mehdi, Claudia Der-Martirosian and Georges Sabagh (1996) "Middle Easterners: A New Kind of Immigrant," pp. 345–378 in Roger Waldinger and Mehdi Bozorgmehr (eds) *Ethnic Los Angeles*. New York: Russell Sage Foundation.

Breton, Raymond (1964) "Institutional Completeness of Ethnic Communities and the Personal Relations of Immigrants." *American Journal of Sociology* 84: 293–318.

Broder, Jonathan (1999) "Heeding the Call." *Jerusalem Report* (March 29): 34–5.

Burawoy, Michael (1976) "The Function and Reproduction of Migrant Labor: Comparative Materials from Southern Africa and the United States." *American Journal of Sociology* 81: 1050–87.

Burston, Bradley (1990) "Consulate General in LA Reports: Over 400 Israelis in LA Return for Army Service." *Jerusalem Post*, December 28.

Burt, Ronald S. (1992) *Structural Holes*. Cambridge: Harvard University Press.

—— (2000) "The Social Capital of Structural Holes." http://gsbwww.uchicago.edu/fac.ronald.burt/research

Byron, Christopher (1992) *Skin Tight: The Bizarre Story of Guess v. Jordache*. New York: Simon and Schuster.

Calavita, Kitty (1992) *Inside the State: The Bracero Program, Immigration and the I.N.S.* New York: Routledge.

Calhoun, Craig (ed.) (1994) *Social Theory and the Politics of Identity*. Oxford: Blackwell.

Castells, Manuel (1989) *The Informational City*. Oxford: Basil Blackwell.

Castles, Stephen and Godula Kosack (1973) *Immigrant Workers and Class Structure in Western Europe*. Oxford: Oxford University Press.

Castles, Stephen and Mark J. Miller (1998) *The Age of Migration*, 2nd edn. New York: Guilford.

Central Bureau of Statistics (of Israel): www.cbs.gov.il

Chabin, Michele (1997) "Behind the Headlines: Israelis Living Abroad Wooed to Return by Government Firms." Jewish Telegraphic Agency On Line (March 2).

Cheng, Lucie and Philip Q. Yang (1998) "Global Interaction, Global Inequality, and Migration of the Highly Trained to the United States." *International Migration Review* 32(3): 626–53.

Chiswick, Barry R. (1988) "Differences in Education and Earnings Across Racial and Ethnic Groups: Tastes, Discrimination, and Investments in Child Quality." *Quarterly Journal of Economics*, Vol. CIII No. 3 (August): 571–97.

—— (1991) "An Economic Analysis of Philanthropy," pp. 2–16 in Barry A. Kosmin and Paul Ritterband (eds) *Contemporary Jewish Philanthropy in America*. Savage, MD: Roman and Little Field.

Clifford, James (1994) "Diasporas." *Cultural Anthropology* 9(3): 302–38.

Cohen, Abner (1969) *Custom and Politics in Urban Africa*. Berkeley: University of California Press.

Cohen, Rina (1999) "From Ethnonational Enclave to Diasporic Community: The Mainstreaming of Israeli Jewish Migrants in Toronto." *Diaspora* 8(2): 121–36.

Cohen, Rina and Gerald Gold (1996) "Israelis in Toronto: The Myth of Return and the Development of a Distinct Ethnic Community." *Jewish Journal of Sociology* 38(1): 17–26.

—— (1997) "Constructing Ethnicity: Myth of Return and Modes of Exclusion among Israelis in Toronto." *International Migration* 35(3): 373–94.

Cohen, Robin (1997) *Global Diasporas*. Seattle: University of Washington Press.

Cohen, Steven M. (1986) "Israeli Émigrés and the New York Federation: A Case Study in Ambivalent Policymaking for 'Jewish Communal Deviants.'" *Contemporary Jewry* 7: 155–65.

—— (1991) "Israel in the Jewish Identity of American Jews: A Study in Dualities and Contrasts," pp. 119–35 in David M. Gordis and Yoav Ben-Horin (eds) *Jewish Identity in America*. Los Angeles: Wilstein.

Cohen, Yinon (1988) "War and Social Integration: The Effects of the Israeli-Arab Conflict on Jewish Emigration from Israel." *American Sociological Review* 53 (December): 908–18.

—— (1989) "Socioeconomic Dualism: The Case of Israeli-Born Immigrants in the United States." *International Migration Review* 23(2): 267–88.

—— (1996) "Economic Assimilation in the United States of Arab and Jewish Immigrants from Israel and the Territories." *Israel Studies* 1(2): 75–97.

Cohen, Yinon and Yitchak Haberfeld (1997) "The Number of Israeli Immigrants in the United States in 1990." *Demography* 34(2): 199–212.

Coleman, James S. (1988) "Social Capital in the Creation of Human Capital." *American Journal of Sociology* 94 (Supplement) S95–S120.

Council of Europe (1998) *Recent Demographic Developments in Europe*. Strasbourg: Council of Europe.

Curtius, Mary (2001) "Tech Slump is Just Leading Edge of Israel's Misery." *Los Angeles Times* (June 22).

Danet, Brenda (1989) *Pulling Strings: Biculturalism in Israeli Bureaucracy*. Albany: SUNY Press.

Dapey Assaf (2000) *The Jewish Israeli Yellow Pages*. New York City.

Davis, Nira Yuval (nd) *Israeli Women and Men: Divisions Behind the Unity*. London: Change International Reports.

DeJong, Gordon F. and James T. Fawcett (1981) "Motivations for Migration: An Assessment and Value-Expectancy Research Model," pp. 13–58 in Gordon F. De Jong and Robert W. Gardner (eds) *Migration Decision Making: Multidisciplinary Approaches to Microlevel Studies in Developed and Developing Countries*. New York: Pergamon.

DellaPergola, Sergio (1992) "Israel and World Jewish Population: A Core-Periphery Perspective," pp. 39–63 in Calvin Goldscheider (ed.) *Population and Social Change in Israel*. Boulder: Westview.

—— (1994) "World Jewish Migration System in Historical Perspective." Paper presented at International Conference Human Migration in a Global Framework, University of Calgary, Alberta, Canada, June 9–12.

—— (2000) Personal Communication, March 12.

Derfner, Larry (2000) "A New Left." *The Jerusalem Post*, Tuesday August 15.

—— (2001a) "Israel's Alien Nation." *Internet Jerusalem Post*, January 28.

—— (2001b) "Waiting for a Better Home." *Internet Jerusalem Post*, August 26.

Detroit Jewish News (1998) July 10.

De Vos, George and Lola Romanucci-Ross (1982) *Ethnic Identity: Cultural Continuities and Change*. Chicago: University of Chicago Press.

Dinnerstein, Leonard, Roger L. Nichols and David M. Reimers (1990) *Natives and Strangers; Blacks, Indians and Immigrants in America*, 2nd edn. New York: Oxford University Press.

Dowty, Alan (1998) *The Jewish State: A Century Later*. Berkeley: University of California Press.

Dubb, Allie A. (1994) *The Jewish Population of South Africa: The 1991 Socio-demographic Survey*. Cape Town: Kaplan Centre For Jewish Studies and Research, University of Cape Town.

Dudkevitch, Margot (2000) "Two Israelis Suspected in Los Angeles Murder." *Jerusalem Post*, May 18.

Eisenbach, Zvi (1989) "Jewish Emigrants from Israel in the United States," pp. 251–67 in U.O. Schmelz and S. DellaPergola (eds) *Papers in Jewish Demography* 1985. Jerusalem: Institute of Contemporary Jewry, Hebrew University of Jerusalem.

Elazar, Daniel J. (1986) "The Jewish People as the Classic Diaspora: A Political Analysis," pp. 212–257 in Gabriel Sheffer (ed.) *Modern Diasporas in International Politics*. New York: St Martins.

Elizur, Dov (1980) "Israelis in the U.S." *American Jewish Yearbook* 1980: 53–67.

Espiritu, Yen Le (1989) "Beyond the Boat People: Ethnicization of American Life." *Amerasia* 15(2): 49–67.

Etzioni, Amitai (1996) *The New Golden Rule: Community and Morality in a Democratic Society*. New York: Basic Books.

Etzioni-Halevy, Eva (1998) "Collective Jewish Identity in Israel: Towards an Irrevocable Split?" pp. 65–76 in Ernest Krausz and Gitta Tulea (eds) *Jewish Survival: The Identity Problem at the Close of the Twentieth Century*. New Brunswick, NJ: Transaction Publishers.

Evron, Boas (1995) *Jewish State or Israeli Nation?* Bloomington: Indiana University Press.

Faist, Thomas (2000) *The Volume and Dynamics of International Migration and Transnational Social Spaces*. Oxford: Oxford University Press.

Findlay, Allan M. (1995) "Skilled Transients: The Invisible Phenomenon," pp. 515–22 in Robin Cohen (ed.) *The Cambridge Survey of World Migration*. Cambridge: Cambridge University Press.

Findlay, Allan M. and F.I.N. Li (1998) "A Migration Channels Approach to the Study of Professional Moving to and from Hong Kong." *International Migration Review* 32(3): 682–703.

Finkielkraut, Alain (1994) *The Imaginary Jew*. Lincoln and London: University of Nebraska Press.

Fish, Neal S. (1984) "Israelis in America: Migration Decision Making and Its Consequences upon Adaptation to the American Jewish Community." Unpublished Doctoral Dissertation, New York: Yeshiva University.

Fishkoff, Sue (1994) "Don't Call us Yordim." *Jerusalem Post*, March 4.

Foner, Nancy, Rubén G. Rumbaut and Steven J. Gold (eds) (2000) *Immigration Research for a New Century: Multidisciplinary Perspectives*. New York: Russell Sage Foundation.

For Those Returning Home (1995) [Hebrew] Supplement to Yisrael Shelanu.

Frankental, Salley (nd) "Israelis Encounter Diaspora." Paper for Conference "Jewries at the Frontier" University of Cape Town.

—— (1998) "Constructing Identity in Diaspora: Jewish Israeli Migrants in Cape Town, South Africa." Doctoral Dissertation, Department of Anthropology, University of Cape Town.

Freedman, Marcia and Josef Korazim (1986) "Israelis in the New York Area Labor Market." *Contemporary Jewry* 7: 141–53.

Freedman, Samuel G. (2000) *Jew versus Jew*. New York: Simon and Schuster.

Gabaccia, Donna (1994) *From the Other Side: Women, Gender and Immigrant Life in the U.S., 1820–1990*. Bloomington and Indianapolis: Indiana University Press.

Galchinsky, Michael (1998) "Scattered Seeds: A Dialogue of Diasporas," pp. 185–211 in David Biale, Michael Galchinsky and Susannah Heschel (eds) *Insider/Outsider: American Jews and Multiculturalism*. Berkeley: University of California Press.

Gardner, Gregg Shai (2000) "Nobel Prize Winner sees Israel as a 'locomotive power.'" *Internet Jerusalem Post*, Monday June 12.

Gerstenfeld, Manfred (1991) "The Pessimists' Optimist." *Jerusalem Post*, August 9.

Gilbertson, Greta A. (1995) "Women's Labor and Enclave Employment: The Case of Dominican and Colombian Women in NYC." *International Migration Review* 29(3): 657–70.

Gitlin, Todd (1994) "From Universalism to Difference: Notes on the Fragmentation of the Idea of the Left," pp. 150–74 in Craig Calhoun (ed.) *Social Theory and the Politics of Identity*. Oxford: Blackwell.

Glazer, Nathan and Daniel Patrick Moynihan (1963) *Beyond the Melting Pot*. Cambridge, MA: MIT Press.

Gleason, P. (1981) "American Identity and Americanization," pp. 31–58 in Stephen Thernstrom (ed.) *Harvard Encyclopedia of American Ethnic Groups*. Cambridge, MA: Harvard University Press.

Glick-Schiller, Nina, Linda Basch and Cristina Blanc-Szanton (1992) "Transnationalism: A New Analytic Framework for Understanding Migration," pp. 1–24 in Nina Glick Schiller, Linda Basch, and Cristina Blanc-Szanton (eds) *Towards a Transnational Perspective on Migration: Race, Class, Ethnicity and Nationalism Reconsidered*. New York: New York Academy of Sciences.

Glick Schiller, Nina and Georges Fouron (1988) "Transnational Lives and National Identities: The Identity Politics of Haitian Immigrants," pp. 130–61 in Michael Peter Smith and Luis Eduardo Guarnizo (eds) *Transnationalism from Below*. New Brunswick, NJ: Transaction Publishers.

Goffman, Erving (1959) *Presentation of Self in Everyday Life*. Garden City, New York: Doubleday Anchor.

—— (1963) *Stigma*. Englewood Cliffs, NJ: Prentice Hall.

Gold, Steven (1992a) *Refugee Communities: A Comparative Field Study*. Newbury Park, CA: Sage.

—— (1992b) "Israelis In Los Angeles." Wilstein Institute Research Note. Susan and David Wilstein Institute of Jewish Policy Studies, Los Angeles.

—— (1994a) "Patterns of Economic Cooperation among Israeli Immigrants in Los Angeles." *International Migration Review* 28(105): 114–35.

—— (1994b) "Israeli Immigrants in the U.S.: The Question of Community." *Qualitative Sociology* 17(4): 325–63.

—— (1994c) "Soviet Jews in the United States." *American Jewish Yearbook* 1994: 3–57.

—— (1994d) "Chinese-Vietnamese Entrepreneurs in California," pp. 196–226 in Paul Ong, Edna Bonacich and Lucy Cheng (eds) *The New Asian Immigration in Los Angeles and Global Restructuring*. Philadelphia: Temple University Press.

—— (1995a) "Gender and Social Capital Among Israeli Immigrants in Los Angeles." *Diaspora* 4(3): 267–301.

—— (1995b) *From The Workers' State to The Golden State: Jews from the Former Soviet Union in California*. Boston: Allyn and Bacon.

—— (1997) "Transnationalism and Vocabularies of Motive in International Migration: The Case of Israelis in the US." *Sociological Perspectives* 40(3): 409–26.

—— (1999) "From 'The Jazz Singer' to 'What a Country!' A Comparison of Jewish Migration to the US, 1880 to 1930 and 1965 to 1998." *Journal of American Ethnic History* 18(3): 114–41.

—— (2000) "Transnational Communities: Examining Migration in a Globally Integrated World," pp. 73–90 in Preet S. Aulakh and Michael G. Schechter (eds) *Rethinking Globalization(s): From Corporate Transnationalism to Local Intervention*. London: Macmillan.

—— (2001) "Gender, Class, and Network: Social Structure and Migration Patterns among Transnational Israelis" *Global Networks* 1(1): 57–78.

Gold, Steven J. and Bruce A. Phillips (1996a) "Israelis in the United States," *American Jewish Yearbook* 1996: 51–101.

—— (1996b) "Mobility and Continuity among Eastern European Jews," pp. 182–94 in Silvia Pedraza and Rubén G. Rumbaut (eds) *Origins and Destinies: Immigration, Race and Ethnicity in America*. Belmont, CA: Wadsworth.

Goldring, Luin (1996) "Blurring Borders: Constructing Transnational Community in the Process of Mexico–U.S. Migration." *Research in Community Sociology* 6: 69–104.

—— (1998) "The Power of Status in Transnational Social Fields," pp. 165–195 in Michael Peter Smith and Luis Eduardo Guarnizo (eds) *Transnationalism from Below*. New Brunswick, NJ: Transaction Publishers.

—— (1999) "The Gender and Geography of Citizenship Practices in Mexico-U.S. Transnational Spaces." Paper presented at ASA Annual Meeting, Chicago, August 10.

Goldscheider, Calvin (1996) *Israeli's Changing Society: Population, Ethnicity and Development*. Boulder: Westview Press

Goldscheider, Calvin, and Francis E. Kobrin (1980) "Ethnic Continuity and the Process of Self-Employment." *Ethnicity* 7: 256–78.

Goldscheider, Calvin and Alan S. Zuckerman (1984) *The Transformation of the Jews*. Chicago: University of Chicago Press.

Goldstein, Joseph (1995) *Jewish History in Modern Times*. Brighton, UK: Sussex Academic Press.

Gordis, David M. and Yoav Ben-Horin (1991) "Preface," pp. vii–xv in David M. Gordis and Yoav Ben-Horin (eds) *Jewish Identity in America*. Los Angeles: Wilstein.

Gordon, Buzzy (2000) "Kodak Purchases Rest of PictureVision." *Internet Jerusalem Post*, May 17.

—— (2001) "Israel would rank in top 10 US tech regions." *Internet Jerusalem Post* (March 23).

Gordon, Milton (1964) *Assimilation in American Life*. New York: Oxford University Press.

Goren, Arthur A. (1980) "Jews," pp. 571–98 in Stephen Thernstrom (ed.) *Harvard Encyclopedia of American Ethnic Groups*. Cambridge, MA: Harvard-Belknap Press.

Granovetter, Mark S. (1973) "The Strength of Weak Ties." *American Journal of Sociology* 78 (6): 1360–80.

—— (1995a) *Getting a Job: A Study of Contacts and Careers*, 2nd edn. Chicago: University of Chicago Press.

—— (1995b) "The Economic Sociology of Firms and Entrepreneurship." pp. 128–65 in Alejandro Portes (ed.) *The Economic Sociology of Immigration: Essays on Networks, Ethnicity and Entrepreneurship*. New York: Russell Sage Foundation.

Grasmuck, Sherri and Patricia Pessar (1991) *Between Two Islands: Dominican International Migration*. Berkeley: University of California Press.

Greenberg, Harold (1979) *Israel: Social Problems*. Tel Aviv: Dekel.

Gross, Netty Chappel (1990) "Hacking in New York." *Jerusalem Post*, October 9.

Guarnizo, Luis Eduardo (1997) "'Going Home': Class, Gender and House-hold Transformation Among Dominican Return Migrants," pp. 13–60 in Patricia R. Pessar (ed.) *Caribbean Circuits: New Directions in the Study of Caribbean Migration*. Staten Island: Center for Migration Studies.

Guarnizo, Luis Eduardo and Michael Peter Smith (1998) "The Locations of Transnationalism," pp. 3–34 in Michael Peter Smith and Luis Eduardo Guarnizo (eds), *Transnationalism from Below*. New Brunswick, NJ: Transaction Publishers.

Halle, Charlotte (2001) "Factionalism Threatens Israel's Survival, Warns British Chief Rabbi." *Ha'aretz* daily newspaper – English Internet Edition, June 15.

Hartmann, Heidi (1989) "The Unhappy Marriage of Marxism and Feminism: Towards a More Progressive Union," pp. 316–37 in Roger S. Gottlieb (ed.) *An Anthology of Western Marxism*. New York: Oxford University Press.

Hechter, Michael (1987) *Principles of Group Solidarity*. Berkeley: University of California Press.

Heer, David (ed.) (1968) *Social Statistics and the City*. Cambridge, MA: Harvard University Press.

Herman, Pini (1988) "Jewish-Israeli Migration to the United States Since 1948." Paper presented at the Annual Meeting of the Association of Israel Studies. New York, June 7.

—— (1994) "A Technique for Estimating a Small Immigrant Population in Small Areas: The Case of Jewish Israelis in the United States," pp. 81–99 in K. Vaninadha Rao and Jerry W. Wicks (eds) *Studies in Applied Demography*. Bowling Green, OH: Population and Society Research Center.

—— (1998) "Los Angeles Jewish Population Survey '97." Jewish Federation of Los Angeles.

—— (2000) "The Jews of the Jews: Characteristics of Los Angeles Households of Israelis by Birth and Israelis not by Birth." Paper submitted for Division E, Contemporary Jewish Society, the Thirteenth World Congress of Jewish Studies. December 2000.

Herman, Pini and David LaFontaine (1983) "In Our Footsteps: Israeli Migration to the U.S. and Los Angeles." MSW thesis, Hebrew Union College.

Herman, Simon (1971) *Israelis and Jews*. New York: Random House.

Hertzberg, Arthur (1989) *The Jews in American: Four Centuries of an Uneasy Encounter: A History*. New York: Simon and Schuster.

Hiltzik, Michael A. (2000) "Israel's High Tech Shifts into High Gear." *Los Angeles Times*, August 13.

Hirsch, Jennifer S. (1999) "En el Norte la Mujer Manda: Gender, Generation and Geography in a Mexican Transnational Community." *American Behavioral Scientist* 42(9): 1332–49.

Holzer, Harry J. (1987) "Informal Job Search and Black Youth Unemployment." *American Economic Review* 27(3): 446–52.

Hondagneu-Sotelo, Pierrette (1994) *Gendered Transitions: Mexican Experiences of Immigration*. Berkeley: University of California Press.

Hondagneu-Sotelo, Pierrette and Ernestine Avila (1997) "'I'm Here, But I'm There:' The Meanings of Transnational Motherhood." *Gender and Society* 11(5): 548–71.

hooks, bell (1997) "Keeping Close to Home: Class and Education," pp. 126–33 in Virginia Cyrus (ed.) *Experiencing Race, Class and Gender in the United States*, 2nd edn. Mountain View, CA: Mayfield.

Horowitz, Bethamie (1993) *The 1991 New York Jewish Population Study*. New York: United Jewish Appeal – Federation of Jewish Philanthropies of New York.

Howe, Irving (1976) *World of Our Fathers*. New York: Harcourt, Brace, Jovanovich.

Hyman, Paula E. (1998) *The Jews of Modern France*. Berkeley: University of California Press.

Israel Bulletin of Statistics No. 6, June 1994.

Itim (2001) "International Ecstasy Ring Smashed by Police." *Internet Jerusalem Post*, August 2.

Jasso, Guillermina and Mark R. Rosenzweig (1990) *The New Chosen People: Immigrants in the United States*. New York: Russell Sage Foundation.

Jerusalem Post (2001) "Population Reaches almost 6.5 Million." *The Internet Jerusalem Post* (September 16).

Jones, Clive (1996) *Soviet Jewish Aliyah 1989–92: Impact and Implications for Israel and the Middle East*. London, England and Portland, Oregon: Frank Cass.

Kadish, Sharman (1998) "'A Good Jew or a Good Englishman?': The Jewish Lads' Brigade and Anglo-Jewish Identity," pp. 77–93 in Anne J. Kershen (ed.) *A Question of Identity*. Aldershot: Ashgate.

Kafra, Michal and Offer Shelach (1998) "Yordim '98," *MA'ARIV* [Hebrew] (August 7).

Kandel, William and Douglas Massey (1999) "The Culture of Migration: Intergenerational Transmission of Migratory Aspirations." Paper presented at ASA Annual Meeting, August 10, Chicago.

Karklins, Rasma (1987) "Determinants of Ethnic Identification in the USSR: The Soviet Jewish Case." *Ethnic and Racial Studies* 10(1):27–47.

Kass, Drora and Semour Martin Lipset (1982) "Jewish Immigration to the United States from 1967 to the Present: Israelis and Others," pp. 272–94 in Marshall Sklare (ed.) *Understanding American Jewry*. New Brunswick, NJ: Transaction Publishers.

Kelley, Ron and Jonathan Friedlander (eds) (1993) *Irangeles: Iranians in Los Angeles*. Berkeley: University of California Press.

Kershen, Anne J. (1997) *London: The Promised Land? The Migrant Experience in a Capital City*. Aldershot: Avebury.

Kibria, Nazli (1993) *Family Tightrope: The Changing Lives of Vietnamese Americans*. Princeton, NJ: Princeton University Press.

Kim, Dae Y. (1999) "Beyond Coethnic Solidarity: Mexican and Ecuadorian Employment in Korean-Owned Businesses in New York City." *Ethnic and Racial Studies* 22: 581–605.

Kim, Illsoo (1981) *New Urban Immigrants: The Korean Community in New York*. Princeton, NJ: Princeton University Press.

Kimhi, Shaol (1990) "Perceived Change of Self-Concept, Values, Well-Being and Intention to Return among Kibbutz People Who Migrated from Israel to America." Ph.D. Dissertation, Palo Alto, CA: Pacific Graduate School of Psychology.

Kivisto, Peter (2001) "Theorizing Transnational Immigration: A Critical Review of Current Efforts." *Ethnic and Racial Studies* 24(4): 549–77.

Korazim, Josef (1983) "Israeli Families in New York City: Utilization of Social Services Unmet Needs and Policy Implications." Ph.D. Dissertation, New York City: Columbia University.

Kosmin, Barry (1991) *Highlights of the CJF 1990 National Jewish Population Survey.* New York: Council of Jewish Federations.

Kosmin, Barry and Jeff Scheckner (1995) "Jewish Population in the United States, 1994." *American Jewish Yearbook* 95: 181–5.

Kotkin, Joel (1992) *Tribes: How Race, Religion and Identity Determined Success in the New Global Economy.* New York: Random House.

LA Jewish Yellow Pages 1993–1994.

Lahav, Gallya and Asher Arian (1999) "Israelis in a Jewish Diaspora: The Multiple Dilemmas of a Globalized Group." Paper presented for the Annual Meeting of the International Studies Association, Washington, DC (February. 16–20). http://www2.hawaii.edu/~fredr/lahav.htm#end

Lahis, Shmuel (1981) "The Lahis Report." [Hebrew] Jerusalem: The Jewish Agency (Reprinted in *Yisrael Shelanu*, February 1, 1981).

Leba, John K. (1985) *The Vietnamese Entrepreneurs in the U.S.A.* Houston: Zielecks.

Lee, Everett S. (1966) "A Theory of Migration." *Demography* 3(1): 47–57.

Lessinger, Johanna (1995) *From the Ganges to the Hudson: Asian Indians in New York City.* Boston: Allyn and Bacon.

Lev Ari, Lilach (2000) "Who Gains, Who Loses? Gender and Ethnic Position Differences among Israeli Immigrants to the United States." Paper presented at the Annual Pacific Sociological Association Meeting, San Diego, March 23–6.

Levine, Etan (ed.) (1986) *Diaspora: Exile and the Jewish Condition.* New York and London: Jason Aronson.

Levitt, Peggy (1998) "Social Remittances: Migration Driven, Local Level Forms of Cultural Diffusion." *International Migration Review* 32(4): 926–48.

—— (2001a) *The Transnational Villagers.* Berkeley: University of California Press.

—— (2001b) "Transnational Migration: Taking Stock and Future Directions." *Global Networks* 1(3): 195–216.

Lieblich, Amia (1993) "Preliminary Comparison of Israeli and American Successful Career Women at Mid-Life," pp. 195–208 in Yael Azmon and Dafna Izraeli (eds) *Women in Israel.* New Brunswick, NJ: Transaction Publishers.

Liebman, Charles S. and Steven M. Cohen (1990) *Two Worlds of Judaism: The Israeli and American Experiences.* New Haven: Yale University Press.

Liebman, Charles S. and Elihu Katz (1997) *The Jewishness of Israelis: Responses to the Guttman Report.* Albany: SUNY Press.

Light, Ivan (1972) *Ethnic Enterprise in America: Business and Welfare among Chinese, Japanese and Blacks.* Berkeley: University of California Press.

Light, Ivan and Edna Bonacich (1988) *Immigrant Entrepreneurs.* Berkeley: University of California Press.

Light, Ivan and Steven J. Gold (2000) *Ethnic Economies.* San Diego: Academic Press.

Light, Ivan and Stavros Karageorgis (1994) "The Ethnic Economy," Ch. 26 in Neil Smelser and Richard Swedberg (eds) *The Handbook of Economic Sociology.* New York: Russell Sage Foundation.

Light, Ivan, Georges Sabagh, Mehdi Bozorgmehr and Claudia Der-Martirosian (1994) "Beyond the Ethnic Enclave Economy." *Social Problems* 41: 65–80.

Lincoln, Yvonna S. and Egon G. Guba (1985) *Naturalistic Inquiry.* Newbury Park, CA: Sage.

Linn, Ruth and Nurit Barkan-Ascher (1996) "Permanent Impermanence: Israeli Expatriates in Non-Event Transition." *Jewish Journal of Sociology* 38(1): 5–16.

Lipkis, Galit (1991) "Business Envoys Whet U.S. Appetites." *Jerusalem Post,* November 26.

Lipner, Nira H. (1987) "The Subjective Experience of Israeli Immigrant Women: An Interpretive Approach." Ph.D. Dissertation, Washington, DC: George Washington University.

Lipset, Seymour Martin (1990) "A Unique People in an Exceptional Country," pp. 3–29 in Seymour Martin Lipset (ed.) *American Pluralism and the Jewish Community.* New Brunswick, NJ: Transaction Publishers.

Lyman, Stanford (1974) *Chinese Americans.* New York: Random House.

Machlis, Avi (2000) "High-tech Start-ups Leave Israel, Need to Go West to Join Gold Rush." Jewish Telegraphic Agency On-Line, June 18.

Mahler, Sarah J. (1998) "Theoretical and Empirical Contribution Towards a Research Agenda for Transnationalism" pp. 64–100 in Michael Peter Smith and Luis Eduardo Guarnizo (eds), *Transnationalism from Below.* New Brunswick, NJ: Transaction Publishers.

Marable, Manning (1983) *How Capitalism Underdeveloped Black America: Problems in Race, Political Economy and Society.* Boston: South End Press.

Marcus, George E. (1995) "Ethnography in/of The World System: The Emergence of Multi-Sited Ethnography." *Annual Review of Anthropology* 24: 95–117.

Marger, Martin and Constance Hoffman (1994) "Intended Immigrant Entrepreneurs in Ontario: Expanding the Concept of Immigrant Enterprise." Paper presented at the Annual Meeting of the American Sociological Association, Los Angeles (August).

Margolis, Maxine (1994) *Little Brazil: An Ethnography of Brazilian Immigrants in New York City.* Princeton, NJ: Princeton University Press.

Markowitz, Fran (1994) "Soviet Dis-Union and the Fragmentation of Self: Implications for the Emigrating Jewish Family." *East European Jewish Affairs* 24(1): 3–17.

Marx, Karl (1978) "On the Jewish Question," pp. 26–52 in Robert Tucker, (ed.) *The Marx-Engels Reader,* 2nd edn. New York: Norton.

Massey, Douglas S., Rafael Alarcón, Jorge Durand and Humberto Gonzalez (1987) *Return to Aztlan.* Berkeley: University of California Press.

Massey, Douglas, Joaquin Arango, Graeme Hugo, Ali Kouaouci, Adela Pellegrino and J. Edward Taylor (1993) "Theories of International Migration: A Review and Appraisal." *Population and Development Review* 19(3): 431–66.

Massey, Douglas S., Luin Goldring and Jorge Durand (1994) "Continuities in Transnational Migration: An Analysis of Nineteen Mexican Communities." *American Journal of Sociology* 99(6): 1492–533.

MFA (Israel – Ministry of Foreign Affairs) (1999) The Facts, etc. http://www.israel-mfa.gov.il/mfa/go.asp?MFAH0kdr0

Milkman, Ruth and Eleanor Townsley (1994) "Gender and the Economy," Ch. 24, pp. 600–19 in Neil Smelser and Richard Swedberg (eds) *Handbook of Economic Sociology*. Princeton and New York: Russell Sage Foundation and Princeton University Press.

Mills, C. Wright (1940) "Situated Actions and Vocabularies of Motive." *American Sociological Review* (May): 904–13.

—— (1959) *The Sociological Imagination*. New York: Oxford University Press.

Min, Pyong-Gap (1996) *Caught in The Middle: Korean Communities in New York and Los Angeles*. Berkeley: University of California Press.

—— (1998) *Changes and Conflicts: Korean Immigrant Families in New York*. Boston: Allyn and Bacon.

Min, Pyong Gap and Rose Kim (eds) (1999) *Struggle for Ethnic Identity: Narratives by Asian American Professionals*. Walnut Creek, CA: AltaMira Press.

Minster, Ruth (1998) *A Subtitled Life* (Documentary film).

Mittelberg, David (1988) *Strangers in Paradise: The Israeli Kibbutz Experience*. New Brunswick, NJ: Transaction Publishers.

Mittelberg, David and Mary C. Waters (1992) "The Process of Ethnogenesis among Haitian and Israeli Immigrants in The United States." *Ethnic and Racial Studies* 15(3): 412–35.

Moaz, Shlomo and Avi Temkin (1989) "Olim and Yordim." *Jerusalem Post*, May 9.

Nir, Ori (2001) "Violence Sparks Desire among American Jews to Support Israel's Arab Minority." *Ha'aretz* daily newspaper – English Online Edition, January 21.

NJPS (1990) *National Jewish Population Survey*. New York: Council of Jewish Federations.

Nonini, Donald and Aihwa Ong (1997) "Introduction: Chinese Transnationalism as an Alternative Modernity," pp. 3–33 in Ong, Aihwa and Donald Nonini (eds) *Ungrounded Empires: The Cultural Politics of Modern Chinese Transnationalism*. New York: Routledge.

Ong, Aihwa (1999) *Flexible Citizenship: The Cultural Logics of Transnationality*. Durham, NC: Duke University Press.

Ong, Paul, Edna Bonacich and Lucie Cheng (1994) "The Political Economy of Capitalist Restructuring and the New Asian Immigration," pp. 3–35 in Paul Ong, Edna Bonacich and Lucie Cheng *The New Asian Immigration in Los Angeles and Global Restructuring*. Philadelphia: Temple University Press.

Ong, Paul, Kye Young Park and Yasmin Tong (1994) "Korean-Black Conflict and the State," pp. 264–94 in Paul Ong, Edna Bonacich and Lucie Cheng (eds) *The New Asian Immigration in Los Angeles and Global Restructuring*. Philadelphia: Temple University Press.

O'Sullivan-See, Katherine and Wiliam J. Wilson (1988) "Race and Ethnicity," pp. 223–42 in Neil J. Smelser (ed.) *Handbook of Sociology*. Newbury Park, CA: Sage.

Parlin, Bradley (1976) *Immigrant Professionals in the United States*. New York: Praeger.

Patai, Raphael (1971) *Tents of Jacob: The Diaspora Yesterday and Today*. Englewood Cliffs, NJ: Prentice Hall.

Patterson, Orlando (1975) "Context and Choice in Ethnic Allegience: A Theoretical Framework and Careibbean Case Study," pp. 305–49 in Nathan Glazer and Daniel P. Moynihan (eds) *Ethnicity: Theory and Experience*. Cambridge, MA: Harvard University Press.

—— (1977) *Ethnic Chauvinism: The Reactionary Impulse*. New York: Stein and Day.

Pedraza, Silvia (1991) "Women and Migration: The Social Consequences of Gender." *Annual Review of Sociology* 17: 303–25.

Pessar, Patricia R. (1986) "The Role of Gender in Dominican Settlement in the U.S.," pp. 273–94 in June Nash and Helen Safa (eds) *Women and Change in Latin America*. South Hadley, MA: Bergin and Garvey.

—— (1997) *Caribbean Circuits: New Directions in the Study of Caribbean Migration*. New York: Center for Migration Studies.

—— (1999) "Engendering Migration Studies: The Case of New Immigrants in the United States." *American Behavioral Scientist* 42(4): 577–600.

Peterson, William (1958) "A General Typology of Migration." *American Sociological Review* 23(3): 256–66.

Phillips, Bruce A. (1991) "Sociological Analysis of Jewish Identity," pp. 3–25 in David M. Gordis and Yoav Ben-Horin (eds) *Jewish Identity in America*. Los Angeles: Wilstein.

Piore, Michael J. (1979) *Birds of Passage*. New York: Cambridge University Press.

Pollins, Harold (1984) "The Development of Jewish Business in the United Kingdom," pp. 73–88 in Robin Ward and Richard Jenkins (eds) *Ethnic Communities in Business: Strategies for Economic Survival*. Cambridge: Cambridge University Press.

Portes, Alejandro (1995a) "Economic Sociology and the Sociology of Immigration: A Conceptual Overview," pp. 1–41 in Alejandro Portes (ed.) *The Economic Sociology of Immigration: Essays on Networks, Ethnicity and Entrepreneurship*. New York: Russell Sage Foundation.

—— (1995b) "Transnational Communities: Their Emergence and Significance in the Contemporary World System." Working Paper No. 16. Program in Comparative International Development, Department of Sociology, Johns Hopkins University.

—— (1998) "Social Capital: Its Origins and Applications in Modern Sociology." *Annual Review of Sociology* 24: 1–24.

—— (2000) "The Hidden Abode: Sociology as Analysis of the Unexpected." *American Sociological Review* 65(1): 1–18.

—— (2001) "Introduction: The Debates and Significance of Immigrant Transnationalism." *Global Networks* 1(3): 181–93.

Portes, Alejandro and Robert Bach (1985) *Latin Journey: Cuban and Mexican Immigrants in the United States*. Berkeley: University of California Press.

Portes, Alejandro and Jozsef Borocz (1989) "Contemporary Immigration: Theoretical Perspectives on its Determinants and Modes of Incorporation." *International Migration Review* 23(87): 606–30.

Portes, Alejandro and Rubén G. Rumbaut. (1996) *Immigrant America: A Portrait* (Second Edition). Berkeley: University of California Press.

—— (2001) *Legacies: The Story of the Immigrant Second Generation*. Berkeley: University of California Press.

Portes, Alejandro and Julia Sensenbrenner (1993) "Embeddedness and Immigration: Notes on the Social Determinants of Economic Action." *American Journal of Sociology* 98(6): 1320–50.

Portes, Alejandro, Luis E. Guarnizo and Patricia Landolt (1999) "Introduction: Pitfalls and Promise of an Emergent Research Field." *Ethnic and Racial Studies* 22(2): 217–27.

Radler, Melissa (2001) "New York Israelis Fly to Polls – or Don't." *The Internet Jerusalem Post*, January 26.

Raval, Dinker (1983) "East Indian Small Businesses in the U.S.: Perception, Problems and Adjustments." *American Journal of Small Business* 7(3): 39–44.

Razin, Eran (1990) "Immigrant Entrepreneurs in Israeli, Canada and California." UCLA ISSR Working Papers in the Social Sciences, Vol 5, No. 8.

—— (1991) "Social Networks, Local Opportunities and Entrepreneurship among Immigrants: The Israeli Experience in an International Perspective." Mimeo: Hebrew University, Department of Geography.

Regev, Motti (2000) "To Have a Culture of Our Own: On Israeliness and its Variants." *Ethnic and Racial Studies* 23(2): 223–47.

Reid, Anthony D. (1997) "Entrepreneurial Minorities, Nationalism, and the State," pp. 33–71 in Daniel Chirot and Anthony Reid (eds) *Essential Outsiders: Chinese and Jews in the Modern Transformation of Southeast Asia and Central Europe*, Seattle: University of Washington Press.

Richtel, Matt (1998) "New Israelis Get Computers to Aid Assimilation." *New York Times*, January 21.

Ritterband, Paul (1986) "Israelis in New York." *Contemporary Jewry* 7: 113–26.

Ritterband, Paul and Steven M. Cohen (1982) *The Greater New York Jewish Population Study*. New York: Federation of Jewish Philanthropies/United Jewish Appeal.

Ritterband, Paul and Yael Zerubavel (1986) "Introduction": "Special Supplemental Section: Conference Reports on Israelis Abroad." *Contemporary Jewry* 7: 111.

Ritzer, George (1988) *Sociological Theory*, 2nd edn. New York: Alfred A. Knopf.

—— (1990) "Micro-Macro Linkages in Sociological Theory: Applying a Metatheoretical Tool," pp. 347–70 in George Ritzer (ed.) *Frontiers of Social Theory: The New Synthesis*. New York: Columbia University Press.

Rivlin, Paul (1992) *The Israeli Economy*. New York: Westview.

Rosen, Sherry (1993) "The Israeli Corner of the American Jewish Community." Issue Series No. 3. New York: Institute on American Jewish-Israeli Relations. The American Jewish Committee.

Rosenthal, Mira (1989) "Assimilation of Israeli Immigrants." Ph.D. Dissertation, New York: Fordham University.

Rosenthal, Mira and Charles Auerbach (1992) "Cultural and Social Assimilation of Israeli Immigrants in the United States." *International Migration Review* 99(26): 982–91.

Rumbaut, Rubén G. (1994) "The Crucible Within: Ethnic Identity, Self-Esteem, and Segmented Assimilation Among Children of Immigrants." *International Migration Review* 28(4): 748–94.

Sabar, Naama (1989) "This is Not My Home: It is Just a House – Kibbutz-Born Immigrants in Los Angeles," pp. 68–85, in J.B. Allen and J.P. Goetz (eds), *Qualitative Research in Education: Teaching and Learning Qualitative Traditions*. Athens, GA: College of Education, University of Georgia.

—— (1996) *Kibbutz L.A.* Tel Aviv: Am Oved Publishers [Hebrew].

—— (2000) *Kibbutznicks in the Diaspora*. Albany: SUNY Press.

Sachal-Staier, Michal (1993) "Israelis in Los Angeles: Interrelations and Relations with the American Jewish Community." MBA Thesis, Los Angeles: University of Judaism.

Safran, William (1991) "Diasporas in Modern Societies: Myths of Homeland and Return." *Diaspora* 1(1): 83–99.

—— (1999) "Comparing Diasporas: A Review Essay." *Diaspora* 8(3): 255–91.

Sassen, Saskia (1991) *The Global City: New York, London, Tokyo*. Princeton, NJ: Princeton University Press.

Schiller, Nina Glick, Linda Basch and Cristina Blanc-Szanton (1992) "Transnationalism: A New Analytic Framework for Understanding Migration," pp. 1–24 in Nina Glick Schiller, Linda Basch and Cristina Blanc-Szanton (eds) *Towards a Transnational Perspective on Migration: Race, Class, Ethnicity and Nationalism Reconsidered*. New York: New York Academy of Sciences.

Schmool, Marlena and Frances Cohen (1998) *A Profile of British Jewry: Patterns and Trends at the Turn of a Century*. London: Board of Deputies of British Jews.

Schnall, David (1987) *The Jewish Agenda: Essays in Contemporary Jewish Life*. New York: Praeger.

Schuetz, Alfred (1944) "The Stranger: An Essay in Social Psychology." *American Journal of Sociology* 49(6): 499–507.

Shafir, Gershon (1995) "Zionist Immigration and Colonization in Palestinian until 1948," pp. 405–9 in Robin Cohen (ed.) *The Cambridge Survey of World Migration*. Cambridge: Cambridge University Press.

Shain, Yossi (2000) "American Jews and the Construction of Israel's Jewish Identity." *Diaspora* 9(2): 163–201.

Shama, Avraham and Mark Iris (1977) *Immigration without Integration: Third World Jews in Israel.* Cambridge, MA: Schenkman.

Shamir, Shlomo (2001) "U.S. Reform Movement threatens to quit WZO." *Ha'aretz* daily newspaper – English Internet Edition, May 14.

Shavit, Rona (nd) "The Glue That Holds Us Together: Enhancing Community Cohesion Through School Choice. A Case Study on School Choice in a Minority Group." Mimeo, School of Education, King's College, London.

Shavit, Uriva (2001) "Westward Ho!" Ha'aretzdaily.com, August 22.

Sheffer, Gabriel (1986) "A New Field of Study: Modern Diasporas in International Politics," pp. 1–15 in Gabriel Sheffer (ed.) *Modern Diasporas in International Politics.* New York: St. Martins Press.

—— (1998) "The Israeli Diaspora" Yordim (Emigrants) Are the Authentic Diaspora," pp. xix - xxxi in S. Massil (ed.) *The Jewish Year Book.* London: Valentine Mitchell.

Shokeid, Moshe (1988) *Children of Circumstances: Israeli Immigrants in New York.* Ithaca: Cornell University Press.

—— (1989) "From the Anthropologist's Point of View: Studying One's Own Tribe." *Anthropology and Humanism Quarterly* 4(1): 23–8.

—— (1993) "One Night Stand Ethnicity: The Malaise of Israeli-Americans." *Israel Social Science Journal* 8(2): 23–50.

—— (1998) "My Poly-Ethnic Park: Some Thoughts on Israeli-Jewish Ethnicity." *Diaspora* 7(2): 225–46.

Shor, Gil (1998) "Israelis in L.A: Present and Absent." *Israel L.A.*, September 16: p. 5 [Hebrew].

Siegel, Dina (1998) *The Great Immigration: Russian Jews in Israel.* New York: Berghahn Books.

Simmel, George (1971) "The Stranger," pp. 143–9 in Donald Levine (ed.) *George Simmel: On Individuality and Social Forms.* Chicago: University of Chicago Press.

Simon, Rita J. (1985) *New Lives: The Adjustment of Soviet Jewish Immigrants in the United States and Israel.* Lexington, MA: Lexington Books.

—— (1997) *In the Golden Land: A Century of Russian and Soviet Jewish Immigration in America.* Westport: Praeger.

Simon, Rita J., Louise Shelly and Paul Schneiderman (1986) "Social and Economic Adjustment of Soviet Jewish Women in the United States," pp. 76–94 in Rita James Simon and Caroline B. Brettell (eds) *International Migration: The Female Experience.* Totowa, NJ: Rowman and Littlefield.

Sklar, Leslie (1991) *Sociology of the Global System: Social Change in Global Perspective.* Baltimore: Johns Hopkins University Press.

Smith, Dorothy E. (1990) *The Conceptual Practices of Power: A Feminist Sociology of Knowledge.* Boston: Northeastern University Press.

Smith, Michael, Peter and Luis Eduardo Guarnizo (eds) (1998) *Transnationalism from Below.* New Brunswick, NJ: Transaction Publishers.

Smith, Robert C. (1998) "Transnational Localities: Community, Locality and the Politics of Membership Within the Context of Mexico and U.S. Migration," pp. 196–238 in Michael Peter Smith and Luis Eduardo

Guarnizo (eds) *Transnationalism from Below.* New Brunswick, NJ: Transaction Publishers.

Smooha, Sammy (1978) *Israel: Pluralism and Conflict.* Berkeley: University of California Press.

Sobel, Zvi (1986) *Migrants from the Promised Land.* New Brunswick, NJ: Transaction Publishers.

Song, Miri (1999) *Helping Out: Children's Labor in Ethnic Business.* Philadelphia: Temple University Press.

Sowell, Thomas P. (1981) *Ethnic America.* New York: Basic Books.

Soysal, Yasmin N. (1994) *Limits of Citizenship: Migrants and Postnational Membership in Europe.* Chicago: University of Chicago Press.

Statistics Canada (2000) Custom Tabulation from 1996 Census.

Steinberg, Stephen (1989) *The Ethnic Myth,* 2nd edn. New York: Anthenium.

Stern, Geraldine (1979) *Israeli Women Speak Out.* Philadelphia: Lippincott.

Strauss, Anselm (1987) *Qualitative Analysis for Social Scientists.* New York: Cambridge University Press.

Stryker, Sheldon (1980) *Symbolic Interactionism: A Social Structural Version.* Menlo Park, CA: Benjamin/Cummings.

Task Force on Immigrant Integration (1986) *Final Report on the Metropolitan Region: Findings and Recommendations.* Jewish Federation of Los Angeles (July).

Teitelbaum, Sheldon (2001a) "A Normal Israel, in Agoura." *The Jewish Journal* (of Los Angeles) 16(9) April 27–May 3: 25, 27.

—— (2001b) "L.A.'s Hidden Battalions." *The Jewish Journal* (of Los Angeles) 16(24) August 10–16: 14, 39.

Thomas, W.I. and Florian Znaniecki (1920) *The Polish Peasant in Europe and America.* New York: Richard Badger.

Tilly, Charles (1990) "Transplanted Networks," pp. 79–95 in Virginia Yans-McLaughlin (ed.) *Immigration Reconsidered: History, Sociology and Politics.* New York: Oxford University Press.

Tobin, Gary A. (1992) *Trends in American Jewish Philanthropy: Market Research Analysis.* Waltham, MA: Cohen Center for Modern Jewish Studies, Brandeis University.

Tobin, Gary A., Adam Z. Tobin and Lorin Troderman (1995) *American Jewish Philanthropy in the 1990s.* Waltham, MA: Cohen Center for Modern Jewish Studies, Brandeis University.

Toren, Nina (1980) "Return to Zion: Characteristics and Motivations of Returning Emigrants," pp. 39–50 in Ernest Krausz (ed.) *Studies of Israeli Society,* VI, Migration, Ethnicity and Community. New Brunswick, NJ: Transaction Publishers.

Trankiem, Luu (1986) "Economic Development Opportunities for Indochinese Refugees in Orange County." California Community Foundation.

Trofimov, Yarolslav (1995) "Booming Economy Lures Israelis home from U.S.: Jewish State Now More Inviting." *San Francisco Examiner,* October 8.

Tugend, Tom (1989) "Peretz: Integrate Yordim into Jewish Community" *Jerusalem Post*, November 29.

United States Bureau of the Census (1990) Census of Population, 5% Public Use Microsample.

Uriely, Natan (1994) "Rhetorical Ethnicity of Permanent Sojourners: The Case of Israeli Immigrants in the Chicago Area." *International Sociology* 9(4): 431–45.

—— (1995) "Patterns of Identification and Integration with Jewish Americans Among Israeli Immigrants in Chicago: Variations Across Status and Generation." *Contemporary Jewry* 16: 27–49.

Van Hear, Nicholas (1998) *New Diasporas: The Mass Exodus, Dispersal and Regrouping of Migrant Communities*. Seattle: University of Washington Press.

Vega, William A. and Rubén G. Rumbaut (1991) "Ethnic Minorities and Mental Health." *Annual Review of Sociology* 17: 351–83.

Waldinger, Roger (1986) *Through the Eye of the Needle*. New York: NYU Press.

—— (1996) *Still the Promised City? African-Americans and New Immigrants in Postindustrial New York*. Cambridge, MA: Harvard University Press.

Waldinger, Roger and Mehdi Bozorgmehr (eds) (1996) *Ethnic Los Angeles*. New York: Russell Sage Foundation.

Waldinger, Roger, Howard, Aldrich, Robin, Ward and Associates (1990) *Ethnic Entrepreneurs: Immigrant Business in Industrial Societies*. Newbury Park: Sage.

Ward, Robin H. (1986) "Orientation and Opportunity: An Interpretation of Asian Enterprise in Western Society." Paper presented at Annual Meeting of the American Sociological Association, August 30–September 3, New York.

Warner, R. Stephen and Judith G. Wittner (eds) (1998) *Gatherings in the Diaspora: Religious Communities and the New Immigration*. Philadelphia: Temple University Press.

Warnock, Steve (1998) "Israeli Drug Ring Broken." *Sun Herald* (Sydney), March 1.

Waterman, Stanley (1997) "The 'Return' of the Jews into London," pp. 143–60 in Anne J. Kershen (ed.) *London: The Promised Land? The Migrant Experience in a Capital City*. Aldershot: Avebury.

Waterman, Stanley and Barry Kosmin (1986) "The Jews of London." *Geographical Magazine* 58: 21–7.

Waters, Mary C. (1990) *Ethnic Options: Choosing identities in America*. Berkeley: University of California Press.

—— (1999) *Black Identities: West Indian Immigrant Dreams and American Realities*. Cambridge, MA: Harvard University Press.

Weber, Max (1978) *Economy and Society*. Berkeley: University of California Press.

Weinstein, Eugene A. and Judith M. Tanur (1976) "Meanings, Purposes and Structured Resources in Social Interaction." *Cornell Journal of Social Relations* 11: 105–10.

Weiss, Miriam J. (1990) "How Many Leave and Why." *Jerusalem Post*, April 2.

Werthheimer, Jack (1995) "Jewish Organizational Life in the United States Since 1945." *American Jewish Yearbook* 95: 3–98.

Wilensky, Harold L. and Anne T. Lawrence (1979) "Job Assignment in Modern Societies: A Re-examination of the Ascription-Achievement Hypothesis," pp. 202–48 in Amos Hawley (ed.) *Societal Growth: Processes and Implications*. New York: Free Press–Macmillan.

Wilson, William J. (1978) *The Declining Significance of Race*. Chicago: University of Chicago Press.

—— (1987) *The Truly Disadvantaged*. Chicago: University of Chicago Press.

—— (1996) *When Work Disappears: The World of the New Urban Poor*. New York: Knopf

Wirth, Louis (1928) *The Ghetto*. Chicago: University of Chicago Press.

Wolf, Diane L. (1997) "Family Secrets: Transnational Struggles Among Children of Filipino Immigrants." *Sociological Perspectives* 40 (3): 455–80.

Wolitz, Seth L. (1991) "The American Jew is American First." *Jerusalem Post*, February 20.

Yiftachel, Oren (1998) "Nation Building and the Division of Space: Ashkenazi Domination in the Israeli 'Ethnocracy.'" *Nationalism and Ethnic Politics* 4(3): 33–58.

Yoon, In-Jin (1997) *"On My Own". Korean Businesses and Race Relations in America*. Chicago: University of Chicago Press.

Zenner, Walter P. (1991) *Minorities in the Middle: A Cross-Cultural Analysis*. Albany: SUNY Press.

Zerubavel, Yael (1995) *Recovered Roots: Collective Memory and the Making of Israeli National Tradition*. Chicago: University of Chicago Press.

Zhou, Min and Carl L. Bankston, III (1998) *Growing Up American: How Vietnamese Children Adapt to Life in the United States*. New York: Russell Sage Foundation.

Zhou, Min and John R. Logan (1989) "Returns on Human Capital in Ethnic Enclaves." *American Sociological Review* 54(5): 809–20.

Zvielli, Alexander (1989) "The Mark of Cain." *Jerusalem Post*, September 26.

Zweig, Ferdynand (1969) *Israel: The Sword and the Harp*. London: Heinemann.

INDEX